Migration, Minorities and Citizenship

General Editors: **Zig Layton-Henry**, Professor of Politics, University of Warwick; and **Danièle Joly**, Director, Centre for Research in Ethnic Relations, University of Warwick

Titles include:

Muhammad Anwar, Patrick Roach and Ranjit Sondhi (*editors*)
FROM LEGISLATION TO INTEGRATION?
Race Relations in Britain

Naomi Carmon (*editor*)
IMMIGRATION AND INTEGRATION IN POST-INDUSTRIAL SOCIETIES
Theoretical Analysis and Policy-Related Research

Adrian Favell
PHILOSOPHIES OF INTEGRATION
Immigration and the Idea of Citizenship in France and Britain

Sophie Body-Gendrot and Marco Martiniello (*editors*)
MINORITIES IN EUROPEAN CITIES
The Dynamics of Social Integration and Social Exclusion at the Neighbourhood Level

Simon Holdaway and Anne-Marie Barron
RESIGNERS? THE EXPERIENCE OF BLACK AND ASIAN POLICE OFFICERS

Atsushi Kondo (*editor*)
CITIZENSHIP IN A GLOBAL WORLD
Comparing Citizenship Rights for Aliens

Danièle Joly
HAVEN OR HELL?
Asylum Policies and Refugees in Europe

SCAPEGOATS AND SOCIAL ACTORS
The Exclusion and Integration of Minorities in Western and Eastern Europe

Jørgen S. Nielsen
TOWARDS A EUROPEAN ISLAM

Jan Rath (*editor*)
IMMIGRANT BUSINESSES
The Economic, Political and Social Environment

Peter Ratcliffe (*editor*)
THE POLITICS OF SOCIAL SCIENCE RESEARCH
Race, Ethnicity and Social Change

John Rex
ETHNIC MINORITIES IN THE MODERN NATION STATE
Working Papers in the Theory of Multiculturalism and Political Integration

Carl-Ulrik Schierup (*editor*)
SCRAMBLE FOR THE BALKANS
Nationalism, Globalism and the Political Economy of Reconstruction

Steven Vertovec and Ceri Peach (*editors*)
ISLAM IN EUROPE
The Politics of Religion and Community

Östen Wahlbeck
KURDISH DIASPORAS
A Comparative Study of Kurdish Refugee Communities

John Wrench, Andrea Rea and Nouria Ouali (*editors*)
MIGRANTS, ETHNIC MINORITIES AND THE LABOUR MARKET
Integration and Exclusion in Europe

309-507-2947

Migration, Minorities and Citizenship
Series Standing Order ISBN 0–333–71047–9
(*outside North America only*)

You can receive future titles in this series as they are published by placing a standing order. Please contact your bookseller or, in case of difficulty, write to us at the address below with your name and address, the title of the series and the ISBN quoted above.

Customer Services Department, Macmillan Distribution Ltd, Houndmills, Basingstoke, Hampshire RG21 6XS, England

Philosophies of Integration

Immigration and the Idea of Citizenship in France and Britain

Adrian Favell

Second Edition

palgrave

in association with
Centre for Research
in Ethnic Relations,
University of Warwick

First edition 1998
Second edition 2001

Published 2001 by
PALGRAVE
Houndmills, Basingstoke, Hampshire RG21 6XS and
175 Fifth Avenue, New York, N. Y. 10010
Companies and representatives throughout the world

PALGRAVE is the new global academic imprint of
St. Martin's Press LLC Scholarly and Reference Division and
Palgrave Publishers Ltd (formerly Macmillan Press Ltd).

ISBN 0–333–94593–X paperback

This book is printed on paper suitable for recycling and made from fully managed and sustained forest sources.

A catalogue record for this book is available from the British Library.

Library of Congress Cataloging-in-Publication Data
Favell, Adrian.
    Philosophies of integration : immigration and the idea of
    citizenship in France and Britain / Adrian Favell.—2nd ed.
        p. cm. — (Migration, minorities, and citizenship)
    Includes bibliographical references and index.
    ISBN 0–333–94593–X (pbk.)
        1. France—Emigration and immigration—Government policy.
    2. Immigrants—France. 3. Citizenship—France. 4. Great Britain–
    –Emigration and immigration—Government policy. 5. Immigrants–
    –Great Britain. 6. Citizenship—Great Britain. I. Title. II. Series.
    JV7933.F38 1998
    325.41—dc21
                                                            2001021868

10   9   8   7   6   5   4   3   2   1
10   09   08   07   06   05   04   03   02   01

Printed and bound in Great Britain by
Antony Rowe Ltd, Chippenham, Wiltshire

Contents

Preface to the Second Edition

Philosophies of Integration sets itself the task of viewing the politics of race, immigration and citizenship in France and Britain from a vantage point outside the nationally specific debates that dominate discussions within these two countries. It also offers a general approach to doing cross-national comparative research on the integration of immigrants, a research agenda that is everywhere across Europe distorted by local political influences on the way knowledge on the subject is constructed and debates are framed. For this reason, much of what the book says about France and Britain differs sharply from the tone, language and even subject-matter of the best-known work produced internally in the two countries. It may, therefore, puzzle and perplex those who in Britain seek to refer all discussion back to polemics about anti-racism or the politics of identity, or indeed those in France who frame everything in terms of republicanism and *citoyenneté*.

However, it is my hope that in relativising what these two case studies reveal, the text may also provoke in such readers a phenomenological moment of self-consciousness and insight, about just how *context specific* and *nationally peculiar* their often sweeping formulations about race, ethnicity, identity or migration in each country in fact are. Britain and France are two relatively small nations with vastly over-blown self-conceptions about their place in the world. Academics working in the two countries have, by failing to engage in meaningful comparative work, made a bad habit of writing about nationally specific events and forms of immigration politics as if they can be unproblematically generalised into theories and concepts that apply untranslated to the rest of Europe, or indeed, the world. This is exacerbated by the intellectual imperialism of the English-speaking publishing world; as well as the often insular intellectual self-sufficiency of Paris.

The strategy of the book is instead to explore the national idiosyncrasies of these two countries in terms that translate their own particular ways of seeing and talking about immigration and integration, into a general comparative framework that might work for a whole range of other cases. In part this is a historical, interpretative task, paying reflexive attention to the ways in which long-standing national conceptions about liberalism as a political philosophy have shaped the recent production of ideas, debates and scientific knowledge about the subject. Yet I also stress throughout the changeability of the distinct national frameworks: the way in which policy making is forward looking, and inherently normative and creative in its dynamics. Thus, the concept of 'public philosophies' on which my studies relies, should not be read – as some readers have – as the equivalent of a rooted historical tradition which determines the language and outcomes of present-day politics. Rather, the history of immigration politics in the two countries (what I analyse in terms of *path dependency*) provides a series of contingent political constraints, within which policy makers have come up with new and often bizarre solutions to current concerns: sometimes, as I stress, creating all kinds of peculiarly contorted and pathological versions of past policies as they seek to reconcile new circumstances with inherited practices.

The tension of the book, therefore, lies in specifying the degree to which it is possible for policy makers to learn from their mistakes and start behaving outside of the nationally determined railtracks of habit and ideology. One point, obviously, is that rational cross-national learning is blocked – particularly in the context of growing European co-operation – when national politicians and commentators are so resistant to seeing themselves in anything other than nationally specific and nationally self-referential terms. The *dialogue de sourds* (discussion between deaf people) between French and British academics in this field, is a near legendary feature of the mutual miscomprehension of philosophers, sociologists and political scientists that characterises the subject. However, my account is not a deterministic one, and I would be delighted if, five years on from the drafting the first version, I could report many instances of my pessimism on the subject as being wrong. Conversely, I take very little delight in still finding abundant evidence in both countries (particularly in Britain) that I was right.

The first edition was published soon after the coming to power of New Labour. On questions of race and immigration there is not yet any reason to deviate from my conclusion then that we were likely to simply see more of the same nationally specific conservatism on these issues, however radical other parts of the Blair agenda have been. Before the election, one of my PhD examiners and a distinguished former deputy chair of the Commission for Racial Equality, Bhikhu Parekh, told me of his pessimism about the new government seizing the opportunity to reform Britain's existing race relations and multicultural institutions. Parekh now chairs a new Commission on the future of Multi-Ethnic Britain which, along with new efforts by the CRE to review its achievements 25 years on and the Runnymede Trust's campaign on multicultural citizenship, is pushing for some new thinking on the subject, despite the fact that little has been done in the first term of office. This effort, in itself, is a good sign. The most optimistic campaigners see a second term Labour government as a true reformist hope, pushing for a revised fourth Race Relations Act, that will address the *lacunae* about the discrimination of Muslims in Britain (see pp. 217–25), and engage in a broader proactive agenda of positive action on employment, public services and education. One wonders if they will be as disappointed as the teachers, lecturers, nurses and public transport campaigners first time round.

Europe, as a dimension of these issues, hardly ever features in these discussions, except when it is seen as a new 'market' for promoting specifically British ways of dealing with anti-discrimination and multiculturalism. However, on a constitutional level at least, the Blair government has taken steps towards incorporating the Europe Convention on Human Rights within the British legal system, and the new government was swift to reverse years of non-involvement in European level discussions on migration, by offering a green light to new European measures on migrants and minorities towards the end of the 1996–97 Inter-governmental Conference (IGC) on the European Union. This endorsed the incorporation of anti-discrimination measures in the subsequent Amsterdam Treaty and the setting up of a new Monitoring Centre on racism and xenophobia in Vienna: something that had been resisted by the previous Conservative government. These mildly constructive developments prove – as Michael Banton and Randall Hansen have pointed out in reviews – that the isolationist expectations of my account were overly pessimistic.

However, it is still not clear that the normative consequences these developments entail have had the slightest effect on the internal practice and justification of immigration control or race relations in the country. British policy makers argue that Britain already abundantly fulfils these external obligations, having legislation they see as far superior to any other in Europe. The refusal to join the Schengen agreement on the management of borders and immigration control only serves to underline how its sovereign prerogative continues to be the bottom line in this area. More widely, it is possible that the European question in Britain could still go either way. It is unclear where exactly the government stands on joining the single currency, and while Home Office minister Jack Straw has been keen to encourage the involvement of Britain in co-operation on policing and customs control, other aspects of Schengen concerning rights to free movement are subject to the usual British opt out.

The logic of conceiving Britain as a strictly bounded territory within which integration may then take place thus remains firm (see pp. 110–22). What has been going on in Europe – on issues to do with migration, minorities and cultural diversity – has very little impact on the British debate. Internally, however, there are serious developments shaking some of the foundations of the 'multicultural race relations' compromise. *Ethnic Minorities in Britain*, the enormously important 1997 report by the Policy Studies Institute, headed by Tariq Modood, revealed an increasingly differentiated pattern of diversity and disadvantage among Britain's ethnic minorities, putting a final stake through the activist fiction of a common 'black' front in British ethnic minority politics and social behaviour. It also drew vastly different pictures of social success and integration for Britain's Asian population. The relative social mobility of Indians and Sri Lankans in Britain – particularly the East African Gujarati forced out of Uganda by Idi Amin – stands in stark contrast to the continued urban deprivation of Britain's Pakistani and Bangladeshi population. Some integrationists have rather ingenuously celebrated these findings by arguing how Indians are following a 'Jewish' path to socially mobile integration, while West Indians and Pakistanis follow an 'Irish' path into social disadvantage and underachievement. Self-flattering comparisons have also been drawn in new research attempting to link up these findings with integration studies in the USA. However, the misguided turn to North America for self-comparison misses the point about the far more urgent and realistic need to relate British experiences to other European ones.

All is not settled, though, within the patchwork of 'official' ethnic groups established by the ethnic question of the 1991 census (see pp. 119–20). There is strong lobbying going on for the inclusion of white ethnic groups within the controversial ethnic self-identification question: notably, to provide a mechanism for identifying the 'racial' discrimination felt by the Irish-origin population in Britain, and for recognising the large but mostly invisible Jewish population. As in the USA, the opening up of the Pandora's box of whiteness may prove a fatal step in the undermining of existing race relations mechanisms, which depend on identifying racially distinct ethnic groups in relation to norms of social mobility achieved by the majority 'white' population. Nobody denies discrimination against the Irish: but it is sheer foolishness to call this 'racial' in nature, rendering the term meaningless in other cases. Moreover, these ways of identifying the object of integration policies fail entirely to reflect the significant and growing populations of other ethnic groups in Britain, who do not figure among the official, recognised list of minorities: the various South East Asian nationalities lumped together under the category of Chinese; Turkish and Kurdish refugees; the very large Iranian population in London; Bosnians and others from the former Yugoslavia; or indeed the growing population of central European Roma (gypsies). These archetypal consequences of 'new' migration patterns, then, are still those that find little or no recognition within the existing set up, even if they are generating significant social problems that fall outside of the post-colonial race relations paradigm.

It is no surprise then, that the single most significant event to have shaken the race relations scene in Britain was in every way a classic 'race' issue, repeating former patterns of public concern about racial discrimination and inter-racial violence.

The enormous public reaction to police incompetence surrounding the investigation of the death of Stephen Lawrence – a young black teenager murdered in a racial attack in South London – may indeed prove a significant watershed. For the first time, it saw the mainstream media squarely endorse the rage of the black community at the institutionalised racism in the police force it revealed. The day the *Sun* or *Daily Mail* begin to fulminate on the iniquities of racism in Britain is indeed a day when some genuine idea of a multi-racial Britain can be said to be taking hold. Yet, as John Solomos pointed out in a recent commentary on the affair, it was an event very inadequately reflected in the current, abstract concerns of social theorists of race, gender and identity in Britain, centred on cultural studies debates about 'new ethnicities' and celebrations of 'resistance' or 'hybridity'. They had need, he argues, to return to a much more empirical political sociology of race and ethnic relations, that should be charted through the dynamics of political competition and the evolution of public institutions and organisations. *Philosophies of Integration* responds directly to this demand; a response to mainstream academic shortcomings most nakedly exposed, I would argue, by the lack of comparative cross-national knowledge displayed in any of the texts by leading cultural studies theorists in Britain (such as Hall, Gilroy, or Brah).

But perhaps the most glaring symptom of Britain's persistent insularity on questions of immigration and race, is the fact that the affirmative discussions of race after the Lawrence affair continue to be seen as an entirely separate issue from public debates and reflection on immigration issues classified under the heading of asylum and refugees. In the latter half of the 1990s, Britain found itself pressurised to open its doors to new refugee claims, reversing its significant lag *vis à vis* its European neighbours. However, the new *de facto* openness has not seen the policy making atmosphere become any more gracious or constructive, and certainly not any more rights-based in its logic. Rather, acting under presumption of British sovereignty in this matter, recent refugees have been routinely portrayed by the press and government alike as undeserving scroungers, a menace to public order (particularly in local contexts such as Dover and Folkestone) and linked with high profile security concerns about trafficking and international crime networks. The New Labour government has followed its predecessors' populist strategy, pursuing an even stricter Immigration and Asylum Act of its own (1999), that tightens the right of asylum seekers to work or claim benefits, and institutionalises unworkable policies of dispersal around Britain. The failure to match up to international standards on these questions indicates the consequences of Britain's go-it-alone attitude on immigration questions in Europe, and its refusal to recognise 'new' non-Commonwealth, and sometimes temporary migrants, as an integral part of the ethnic minority population in Britain, or a part of the 'multiculturalism in one nation' that progressive post-war policy makers have sought to build (see p. 115).

To all this, British specialists are likely to retort: 'But we *are* different! We are an island after all!'. For sure, one cannot argue with the geographical determinants of Britain's place in Europe. But this does not excuse the persistent British attitude that 'Europe' is something that very easily gets 'cut off by fog in the channel' (to paraphrase a famous old newspaper headline); any more than it excuses the lack of political will that causes the Eurostar train to slow to a third of its top speed – and even be overtaken by local commuter trains – the moment it comes out of the chunnel on the way to London. Britain may be getting a little less 'rabid' in its logic of self-imposed isolation on immigration and integration policy: the Labour government has even begun to address the most absurd of British idiosyncrasies by removing quarantine restrictions for pets from the continent (see pp. 202–3). But there is a long way to go before the British show some intellectual generosity to their neighbours and open themselves to the European-wide experience of migration and ethnic diversity. On these questions, the rest of Europe, ultimately, has as much to teach Britain as Britain has to contribute to the continent, on discussions about anti-discrimination and the management of multicultural diversity.

France's relation to Europe is less ambiguous than the British: it knows, fundamentally, that it has no other option in the long run but to embed itself in the wider European political project. Yet on immigration and integration questions, it too has pursued a defiantly nationalist line: claiming, like Britain, a privileged independence of self-definition on questions relating to the particularities of the French universalist tradition, and its self-styled achievement of a very culturally specific form of *intégration*. So in the last few years, can we still say that it has been a case of *plus ça change* ....?

It is clear that the tone and language of debate in France remains fairly constant. Whether it is the ongoing discussions on nationality and naturalisation, on the place of Islam, or the merits of the French idea of individualist equality *vis á vis* the so-called *communautarisme* of the British, Germans or Americans, the French are still determinedly pursuing issues defined in national rather than internationalist terms. In particular, this has isolated French campaigners from the emerging discussions at the European level on creating anti-discrimination provisions in European legislation, and on the development of multicultural programmes. Here, indeed, it was a specifically Anglo–Dutch coalition (notably the Starting Line Group and the Dutch Standing Committee of Experts on Immigration Law) who made the most decisive interventions into the IGC process. It is also these groups who now monopolise lobbying in Brussels and Strasbourg. The mainstream terms of debate in France remain extremely hostile to the use of what they bizarrely refer to as 'anglo-saxon' terminology on immigration and integration: particularly anything to do with 'multiculturalism' or 'ethnicity'. This is despite the fact that at local levels, communes pursue policies – such as through the *Fonds d'Action Sociale* – which look very much like state-promoted multiculturalism. Moreover, demographers and sociologists are slowly beginning to realise that they need to introduce some sort of 'ethnic' classification, in order to identify the growing population of immigration-origin French nationals of the second and third generation (see pp. 71–3, 161–2). It was remarkable, however, just how much flak a team, led by demographer Michèle Tribalat, encountered in the press for taking a small step in this direction, when completing a state-of-the-art survey by INED (the National Institute for Demographic Studies), *De l'immigration à l'assimilation* (1996).

In other ways, there have been some surprises. First, was the remarkable turn around in political fortunes, with the surprise victory of the Socialist party under Lionel Jospin in the parliamentary elections of 1997, and his strong showing in the presidential election. This forced the right prematurely out of power, pre-empting a dramatic fragmentation of the right wing and conservative parties and leaving Chirac as a rather lame duck *cohabitation* president. Moreover, some real party differences have emerged on the question of immigration and integration, with the open rejection by the new government of the Pasqua laws of 1994 (see pp. 152–9). Characteristically, of course, number one priority – for reasons explained in my study – was to re-open the whole symbolic issue of nationality law once again. This time round, Jospin called on the internationally-minded public policy scholar Patrick Weil to lead the expert reflections, signalling a shift away from the big ideological questions of past proposals to a more pragmatic attitude about the management of migrant demands and the implementations of new laws. At around the same time, Sami Naïr presented a similarly pragmatic report on the need for France to take a positive pro-active role in discouraging migration by increased development aid and trade links to Africa, rather than physical border controls. Weil's report, meanwhile, rejected the accent on voluntarism that was so strong in previous Commissions, arguing forcefully about the failed practicalities and inequalities of this method of attributing nationality. The new laws passed in 1998 reinstated an automatic attribution of *ius soli* to second generation migrant children. At the same time, the *Haut Conseil à l'Intégration* now also chaired by Weil, drew up quite revolutionary plans to introduce new forms of anti-discrimination legislation in France. These began to recognise the need to attack racism as a civil rather than a criminal issue, in which individuals and organisations could be prosecuted for direct and indirect discrimination in areas such as housing and employment.

In this new atmosphere, it is noticeable how public debates on the problems of integration have shifted away, again, from the cultural issues raised by the *affaire du foulard* and Islam in France back towards more socio-economic issues about poverty and exclusion. This displays a growing recognition that the problems of the *banlieues* – particularly the spectacular series of riots seen in provincial cities such as Lyon, Lille and Strasbourg – point towards failures in the philosophy of integration that cannot be put down to cultural differences alone. In the widely seen film by Matthieu Kassovitz, *La Haine* (1995), the mixed race threesome of *banlieue* youth represent a generation socially and spatially excluded from the bourgeois life of the big city, not some cultural stereotypes. Intellectual debate accordingly has focused on addressing the problems of the periphery *cités* with new state interventionist policies. The urban sociologist, Sophie Body-Gendrot, presented a report (1998) which underlined the drift away from cultural concerns to the kind of urban issues that have long preoccupied social policy on inequality in Britain or the USA.

The socio-economic turn also chimes well with the emergence of a new intellectual movement in Paris, led by Pierre Bourdieu, which reaffirms a near-Marxist sociological drive in its thinking. This movement explicitly rejects the whole generation of media *philosophes* – notably those figures associated with the *Fondation Saint Simon*, such as Todd, Taguieff and Schnapper – whose ideology of republican citizenship dominated discussions on integration in the early 1990s. The journal and bestselling series of polemics under the title *Liber* have instigated a small publishing revolution in Paris. The movement's most subversive act has not been its rather naive declarations of solidarity for the trade unions (in which the ghost of Sartre rides again), but the clever way it has engaged the press and television media. Bourdieu and others now only accept interviews on condition that journalists allow the intellectuals to speak and develop arguments on air that are not compressed into the usual 20-second soundbites, and where they have editorial control on the content. The sheer presence of intellectualism in French public life never ceases to impress when compared to other European countries, such as Britain, where the intellectual class are well nigh irrelevant in public political discussions (Anthony Giddens' bland role in the formulation of Blair's ideas on the 'third way' is the weak exception which proves the rule). Yet, objectively, it has to be noted that other forces dictate that the intellectual influence in Paris, as in other national contexts, is in inexorable decline.

The outcome of the grassroots *sans papiers* movement (see p. 172) also revealed a new edge to French immigration politics, introducing significant critical arguments about international human rights and 'personhood' into a French debate normally dominated by nationally-bounded normative considerations. Part of this, has been the growing recognition of racially-inflected integration questions associated with the place of black African migrants, rather than the cultural discrimination directed at Islam and North Africans. In the face of a still popular public backlash against excessively anti-immigrant views on the right, even the *Front national* has found itself divided on its future strategy, with deputy Bruno Mégret splitting with Le Pen over his refusal to move the party towards a less isolated position in the political spectrum. With Le Pen still banging the old anti-immigrant line, it was heartening to see the way in which a victorious France embraced its remarkably multi-racial and multi-ethnic football team in the 1998 World Cup, which was seen as embodying the very spirit and achievement of French ideas of citizenship and integration.

It would be wrong to deny the French their own triumph on this point, just as it is wrong to deny the small miracle by which something like the Notting Hill carnival in London has changed from being a dark threat to national public order, to becoming a tourist board bonanza and symbol of all that is best about the cosmopolitan capital city. Paris matches London all the way in its own startlingly multi-racial feel at the turn of the century. The real challenge here is not to compare them as places which embody the essence of the nations in which they are situated, but rather to understand just how these genuinely global cities have come to coexist in such stark contrast to the provincialism of the rest of the country around them. The gap was never better symbolised than in the ironic discussions about why London should secede from the rest of Britain, when its strongly liberal, cosmopolitan and modernist leanings were rudely challenged by a series of huge protests by 'countryside campaigners' descending on the capital. Similar things might be said about the startlingly reactionary attitudes of French agriculteurs, hunters and lorry drivers in the face of reformist government plans. France, like Britain, is going through a period of intense self-reflection about what it is as a cultural unity. As devolution has proceeded apace in Britain, so France finds itself seeking new self-definitions that square with a less centralised and more globalised world. This is not to deny the continued part that atavistic nationalist reaction plays in the two countries. The food war of autumn 1999, that blocked beef and other products on both sides of the channel, revealed a dramatically isolationist turn in Britain. In the same way, the anti-McDonalds and anti-Americanisation campaigns of 1999 in France, played on the worst kinds of hypocritical French chauvinism. The suspicion still is that both countries may be in fact fair-weather Europeans and internationalists, only too ready to snap back into nationalist self-defensive mode when cross-national co-operation goes wrong in some way.

The European agenda, then, continues to be pushed by other countries, ready to accept that immigration and asylum co-operation has to be the order of the day in an interdependent Europe gearing itself up for further enlargement. The product of these negotiations, traced through the Amsterdam Treaty (June 1997), the Vienna Declaration on migration and asylum (July 1998) and the meeting on Justice and Home Affairs at Tampere (October 1999), has been an ever stronger focus on security and policing issues on immigration and asylum, with some slower progressive developments on the rights of third country nationals in Europe, anti-discrimination and managing labour migration flows. Among academics, there has been much misplaced reflection on the possibilities of 'European citizenship' developing for third country nationals in Europe; in fact, the kinds of rights for such non-nationals envisaged by citizenship-focused scholars are far more likely to be satisfied by easier and more consistent access for resident foreigners to full naturalisation of member states. As widening the community via enlargement becomes the main priority, it is likely that citizenship issues will take a back seat to the more basic questions of free movement of labour and trade, back and forth across newly opened borders in East and Central Europe. The evidence so far is that the prognosis regarding manageable migration is good for Poland, Hungary, the Czech Republic and other countries in the front line to accession. That is, open borders are encouraging more people to return to or stay in these countries rather than join any imagined 'flood' of migrants from East to West and that this will have a significant positive impact on the economic and cultural development of these countries.

As well as underlining a growing concern with these fundamental migration issues, the presidency conclusions of the Tampere meeting also signalled that the Commission intends to take a more direct and active role in the integration of

immigrants across Europe. It is difficult, however, to see how
this might happen either legally or politically. Integration
questions – about culture, language, education, the place of
religion, or anti-discrimination in housing and employment –
are still so clearly the practical domain of national government and their local agencies. The European Union has little
or no competencies in these areas, nor is it likely to be given
to them: they are issues so inevitably connected to nation-
building in the traditional sense. There is no avoiding the conclusion that the nation-state is still the dominant form of social
organisation in Europe; and it is to comprehensive cross-national comparison that most research efforts should still be directed.

The goal of genuinely cross-national comparative work on
integration across Europe is however a distant one. The data
and categories for comparison of migrants and minorities in
each country are still so incompatible and so shaped by local
national debates and considerations, that the field is still a
largely empty one. The most promising development would
seem to be the growing focus, not on comparing nation-states,
but on comparing cities and the migrants who populate them.
Cities are the arena where the newest and sharpest developments are first observed, and where there is a degree of cross-
national convergence on both policy problems and policy
solutions, that belies many of the differences reflected in national ideological debates. It is at this level also that the new
research agenda on transnationalism and the 'globalisation of
place' makes some sense. Paris, London, Amsterdam, Brussels,
Berlin and Milan, among others, have become multicultural
cities in ways quite unexpected and unintended by national
governmental policy makers, and each requires attention to
its specificities within a national, regional and international
context, in order to explain how.

As well as crossing national boundaries, it is also my hope
that this is a work that moves freely across the boundaries of
academic disciplines, and which may speak equally to sociologists, political scientists, anthropologists and geographers interested in seeing these particular national cases within a
wider European and transatlantic context. At the same time, it
is disappointing to note how little interest it has attracted
among what was originally my primary target readership:

moral and political philosophers interested in applying abstract theories on multiculturalism and citizenship to specific case study material from actual existing liberal democracies. It would seem with one or two notable exceptions – Will Kymlicka and Rainer Bauböck, for example – that the current generation of political philosophers are finding it difficult to make the leap into genuinely applying moral and political philosophy to the real world. At best, philosophers tend to only engage in anecdotal debate about how to solve 'hard cases' of multiculturalism, ripping their examples (or 'thought experiments') out of the contextual circumstances that give them meaning. *Philosophies of Integration* was an attempt to do something rather more sustained and empirically systematic. As an invitation to philosophical readers, then, it might be pointed out how a selective reading of the text can systematically relate the evidence from the two empirical studies to the core concerns of political philosophy. The methodology I pursue, in fact explains how abstract philosophical notions can be observed at work in the dynamic of ideas in party politics and policy making. Moreover, the extensive index included with the text has been designed with precisely this in mind: by following up references under the heading of 'ideas in politics' or 'reasoning, forms of', a long line of philosophical themes in action can be traced through my analysis of the French and British cases.

One or two people teased me about the extraordinary length of thank-yous included in the Preface to the first edition. I can offer no excuses or apologies for this: they were all necessary, and I am still very grateful! My point here was that a book such as this, although the product of a long and lonely writing process, is also a hugely interpersonal enterprise, that bears both the obvious imprint and the subtle influence of countless encounters, discussions and moments of behind-the-scenes encouragement, in all kinds of privileged and special academic environments. As well as thanking again those who made it such a formative experience the first time round, I would like to thank a number of other people who have enabled me to take my work further in the last few years. First, my thanks to colleagues at ERCOMER, Utrecht, where I was a funded research fellow of the European Union's Marie Curie Training and Mobility of Researchers programme; to friends in the Netherlands and Belgium who have opened my mind to a whole new set of nationally-specific issues and studies in the last couple of years; to Doug Klusmeyer and Alex Aleinikoff at the Carnegie Endowment for International Peace for asking me to contribute to the 'Comparative Citizenship Project'; and to colleagues, researchers and students at the Sussex Centre for Migration Research and School of European Studies at the University of Sussex, where I have been very happily working since January 1999. I must thank also the numerous individuals who have given me so much support and encouragement during this period: particularly Michèle Lamont, Rogers Brubaker, Cristiano Codagnone, Karen Phalet, Dirk Jacobs, Hassan Bousetta, Randall Hansen, Erik Bleich, Carl-Ulrik Schierup, Martin Schain, Romain Garbaye, Paul Statham, John Solomos, Didier Bigo and Elspeth Guild. Like so many people, I will sadly miss the generosity and spirit of Vincent Wright. Finally, I would like to thank my publishers for all their hard work on my behalf, particularly Tim Farmiloe, Annabelle Buckley and Eleanor Birne who have made this second edition possible.

Preface

This book began life one grey February day in a French *collège* in the inner city ZEP of Châteauroux. A bunch of *beurs gouailleurs*, my *troisième* class of 15-year-olds for the afternoon, rolled into class, laughing and jostling after lunch at home in the nearby housing project. They told me that some Iranian priest had pronounced a world-wide death sentence on an English writer for a book he had written. The kids thought it was hilarious, and asked me what I thought.

I didn't really know then, and several years later, I still don't. Yet I have grown to recognise the confused feeling of angst, ignorance and righteous indignation, as characteristic of the bonfire of liberal certainties that the Rushdie case – and other symbols of the western world's problem with Islam and cultural pluralism in recent years – represented. This is a hellishly difficult subject to come to any kind of ethical or political standpoint on, but it did – as everyone kept telling me – make for excellent PhD material. The philosophical search for a pluralist liberal 'theory of my own' eventually gave way to a more focused, empirical study of national policies and ideas about the issues at stake, and all kinds of other academic interests were plugged in and out of the research problem in the meantime. But I still like to think of this project as some kind of personal response to the original question.

My book also represents a response to the other damaging problem of cultural difference that has preoccupied me increasingly in recent years: the inability of European nations to understand each others' distinct perspectives and patterns of thought about common European problems. Those looking to find fashionably cynical Euro-sceptic conclusions in this book will be disappointed. There can hardly be anything more dismaying for European citizens of Britain than to watch the continual arrogance and stupidity with which the 'European question' is discussed by all sides there. France, in recent years, has not been far behind in its inward-looking obsessions with archaic post-colonial myths and self-conceptions. My effort to translate comparatively the French and British viewpoints on citizenship and immigration is then my own little gesture of European harmonisation. I can at least hope it might help stop French and British commentators on the subject talking straight past each other.

As befits the scope of the subject, this is a wilfully interdisciplinary piece of work that I have carried with me through all kinds of seminars and venues. Many of the people I talked to about it were unclear what it was I was trying to do, but it is highly symptomatic of the question that all were able to call upon their own concerns and reflections on the issues involved. The work first took shape at the University of East Anglia, Norwich, as part of my attempt to combine a degree in comparative literature and philosophy. I owe much to my teachers there for the subsequent course of my academic research, particularly Martin Scott-Taggart, Martin Hollis, Tim O'Hagan, Peter Hobbis, Robert Clark, Neil MacMaster, Elinor Shaffer and Dani Limon. In the years since, all kinds of other people made important suggestions and comments on the work in progress. I am particularly grateful for the encouragement I received in the early stages from John Dunn, Avishai Margalit, David Nicholls, Rainer Bauböck and Tom Heller. Meetings with Katherine O'Donovan, Giovanna Zincone, Françoise Lorcerie, Yasemin Soysal, Miriam Feldblum, Marco Martiniello, Anne Phillips, John Crowley, Will Kymlicka, Wayne Norman and Richard Tuck added significant elements to the finished work. I also owe a special word of thanks to Bhikhu Parekh, Jean Leca and John Rex for their longstanding support.

A period spent in the United States was of critical importance to the final direction the research talk. I am very grateful for the discussions I had with the late James Coleman, William Julius Wilson, Clifford Geertz, Russell Hardin, Rosemary Taylor and Todd Gitlin, and the many people I met at the University of California, Berkeley, particularly, Loïc Wacquant, Neil Fligstein, Troy Duster, Michael Omi, Hanna Pitkin, Robert Bellah, Paul Rabinow, Sam Scheffler, Beth Bernstein and Chris Rhomberg. In France, I owe thanks to Michel Oriol, Jean-Marc Zaïdi, Riva Kastoryano, Jean-Pierre Worms, Jacqueline Costa-Lascoux, Sophie Body-Gendrot, Eleni Varikas, Michel Wieviorka, Albano Cordeiro and Catherine Neveu. I hope my French readers will not be too dismayed by what I have to say about France: a country I love and am exasperated by in about equal proportion. Towards Britain, I feel even more 'conflicted' – although rather less indulgent about its European nation-state idiosyncrasies. I am grateful to Shamit Saggar, Tariq Modood, Malcolm Cross, Harry Goulbourne, Michael Banton and Andrew Geddes for their help.

And then there are my many 'institutional' debts. The final version was written as a *chercheur invité* of the Centre d'étude de la vie politique française (CEVIPOF), Paris, a very kind invitation for which I must thank Pascal Perrineau. I am also grateful to Patrick Weil for his help at the Institut d'études politiques. I would like to acknowledge the funding of the Leverhulme Trust, London for the year spent in Paris. For the period prior to this, I must thank Philippe van Parijs and everyone at the Chaire Hoover d'éthique économique et sociale, Louvain-la-Neuve, for six very enjoyable months in Belgium as a fellow there. These travels have made it a little easier to stop missing my home before this. The European University Institute, Florence was a wonderful place to spend four years. It provided me with the mental distance needed to write with a new perspective on the internal politics of France and Britain, and a great deal of support for research abroad. It is also a uniquely international and co-operative graduate school. Numerous friends read the work in progress, and questioned or commented on it. Thanks especially are due to Simon Hix, Damian Tambini, John Stanton-Ife, Davide Sparti, Chris Woodard, Ben Crum, Benoît Guiguet, Beth Ginsburg, Ferruccio Pastore and Vladimir Gradev. I must also thank Eva Breivik, Marie-Ange Catotti and Nancy Altobelli for all the help they gave me during my time there. Christian Joppke was, as well as being my toughest critic, an enormously encouraging and attentive reader. Giandomenico Majone and Yves Mény both helped me greatly with detailed critical readings. And a special thanks is due to my two main mentors there – Steven Lukes and Alessandro Pizzorno – in whose brilliant seminars most of my main ideas and interests took shape.

Finally, a special *merci* to Virginie Guiraudon, who made the single biggest difference to my work and had the last word.

ADRIAN FAVELL

Glossary

a priori	reasoning by principles alone, not empirical consequences
affaire du foulard	the headscarves affair, Autumn 1989
alterité	otherness
ancien régime	pre-revolutionary royalist regime
anomie	anomie, lit. without norms (cf. Durkheim)
auto-da-fé	book-burning, lit. burning of heretics
antillais	French West Indian
banlieues	suburbs, often deprived housing projects
beurs	young North African French (*verlan*)
bicentenaire	200th anniversary of 1789 revolution
brassage	intermixing, lit. brewing
cadre	frame
carte d'identité	identity card
charif	Muslim head of mosque
citoyen	citizen
citoyenneté	citizenship
clandestins	illegal immigrants/aliens
cohabitation	period of mixed left/right political power
communautarisme	communitarianism, allowing distinct ethnic minorities
creuset français	French melting pot

décalage	gap, discrepancy, inconsistency
département	French region/county (for example, la Creuse)
dérapage	slipping and sliding, lit. skid
dictats	imposed rules from on high
différence	difference, for example, cultural (also phil. sense)
distinction	self-distinction, for example, by education (cf. Bourdieu)
droit	right, law
droit à la différence	the right to be different
émigré(s)	emigrants
énarques	graduates of l'Ecole nationale d'administration (ENA)
encadrement	framing, fixing
enracinement	the putting down of roots
enjeu	the thing at stake
étranger	foreigner, stranger, outsider
excision	female circumcision
foulard	Islamic headscarf
grandes surfaces	large warehouse-type shopping store
Hexagone (l')	France, lit. the hexagon-shaped country
immigré(s)	immigrants
insertion	socio-economic insertion into society
ius sanguinis (droit du sang)	citizenship by bloodline
ius soli (droit du sol)	citizenship by birth on territory
jihad	Islamic struggle or holy war

jusqu'au bout	to the end
laïcité	secularism, separation of church and state
laissez faire	non-interventory state policies
langue de bois	inflexible ideological language, lit. wooden language
libéralisme	free market liberalism (not American sense)
longue durée	the historical long run, long tradition (cf. Braudel)
lumières (les)	the enlightenment tradition
mauvaise foi	self deception, lit. bad faith (cf. Sartre)
modèle (français; anglo-saxon, etc.)	political model/idea (French, Anglo-American, etc.)
modus vivendi	live and let live social arrangement (cf. Hobbes)
nationalité réussie	proven and successful nationality status
pieds noirs	white French settlers in Algeria
problématique	intellectual problem
rapports	official government reports
repli sur soi-même	turning in on oneself (e.g. on one's own culture)
République du centre	centrist republic (end of left/right ideological clash)
ressentiment	resentment of those of power (cf. Nietzsche)
sans domicile fixe	homeless
sans papiers	illegal residents, lit. without papers
seuil de tolérance	limit of toleration, lit. threshold

Glossary

soixante-huitards	generation of 1968
surenchère	double or quits strategy, lit. bid higher
telos	historical line to pre-destined future
umma	worldwide Muslim community
verlan	North African French backwards slang
volonté	free will/choice
zeitgeist	spirit of the times

1 Liberal Democracies and their Ethnic Dilemmas

One of the defining characteristics of the 1980s and 1990s has surely been the dramatic emergence of various 'ethnic dilemmas' across western society, that appear to challenge the theory and practice of liberal democratic politics.[1] There are numerous different problems of a racial or cultural origin that could be thought of in this way: the emergence or reemergence of ethnic, cultural or religious movements among minority groups; the reappearance of overtly racist and xenophobic attitudes among majority populations; the continuing difficulties of race relations, and the appearance of the so-called multicultural society; and, at the strongest extreme, the threat of separatist movements and claims of self-determination to the integrity of federal or nation-states. In the countries of Western Europe, many of these problems have been brought on by post-war immigration, and the integration of new ethnic groups who came and stayed.

In response to these developments, there has been a spate of public and intellectual debate across the western world about the meaning and content of *citizenship*. Everybody is talking about citizenship because these problems pose very fundamental questions about the unifying values, cohesion and identity of liberal democratic states. They also challenge the liberal standards these societies are supposed to live up to. Does the treatment of distinct ethnic groups match up to the ideals of liberty, equality, toleration or justice that liberal democracy is meant to embody? Or are these ideals far from the reality of political practice? Put this way, there ought to be a way of 'reading' the policy challenges that ethnic dilemmas pose – and the applied 'solutions' found by different liberal democratic states – as a kind of litmus test of the nature of liberal democracy generally. The reaction of liberal democracies to these problems will reveal the grounds on which they may fairly claim to have political *legitimacy* as tolerant, open or pluralist

1

states. At the same time, practical liberal democratic responses will also highlight the constraints of open party politics or legal and technocratic intervention, and hence the harsher realities and failures of the liberal democratic ideal. With these thoughts in mind, how might such a reading be made?

COMPARING PHILOSOPHIES OF INTEGRATION: FRANCE AND BRITAIN

My idea is to take as examples of pluralist liberal democracy in practice, the distinct political responses that two West European societies – France and Britain – have developed. These are responses designed to deal with the political, social and moral dilemmas posed by the integration of various ethnic and racial groups, particularly those of Muslim origin. I focus on the politics and policy-making process that have taken place in the two countries over these questions during the last thirty years or so, and the central institutions that have emerged for dealing with them. In France, the dominant policy framework addresses the country's ethnic dilemmas in terms of republican ideas of *citoyenneté* and *intégration*. Britain, meanwhile, addresses similar problems in terms of the management of *race relations* and *multiculturalism*.

These two frameworks can be found to rest on rather different 'philosophies', based on contrasting understandings of core concepts such as citizenship, nationality, pluralism, autonomy, equality, public order and tolerance. These elements fit together as a kind of underlying public political theory – a 'public philosophy' – founded on a set of consensual ideas and linguistic terms held across party political lines, that can be analysed into its respective normative and explanatory goals and assumptions. Essentially then, the two nations' political solutions can be read as distinct applied versions of philosophical liberalism, which both, in their own way, respond to a very fundamental question of social and political theory. This question is of Hobbesian vintage. How can a political system achieve stability and legitimacy by rebuilding communal bonds of civility and tolerance – a moral social order – across the conflicts and divisions caused by the plurality of values and individual interests?[2] It is this that I define as the problem of *integration*. This is an area of public policy characterised both by the paradoxical dilemmas it sets for the conventional principles of western liberal democracy, and the controversy and under-determination of scientific knowledge about race, culture and ethnicity or the securing of social order in pluralist societies.

I use the term 'integration' mainly because it has been used publicly in both France and Britain to characterise their progressive-minded, tolerant and inclusive approaches to dealing with ethnic minorities. As a concept, its theoretical origins run deep. It dates back to the American functionalist solution to the Hobbesian problem of value pluralism, worked out in the sociology of Talcott Parsons, which synthesised the sociological traditions of Weber and Durkheim. Here, the society's need for an order that overcomes conflict and differences pulls a harmonious, socially inclusive unity based on 'value integration'. The Chicago school of urban sociology then popularised the application of the idea of integration to the study of race and ethnicity, and its use as a conceptual framework for public policies.[3] In their use, however, it has a predominantly assimilatory sense, describing the integration achieved through neutral 'colour blind' institutions, which work as a machine-like 'system': imposing unity through a process which passes from initial contact between minority and majority groups, through conflict and transformation, to the final goal of assimilation. It is not without irony, then, that the term has been picked up in the recent French and British debates.

As my formulation suggests, the fundamental theoretical question concerns more than just the integration of new ethnic minorities. It is as much a general question about the 'glue' of a particularly society – in each case here, a nation – across its wider cultural, regional and class divisions. The problematic of immigration has indeed been highly symbolic in raising, as a live political issue, this more general question about the unity and order of the nation, and the public myths and traditions that hold it together. This is partly to do with the new kinds of cultural and political behaviour new immigrants have been seen to introduce; partly to do with the inherently international dimension of migration and the social change it provokes. The responses of France and Britain, as befits their respective colonial reputations, appear to be almost reversed mirror images of one other: France emphasising the universalist idea of integration, of transforming immigrants into full French *citoyens*; Britain seeing integration as a question of managing public order and relations between majority and minority populations, and allowing ethnic cultures and practices to mediate the process.

I take it as axiomatic that ethnic dilemmas are not just a political *problem*, but that, dealt with in the right way, they can be a resource of social progress and diversity. The thought is that a feasible multi-ethnic diversity makes everyone better off. Failure to achieve the right framework for integration, however, will lead to an increase in intolerance and xenophobia among majority populations, and a loss of 'moral social order'. This raises the comparative question: which national framework is the better way? This is a valid question, but not necessarily one with a direct answer. Britain and France's rather comparable levels of development and experience would need to be compared with a broader canvas of liberal institutional solutions to the same questions: with other post-colonial nations such as Germany and the Benelux countries; new immigration countries in Scandinavia or Southern Europe; and traditional settler countries such as Canada, Australia or the USA. My conclusions here, in fact, consider Britain and France in relation to potential international solutions to the same questions that might yet be developed at a co-operative European level. Their peculiar, nationally bounded solutions have indeed been rather resistant to this line of development, and they have rather arrogantly tried to impose their national policy frameworks on the less-compatible new dilemmas emerging across Europe. It is both ironic and disconcerting that the two states most 'experienced' in problems of immigration and integration have proved to be those most obstructive to the co-operation and development of policies on these questions at the European level.

A NOTE ON THEORY AND METHODOLOGY

This is a determinedly *interdisciplinary* study. In its appropriation of theoretical tools for the comparative study of public policies in this field, I range across questions often considered in very different ways by social and political theorists, sociologists or political scientists. What I hope to have established in the theoretical approach I set up is a framework for an important but missing academic dialogue between these different disciplinary approaches. The empirical field of study I use – the contemporary politics of immigration and citizenship in Europe – is thus an illustration of an approach that might potentially be applied to other areas of public policy. I have, however, kept the theoretical frame as informal and accessible as possible, while indicating the range of works it is built up on. In order to enable a sensitive comparison of the two national cases, I have also sought to illustrate my recognisably general theoretical model with an approach based on the kind of interpretative 'thick description' – combining textual analysis and phenomenological detail – more familiar to comparatist studies in the humanities. The ongoing trench warfare in the social sciences between quantitative and qualitative methods or scientific and humanistic approaches is, I believe, to the impoverishment of all. Any adequate comparative work in fact needs to be highly flexible and fraternal in its methodological approaches, if it is not to denature the case study material it seeks to compare.

My main effort then has been to make sense of the conceptual terms and language which constitute the medium of the public policies in each case, and translate them into a simple theoretical frame that might enable wider comparison with other national or international cases. The policy frameworks in each country are thus 'read' in my analysis from the kind of public ideas and justifications used by political actors and commentators to create and maintain coherent political solutions. I draw upon the work of influential intellectuals and academics, high-level political discussion and formulation, legal jurisprudence and, where appropriate, the reflection of these arguments in public discourse. Clearly, I have had to use a good deal of interpretative judgement in deciding which texts or documents are the most revealing and representative. Those I use are in fact all very familiar and oft-quoted texts in the two countries. My main justification for this is a heuristic one. I also concentrate throughout, therefore, on re-organising and making sense of the large amount of available secondary literature and documentation in a way that might finally enable meaningful comparison and criticism of French and British perspectives. As I will indicate throughout, the vast majority of secondary works in fact simply confirms and reproduces the nationally bounded perspectives on the policy questions at stake. It is in fact often necessary to read these 'scientific' works against the grain, as both carriers and symptoms of the ideas and conceptualisations found in the two countries. I have indicated throughout, however, works which do manage to transcend the bounded national perspectives, and thereby contribute to a better cross-national comparative understanding. With all this put together, I believe the general comparative framework I offer not only makes better sense of the dominant policies in the two countries, but also illustrates the theoretical usefulness of combining normative and explanatory concerns.

OUTLINE OF CHAPTERS

This study is made up of two rounds of case study material, prefaced by a theoretical introduction. General readers, less interested in comparative problems or the reasoning behind my theoretical approach, might wish to pass straight on to the case study chapters. They can easily be read as self-contained essays. In Chapter 2, my theoretical introduction, I set out my reasoning for combining normative and explanatory concerns in the study of public policy, and how philosophical issues can be brought closer to the empirical study of politics and institutions. I go on to set out a simple general model of the evolution of policies of immigration and integration in the two countries, and the emergence of a dominant political consensus in each case. I then introduce the theoretical apparatus for studying how such a consensus can have negative effects over time, through an application of the concept of 'path dependency': what I call the study of 'institutional pathologies'. In Chapters 3 and 4, the first round of case studies, I seek to narrate sympathetically the party politics and institutional dynamics by which a dominant policy framework was established in the two countries, and analyse the core foundational ideas, theoretical assumptions and end-goals that make up the respective 'public philosophies'. In Chapters 5 and 6, the second round, I then go on to explain recent developments or problems that have been caused in some way by the terms of the existing framework, notably heated discussion about reform of immigration and nationality law, and high profile events such as *l'affaire du foulard* and the Rushdie affair. My aim here is to question the continued effectiveness and sensitivity of the policy frameworks to new and unexpected circumstances. My reading is mainly critical and indeed punctures the ideal that I have earlier built up in each case. In Chapter 7, the conclusion, I step back from the two cases and consider the general convergent or divergent tendencies in the two countries, and how they look from a wider European perspective.

Notes

1. I borrow the term 'ethnic dilemmas' from Nathan Glazer, *Ethnic Dilemmas 1964–1982* (Cambridge, Mass.: Harvard University Press, 1983).

2. On the Hobbesian problematic, see Jon Elster, *The Cement of Society* (Cambridge University Press, 1989); Michael Taylor, *The Problem of Cooperation* (Cambridge University Press, 1989); and, closest to my approach, Alessandro Pizzorno, 'On the individualistic theory of social order', in P. Bourdieu and J. S. Coleman (eds), *Social Theory for a Changing Society* (Boulder, Colo.: Westview, 1991). My understanding of the concept of 'value pluralism' is the broadly Weberian one, used as a foundational concept in Joseph Raz, *The Morality of Freedom* (Oxford: Clarendon, 1986); and John Rawls, *Political Liberalism* (Princeton, NJ: Princeton University Press, 1993).

3. Talcott Parsons, *The Structure of Social Action* (New York: Free Press, 1937), discussed in Pizzorno, 'On the individualistic theory of social order'. On the Chicago School, see Nathan Glazer, 'The problem of ethnic studies', in his *Ethnic Dilemmas*, pp. 99–100; and Barbara Ballis-Lal, *The Romance of Culture in an Urban Civilization: Robert E. Park on Race and Ethnic Relations in Cities* (London: Routledge, 1990).

2 Public Philosophies as Normative and Explanatory Theories

Like all genuine comparative works, this is a study which aims – via the comparison of two archetypal case studies – to offer very general insights about politics and society in western liberal democracies. The choice of cases could in fact be made from a range of major western societies – a 'G8' as it were of pluralist liberal democracies – that have faced ethnic dilemmas caused by immigration and integration in recent decades. However, France and Britain are an obvious choice of 'most similar cases': two old nations with comparable national political traditions, colonial involvements and post-war immigration. Historically speaking, they are also two countries whose political experiences have been central to the evolution and development of liberal democratic ideas and practice.

Given these similarities, what is most striking about the French and British perspectives is the *prima facie* differences between their respective policy frameworks. There is in both countries a large indigenous social scientific literature, which documents the political and social origins of the current policies, and often engages prescriptively in the ongoing debate about their reform. This literature follows and reflects the very distinct practices and political rhetoric characteristic of the French and British cases. Crudely speaking, French writing follows the republican agenda of citizenship and questions about the political assimilation of culturally distinct *immigrés*; while British writing is concerned with issues of race and racism, the definition and operation of anti-discrimination laws, and the idea of multiculturalism as the best means of accommodating Britain's distinct *ethnic minorities*. The differences in approach make the two cases difficult to bring together in a single comparative focus. To make sense, each needs to be translated into the terms and language of the other.[1]

The comparison must above all be *interpretatively* sensitive because it is more than a question of simply describing the formal laws, policies and institutions found in France and Britain. Politics takes place within language: within argument and rhetoric which divide up, categorise and bound the social and cultural context of the policies, and which constrain and shape their development over time.[2] No study of the policies in France and Britain, for example, could go without reflecting on the significance and consequences of the political taboo in France against distinguishing and counting its immigrant population as 'ethnic minorities' of distinct racial or cultural origin; or the equally extraordinary 'racial' categories that make British anti-discrimination legislation operational. Such factors play integral, *structural* roles in the policy practices of the two countries, and they are not isolated elements. Rather, they are part of a complex framework of ideas and justifications that sustains the policies, and, in some way, is cognitively held and understood by a political consensus in each country which upholds and works within the dominant framework.

Within each country, political actors and commentators are apt to say that there is no consensus on the policies of immigration and integration. Their perspective is, of course, dominated by the local political agenda as they see it, and the need to fight against and distinguish themselves from other actors' political agendas. That there is a consensus, however, in France and in Britain is testified by two otherwise puzzling facts.

First, viewed from the *outside* – a French observer trying to make sense of Britain's idiosyncratic racial and ethnic classification, for example – it is clear that political adversaries in the British debates do in fact agree on the basic terms for identifying the objects and issues of public policy: the existence of distinct racial groups and ethnic minorities, the need for some kind of public recognition of 'multicultural' Britain, and so on. However much they argue, both British Conservatives and Labour Party activists are also likely to agree that the French model of assimilatory republicanism is in *any* case wrong and inferior to the British approach. For this reason, politicians in both countries rarely fail to defend their national 'model' as the best one internationally speaking.

Second, once in place, policy frameworks for ethnic minority policies in both countries have remained remarkably stable.

There would appear to be some deep stakes for all parties concerned in maintaining the overall framework over time, de-
politicising the issue as far as possible, and eliminating wider
political dangers that a new destabilisation or fundamental
change might bring. As I will show, the dominant British framework was able to hold ground in a decade–the 1980s–riven by
political conflict and the breakdown of the post-war political
consensus over many other issues; equally, a new framework
came together in France in nationally unifying terms that over-
came centuries of traditional ideological conflict over the same
ideas. The liberal *settlement* on ethnic minority policies reflects
the threat that the issue of integrating culturally or ethnically
distinct immigrants might expose the fragility of other social
and political ties that keep the whole order of the nation together. This can have both negative and positive effects on the
success of the policy framework. What will be revealed is both
the necessity of an underlying consensus to build progressive
public policy frameworks, and the problems that maintaining a
political consensus can cause over time.

    In this chapter, then, I aim to build a framework that can
make sense of these observations. In the first two sections, I
begin with a review of the literature for this kind of study, from
which I will build my own theoretical approach. I consider the
existing normative and explanatory approaches to the study of
ethnic dilemmas, and then go on to look at the theoretical resources for studying the 'public philosophies' behind politics
in western liberal democracies. In the latter sections, I offer my
own approach. This is in two parts: each section corresponding
roughly to the first and second round of case studies. The first
offers a simple theoretical model of the emergence and recognition of immigration and integration as an important public
problem in contemporary western societies. The second then
goes on to discuss the tools for analysing 'institutional performance' and the phenomenon of 'path dependency' in the evolution of ethnic minority policies.

NORMATIVE AND EXPLANATORY APPROACHES TO THE
STUDY OF ETHNIC DILEMMAS

To build an adequate frame for comparing and evaluating
national public policies of immigration and integration, it is

necessary to step beyond the habitual theoretical and method-ological barriers that prevent the useful combination of differ-ent disciplinary perspectives. The kinds of question I wish to ask are the following. What is the rationale for the policy insti-tutions for dealing with ethnic dilemmas that exist in each country? What are the grounds for their legitimacy as living examples of liberal democracy in practice? In what sense can they be read as progressive institutions, but how can they also be critiqued? How did they emerge from the crucible of party politics? What are their evolutionary dynamics? Is the evolu-tion of policy in different liberal democracies on a convergent or divergent path?

These theoretical questions are my starting point. At a general *normative* level, there is indeed no shortage of recent reflection on the question. Philosophers and theorists have been quick to respond to the new ethnic dilemmas, and have formulated a range of theoretical interpretations. Contemporary political philosophers have approached the dilemmas as problems of 'cultural pluralism': as a classic problematic of liberalism, which reveals the distinctive basic normative requirements of liberal polities in terms of rights, recognition, liberty or equality. The liberal-communitarian debate, in particular, has applied itself to many of these problems, framing them as a question essentially about the reconciliation of cultural diversity and political unity.[3] Democratic theorists, meanwhile, have seen in the same dilem-mas challenges to the limitations of liberal practice, which suggest how a more radical development of citizenship, partici-patory democracy, civil society or social movements might over-come the injustices and exclusions said to be inherent in current liberal democratic forms.[4] If pressed, many philosophers working within these theoretical debates would defend their work as applied 'philosophy and public affairs', in the manner of the famous journal that has been at the heart of the contempo-rary resurgence of political philosophy. Its bold opening 'state-ment of purpose' sums up well the general attitude of theorists towards the idea of applied normative political theory: 'Issues of public concern often have an important philosophical dimen-sion. *Philosophy and Public Affairs* is founded in the belief that a philosophical examination of these issues can contribute to their clarification and their resolution'.

This is certainly a laudable manifesto. However, while many of these theoretical discussions are staged in the light of current political concerns about immigration and integration in different liberal societies, hardly any offer a systematic empirical connection to current political practices and institutions, or the political dynamics which produce them. This is partly because the range of policy frameworks and public conceptualisations found across western societies is too diverse to be captured by any one single theory of pluralist liberal democracy; partly also because philosophers prefer to maintain a critical, *ideal* distance from the societies they have in mind. Critics of the dominant currents of political philosophy have been quick to point out the costs involved in this distance. There is a notorious disconnection between the ideal world of contemporary political philosophy – its happy discourse of rights and justice, or the idealisations of cultural difference and radical democracy – and the actual institutional and technocratic practice of liberal politics. Liberal democracy in reality is a tough and complex world of social policy dilemmas, legal technicalities, border control and census questions.[5] An explicit connection between liberal reflection and liberal practice is generally missing, a fact which distorts the reality philosophers see through their theory.

At the same time, it is far from clear that the current state-of-the-art in the empirical social and political sciences is equipped to address the big and most interesting questions about liberal democracies in the face of their ethnic dilemmas. There are no generally accepted scientific concepts and theories concerning race, ethnicity, nationality or citizenship.[6] The most developed discipline to deal with these questions – the sociology of race and ethnicity – has become increasingly fragmented in recent years. It has seen its empirical core concerns compromised by the growing influence of postmodern 'cultural studies', particularly its post-Marxist, anti-racist and feminist *critique*. These heavily politicised works preach anti-system 'identity politics' and an unmasking of the omnipresent racial, gendered or cultural oppression of familiar liberal politics and institutions. They are thus by definition unable to make anything other than negative and destructive readings of their object of study, and their concerns are disconnected from mainstream empirical approaches to studying the welfare state, party politics or institutional and legal evolution.[7] Moreover, despite a growing focus on studying the

European dimensions of the subject, their theoretical and political conceptualisations often remain rooted in nationally
specific ethnic and racial politics – particularly the anti-racist
concerns of British activists – and are difficult to translate
meaningfully into other national contexts.[8] As such, this has
contributed to the significant lack of reliable and systematic
comparative cross-national studies.

New opportunities for this kind of work have, however,
been opened up by the distinctive research programme
emerging out of the growth in interest – predominantly
among scholars of an American background – in the comparative politics and sociology of immigration and citizenship in
Western Europe. Importing theoretical and methodological
approaches from mainstream comparative disciplines, many
of these works have been able to provide systematic comparisons of European national cases that go a long way to explain
both the existence of national political differences and peculiarities, and the fundamentally similar and convergent mechanisms of policy evolution.[9]

It is perhaps fair to say that these works are still at a first
stage of development. Comparisons have often been made operational by the use of somewhat crude ideas of fixed national
'models' or typologies, and they are on the whole some way
from developing enough interpretative sensitivity to make
fully contextualised comparative studies.[10] Moreover, with one
or two exceptions, these works have to yet to go on to make
connections that need to be made between the politics of immigration and integration, and wider questions of political
economy, welfare, inequality and democracy in Europe. There
is a need to extend their strictly explanatory concerns to ask
what their findings might suggest about the functioning and
evolution of liberal democracy generally, particularly the political dynamics and institutional mechanisms by which 'progressive' policy innovations have been achieved.[11] Typically,
however, these studies bracket off normative questions, and
are comfortable working with the habitually disaffected approach of positive social scientists: that reads policies and institutions as no more than the residual outcome of strategic
interaction between self-interested power and resources
seeking actors. Yet, increasingly, in this subject area as in
others, the role of ideas, universalistic norms and political

argument – for example, justificatory appeals to human rights standards or the pull of national political traditions and ideals – is being cited as an important explanatory factor in political developments.[12] There is therefore a need to account for the distinct normative dimension of such ideas and argument in the emergence of national policy frameworks. In explanatory terms, these amount to springs of political action that cannot be reduced to interest-based motivation alone. In other words, it means reintroducing into an empirical context the kind of considerations political philosophers have always believed shape and motivate 'ideal' liberal democratic politics.

Very generally speaking then, my study is an attempt to go beyond these various limitations and marry the language of contemporary political philosophy with a thoroughly empirical study of the liberal politics of immigration and integration. It is, I hope, a distinctive form of philosophy and public affairs, applied to a specific area of importance in public policy in Europe: with its starting point the rough ground of 'actual existing liberalism' rather than the building of ideal theory. It pays close attention, therefore, to the origins, evolution and content of liberal practices and the constraints that contingent political circumstances impose on policy-making. However, I hope to uphold the belief of political philosophers that liberal politics and institutions can and do have legitimacy in normative terms, while developing a critical stance from a contextual position close to the existing practices.[13]

AMATEUR POLITICAL THEORIES AND PUBLIC PHILOSOPHIES

The study of political ideas and justifications in action, sustaining particular policies or pushing them in new directions, is at the heart of my approach: political argument, in other words.[14] Its focus and raw material are the arguments found empirically in the political reflections surrounding policies and their application in France and Britain. The terms of familiar political discourse in the two countries can thus be analysed for their descriptive and prescriptive force, and the effect that they have in creating the political 'reality' of the situation. Many of the ideas and justifications given to uphold particular policy lines refer to abstract principles, invented conceptualisations, or complex quasi-scientific claims about the functioning or order of society. They testify to the inescapable interpenetration of knowledge and politics in western liberal democracies: something which in effect calls for a 'sociology of political knowledge', to which I contribute here.[15]

A worked-out argument about the question of immigration and integration in a western liberal democracy – a manifesto statement, a public policy document, an editorial comment – is an example of what can be called an 'amateur political theory'. Some such conceptualisation is a necessary cognitive prerequisite for any political actor to grasp causally a political situation and formulate action within it.[16] If an amateur political theory of this kind can be shown to have been accepted consensually as the overall dominant theory justifying public policies in the country, it can be read as a kind of 'official' public theory. Such a theory would have three sorts of components: it would describe and conceptualise the basic facts and reality of the social situation it applies to (epistemological claims); it would theorise the means and application of any political intervention, and thus make assumptions about the causality of political and social processes (explanatory claims); and finally, it would embody some kind of core value or values which spell out the ideal end-goal of the policies, and what their underlying philosophical justification is (normative claims). If successful in becoming the dominant framework for particular policies – and hence establishing itself as the dominant picture of political reality – it can also be predicted that the public theory may lead to certain characteristic problems, if over time it proves to apply badly to certain types of dilemma or new cases that arise.

The essential thing to note about such an 'official' public theory is that it is inherently both explanatory and normative in nature, combining these two dimensions as an automatic condition of its political contextualisation and application. A political argument is unlikely to set the agenda and begin to define the salient facts and elements in a given situation, if it cannot convince that it proposes a plausible and applicable explanation of how an ideal outcome can be arrived at; similarly, however, it is unlikely to inspire or gain political currency if it cannot propose and defend desirable end-goals. Moreover, an official public theory is fundamentally different from an 'ideal' political or philosophical theory because it is not the product of *a priori* reflection. Rather, it is the outcome of a political process that has fashioned a dominant, publicly recognised and understood theory for dealing with the public problems in question, under a series of empirical constraints. These are constraints imposed by the rules of democratic deliberation, the existing institutional conditions with which it has to fit, and the inherent limitations of resources, information and public altruism.

What kind of approaches can be found among contemporary social and political theorists for revealing these underlying public theories? A number of writers have recently revived the idea of 'public philosophy' as a way of characterising the widespread political beliefs and ideas that underpin everyday politics in western liberal democratic societies. The most prominent of these have been the group of American communitarian writers, such as Robert Bellah, Philip Selznick, Amitai Etzioni, Michael Sandel and Robert Putnam, concerned with the individualistic fragmentation of citizenship, and extraordinary levels of social conflict in American public life.[17] In their analysis of American social and political institutions, they uncover an underlying public philosophy of commitment, civic participation and shared understandings which has been battered and undermined by recent social developments. It is thus both a description of an idealised past, and a prescription of what needs to be recognised and affirmed in the present. The civic public philosophy is in effect their answer to the question of integration: of identifying the threatened source of moral social order. Here, the public philosophy exists as a kind of Durkheimian root of the organic communal 'value integration' required for an apparently individualist society such as America to be possible.

The consensus that these writers express is one rooted in history and social traditions. While they are right to point out the structural need for stable social institutions and a degree of political consensus in order to prevent individualistic liberal rights and entitlements working in a conflictual, fragmentary way, their nostalgic, historical focus limits the usefulness of their insights. Does the public philosophy float in the air waiting to be rediscovered by misguidedly individualistic citizens? Does it exhort the blind reproduction of tradition? What is clearly missing from their account of the source of moral order are the forward-looking political dynamics of policy-making and new institution-building. They miss the sense that the good health of liberal democratic politics must in part depend on the fact it has continually to *re-*create and *re-*build a political consensus for dealing with public problems, out of the crucible of democratic political conflict. Progress in these matters is thus connected to the kind of constructive, *evolutionary* responses to problems that the political system is able to produce. Political actors might indeed evoke past experiences and social forms as an argumentative resource in the present, but this kind of justification can only be meaningful if it is adapted to the new and different conditions of the present and future. The idea that the true answer to the problem of integration lies in the rediscovery of some kind of traditional public philosophy, might in fact threaten the possibility of critique and innovation in new policy responses.

Different limitations mark the applications that might be made of the most famous and influential contemporary liberal 'public philosophy' of recent years: that of John Rawls.[18] Rawls's work certainly does take consensus-building and value pluralism as a problem. His theory is based around spelling out the 'just' institutional first principles – in terms of basic rights, liberties and entitlements – that all members despite their differences could, in an ideal situation of deliberation, agree to as the mode of organising the basic public institutions of that society. This would spell out what he calls the 'basic structure' of liberal democratic societies. As his work has developed it has turned increasingly towards the problem of integration as I define it: a search for the 'overlapping moral consensus' that citizens with conflicting cultural and ethical beliefs could agree to as the principles for regulating their social and political interaction. A number of notable recent works have also sought to go further and apply a broadly speaking 'Rawlsian' approach to particular areas of policy reflection, with one or two works going on to apply it directly to the problematic of ethnic dilemmas in liberal societies.[19]

The essential problem with Rawls's work as a starting point for revealing liberal democratic public theories, lies in the rarefied level of its analysis and the impractically high standards of consent and transparency it imposes on 'just' institutions. If institutions can only be considered just if they could be notionally agreed to by all interested parties under ideal conditions, it would rule out from normative endorsement a vast majority of progressive and well-functioning liberal institutions: for example, those based on a paternalist rationale, democratic compromise and trade-off, or simple efficiency and expediency. With this in mind, it is often more realistic to think of liberal political institutions as artificial inventions for dealing with the limitations of finite, morally limited individuals: the kind of things discussed in the literature on prisoner's dilemmas and other collective action failures by rational choice theorists.[20] At a more contextualised, interpretatively sensitive level, it can be found that there are all kinds of institutional forms in liberal democratic societies – with a strong rationale and justification – that are normatively justifiable, not because of the principles they embody, but according to the manner in which they are organised and structured.[21] Empirically speaking, this would certainly apply to the institutional solutions that have been devised in France and Britain for dealing with their ethnic dilemmas: none of which would pass the test of 'overlapping moral consensus'. Yet these solutions are clearly authentic liberal 'philosophies of integration' in some way. There are, in other words, oversights involved in fetishising a political philosopher's view of how liberal democratic systems can and should work. Indeed, lurking behind this is the suspicion that the Rawlsian answer to the problem of moral social order – that the source of a 'well-ordered society' is a set of basic liberal ideals that all citizens could agree to – would be a wholly functionalist and static social theory. This is because it is a theory which pictures consensus as the fruit of idealised consent rather than the outcome of empirically observable political behaviour. It thus eliminates the possibility that moral social order could be something that is the product – not necessarily intended – of the dynamic political interaction of individuals and the institutions that structure their social lives.

A way forward beyond the applied limitations of these strictly normative theories can be found by utilising some of the explanatory theoretical work described as the 'new institu-

tionalism' in political science and sociology. These offer resources for analysing both the organisational rationality of existing political institutions, and the dynamics of political
conflict and consensus-building in the emergence of new institutions.[22] The emphasis of institutional analysis is to show how
past and existing institutional forms and decisions constrain
and shape the choices and behaviour of political actors in the
present; and then how in turn these actors re-shape and revise
the political institutions within which they work. It emphasises
the continual interaction and causal interpenetration of
agency and structure in explaining political outcomes. Such a
theoretical language provides a means for tracking the political construction of institutional responses to public problems,
and the course of political developments within these new institutions once they are in place. It represents a kind of 'rational reconstruction' of the dominant policy formation, using a
mechanistic theory to show how political actors actively col-
luded in constructing the norms and structures they adhere
to; outcomes which might otherwise be explained solely as the
reproduction of political tradition or unquestioned habit.[23]

A number of new institutionalist writers have been concerned with showing how ideas and political argument can
work as institutional structures that shape the interaction of
interests-driven political actors or parties in the policy
process.[24] Typically, ideas come into play in situations where
collective agreement is required but made impossible by interests-based disagreements. The mounting costs of failing to
agree and the uncertainty of having no fixed set of rules for
future bargaining – the 'transaction costs' involved – may push
the parties to seek some grounds for agreement other than
the particular interests they are seeking. It is here that ideas
may enter to solder a wider agreement than might have been
possible. Ideas can act as a focal point which brings together
different policy positions over what they have in common;
they can act as inventions or idealised abstractions that break
the deadlock; they may work as a *post hoc* rationalisation of previous *ad hoc* decisions, and hence provide a structure, sense
and continuity that was missing; or they may work to project
common long-term identity between competing partners on
to the past or future.[25] All of these different ideas-based mechanisms for building a political consensus can be found in the

development of French and British policies on immigration and integration.

The entry of ideas-based explanations into policy-making situations that would normally be accounted for in strictly interests-based terms alone, is also indicative of the special normative pressures political actors come under in crisis situations where some kind of new political agreement or institutional solution has to be reached. In his well-known analysis of the triumph of monetarist ideas over Keynesian economics in 1980s Britain, Peter Hall underlines how the terms of the debate shifted up to the level of fundamental ideas and concepts, because of the crisis and breakdown in the existing 'paradigm' for economic policy (borrowing the famous term from Kuhn), within which all parties had worked during previous decades.[26] That is, their habitual political disagreements about the applied detail of policies and their emphasis were only made possible because of a 'fundamental' agreement on the underlying terms and language of policy. As these terms broke down, actors within the state machinery were engaged in a process of normative and scientific 'puzzling' in search of a new and better underlying public theory for economic policy, a process that raised bitter political conflict until all sides were again ready to resume 'normal' political debate within the terms of a new dominant paradigm. Such a process illustrates how politics, in addition to being a game of power and political competition, may also under certain conditions be a process of collective 'social learning'. A better metaphor, however, than a Kuhnian 'paradigm' for the analysis of policy frameworks as theories is perhaps Lakatos' idea of a 'research programme'. This incorporates a more detailed sense of the internal evolutionary dynamics of a theory over time. A policy framework viewed in these terms can be seen to be made up of both core and peripheral elements, that allow for *ad hoc* adaptations of its less-essential terms in order to protect the 'sacred' assumptions and goals of the core.[27] It will be found that this kind of analytical perspective helps illuminate many of the ongoing problems in the public policy frameworks of integration in France and Britain.

Other institutionalist writers who focus on the complex organisation of institutional forms provide tools for spelling out the various structural elements that make up the core and periphery of public policy frameworks. These writers have demonstrated how, even in the most instrumentally-based forms of organisation such as firms, institutional rule-based structures require all kinds of complex symbolic, linguistic and artificial devices in order to function efficiently.[28] Institutional forms often display isomorphic tendencies as they evolve in relation to others. Or, conversely, they may often get constructed in self-conscious distinction from competing solutions. As we move from economic organisation to political organisation, this kind of analysis in fact becomes increasingly useful in helping to lay out the characteristic blend of elements that make up the average western liberal political system. Typically, these combine formalised legal or institutional structures, on the one hand, with all kinds of idiosyncratic national myths, rituals and conventions, on the other. It reminds us that it is not only the formal content of a public policy that counts, but also its symbolic form and rhetorical packaging.

With these analytical tools in hand, it is possible to start thinking about how the particular public policy domain of immigration and integration – and its evolution over time – might be modelled. I am interested in how and why this particular public problem emerged as a salient political issue, how it was competed over by mainstream political parties, and how and why they found ways of building a consensus on a new institutional framework for dealing with the dilemmas raised. In this process, the entrance of ideas – in the shape of public philosophies or theories – needs to be considered. They have been a contingent factor brought on by the political situation; however, they can also prove to be the decisive element in achieving a solution. The triumph of a public philosophy is not an example of some timeless political 'tradition' imposing itself; it is the outcome of a political process and constructive dynamic of forward-looking policy-making. It is thus essential to focus on explaining the timing of the entry of ideas into the process, and the reasons for the political crisis that inspires a search for a new fundamental framework. This may then offer a clue to the power of ideas over time as an institutionalised structure for ongoing political developments; and secondly, open a way for considering the performance of

ideas as a policy framework, in terms of the positive and negative effects and adaptations it enables as the dominant public
philosophy.

IMMIGRATION AND INTEGRATION: THE EMERGENCE OF A PUBLIC PROBLEM

In recent decades, immigration and the integration of distinct ethnic groups has become a prominent and 'hot' political issue in nearly all of the countries of Western Europe.
The question of 'citizenship' – framed, in particular, as the
reconciliation of cultural pluralism and political membership – has emerged on to political agendas everywhere in
this connection. Immigration, and the citizenship questions
it invites, is a political issue that can, if it unsettles any of the
other social, class or regional divisions that characterise
these societies, rapidly throw into doubt much broader assumptions about the bases of social and political integration
in a nation: its moral and cultural identity, in short. This suggests why mainstream politicians have often been preoccupied with finding constructive political solutions to the
problems immigration raises; and secondly, why responses to
this issue are so revealing of the essential contrasts in the
general 'political culture' or 'national identity' of distinct
western nation-states.

However, viewed over a period of time, it is essential to note
that immigration is not necessarily an important or salient political issue. Indeed, it need not even be recognised as a distinct problem for public policy to address. Immigration *emerges*
as a political issue, according to a 'cycle' of immigration politics. It is picked up as an issue, and blown centre stage; it inspires mainstream political conflict over its terms and issues,
across different institutional arenas; and then the outcome of
these developments goes on to determine the construction
and future course of political and institutional responses to
the integration dilemmas raised. If a successful 'solution' has
been found, the salience of the problems as political issues
may then decline again. It is these political dynamics, common
to many national cases, which suggest that a general 'model'
for western liberal democratic states might be formulated, that

identifies the emergence and evolution of immigration and integration as a public problem.[29] Within such a model, the timing and impact of the entry of ideas into the policy process – for example, a full-scale public debate about the idea of national citizenship, in order to accommodate newcomers – can also be pinpointed. Variation across different national cases in the timing of immigration becoming a hot and salient political issue or the coming together of a political solution, and wide contrasts in the rhetorical terms and justification of these policy frameworks, might then all be accounted for in the same general explanatory terms.

The model begins in the post-war period. A relatively limited amount of immigration to the different nation-states takes place – perhaps through a licensed guest-worker system or because of post-colonial ties – and despite visible cultural and racial differences the immigration is initially negligible as the source of salient political problems. The migration is voluntary and economic in nature, and widely perceived as beneficial to the nation. In so far as it causes social order or integration problems, they are subsumed under the general problematic of class conflict and inequality. Immigrants, indeed, are associated as new members of the working classes. The politics of immigration is thus entirely governed by political economy and welfare concerns, and not thought to disrupt the order or 'identity' of the nation in any way. It is not seen as a separate policy domain. In some cases, 'commonwealth' and colonial ties mean that the immigrants are considered part of the 'nation' in any case. In other cases, guest-workers are there on a contractual basis, and expected to return home after.

Political problems begin to arise within this frame only when there is a conjunction of contingent political economic factors. An economic crisis, which leads to social competition over work and deprived urban spaces and the rejection of new immigrants by the working classes and unions, may then combine with the wider sea-changes of post-industrial societies: the decline of the state, the breaking-up of unified national political culture, the rise of post-national and regional forces. Within this context, immigration can become an effective salient issue, taken up by right-wing traditionalist or working-class parties, and used as a focus for wider grievances. Under these conditions, it can be plausibly pictured as a cause of other problems, rather than being viewed as a symptom. Left-wing social movements may contribute to the heating-up of the issue by taking up the cultural or anti-racist cause of ethnic minorities as a challenge to the dominant political culture. In short, the issue is a good vehicle for 'debate expansion' by weaker, marginalised and non-elite political groups seeking a voice. The issue is thus carried away from a technical, elite question of political economy and welfare management, towards more fundamental, symbolic public issues. It is used as a focus of rhetoric that identifies it as a challenge to the order and identity of the nation.[30] Immigration is now seen to pose a 'fundamental' social order problem, and the political debates start to speak of the loss of national identity, the dilemmas of cultural pluralism, or the problem of a multi-cultural society.

It is here that the destabilising nature of these concerns may cause the idea of citizenship and integration to be raised as a stake. If the militant groups can get the issue on to the mainstream political agenda, there might indeed be a suspension of the existing framework for conceiving citizenship and nationality and the onset of a wider political crisis: the politics of *reconceptualising community*. In these debates, ideas are initially introduced for instrumental reasons by all parties, since they carry with them politically dramatic questions about the order and identity of the nation. Yet once introduced, the ideas are significantly beyond individual actors' control. They can be used by all sides, in defence of an exclusionary idea of the nation or as an argument for a more multicultural one. Within the political history of the nation, the national idea of citizenship is a floating and vaguely defined concept: rooted in some sense but open to varied interpretation and use, while nevertheless containing a certain bundle of connected concepts and connotations.[31] The invocation of citizenship may thus encompass a recognition of the artificial, constructed order of society and political institutions in the modern age, with a mythical affirmation of the nationally particular origins of cultural unification and the nation-state.

In such a situation, it is not only party political interests that are put at stake, but wider epistemological ones about the continuing basis and viability of existing political and social institutions. This is why, even though the mainstream right might, for example, be tempted to benefit politically from the populist concerns of the extreme right, it does so at the cost of perpetuating the fundamental conflict and uncertainty about the encompassing framework of social order and integration. This is likely to pull them towards the centre and make them seek a more consensual 'inclusionary' resolution and new solution to the crisis: a national response to a national dilemma. The language of citizenship, integration and national identity will be taken up by the mainstream policy-makers and used to provide a focal point for a new elite formulation that can secure a more democratic society-wide agreement on a new framework of institutions.[32] It might seek to achieve consensus by projecting a convergence of conflicting interests forward into the future; or back via the (re)invention of a historical myth of the nation as the founding source of these new institutions: the rhetoric of community destiny and tradition. These techniques of history manipulation are often supplemented by methods of national 'self-distinction', in comparison with other national models; or methods of 'self-effacement', hiding the elite paternalist logic of the institutions behind a justificatory veneer which claims they are the outcome of democratic deliberation or an ideal, Rawlsian-style expression of public reason.

If a consensus point can be found, a new policy framework for immigration and the integration of ethnic or cultural minorities may then be established as a policy domain. The new institutional framework may then provide a stable frame for dealing with immigration problems. 'Normal' politics can resume, with a tendency to defuse the saliency of immigration issue again. The issue is now, however, perceived as a separate one, encompassing cultural and ethnic dimensions. It is quite distinct from the general social problems of political economy, welfare and class under which it was once subsumed. All of these elements in the reconceptualisation of community can have consequences in terms of actual policy changes or innovations: changes to nationality law; new specific cultural or anti-discriminatory policies or legislation for the identified minority groups; the firming-up and redefinition of the place of social institutions between the public and private spheres (that is, schools or churches); or new nationalist policies on international migration policy and co-operation. What is important is that these changes will all be framed within the coherent terms of the new framework, and justified as sustaining it into the future.

Despite different timing, and rather distinct linguistic and symbolic content in the ideas of citizenship and integration that were used to justify them, the political developments in both France and Britain substantiate this general model. Using it as a key in Chapters 3 and 4, I will offer a reading and interpretation of the two cases that narrates them in these terms, and spells out the content – the core assumptions, goals and causal mechanisms – of the public philosophy of integration in each case. These form two contrasting and seemingly incompatible sets of ideas about the correct frame for policy responses to ethnic dilemmas in liberal democracies: the integration of *immigrés* into the universalist national community, via access to full participatory political *citoyenneté* in France; the integration of *ethnic minorities* into the tolerant multi-national state, via the management strategy of *race relations* and *multiculturalism* in Britain.

THE EVOLUTION OF POLICY FRAMEWORKS: PATH DEPENDENCY AND INSTITUTIONAL PERFORMANCE

Once a dominant institutional framework of public policy has been identified, it is possible to trace over time the evolution of politics and policies within this framework, and thereby to address the question of 'institutional performance'. The policy framework imposes a language, epistemology and theoretical scheme on the ongoing treatment and debate of policy problems. By this it structures and constrains political actions and policy interventions that take place within the accepted frame. What needs to be explained is why these frameworks have such *prima facie* durability and stability. As I will show the tenacity of the nationally particular and idiosyncratic terms and ideas by which immigration and integration questions have been answered – and are still discussed – has over time clearly created a series of anomalies in policy practice, and hence new political problems. The obvious thing for policy-makers would have been to rethink fundamentally the terms of the policy framework to meet new requirements. Yet more often than not, the frameworks have stayed fixed, and the new questions have instead been approached by a difficult and inappropriate contortion of the original terms and language.

I will analyse these problems with the concept of 'path dependency'. Path dependency is a concept developed in organisational economics to describe apparently 'sub-optimal' behaviour by the market in its 'choice' of successful products competing against each other. Two of the most well-known examples are the adoption of the QWERTY keyboard on typewriters, and the triumph of VHS over BETAMAX video technology. In both cases, the successful product was originally the one widely thought to be inferior: in the long run its triumph has been increasingly costly for consumers and held back technological progress. Once the choice was made, the very large short-term costs of abandoning the decision and investments made stopped firms from breaking out on to the better path of development offered by the other product. Yet a look at the particular contingent circumstances and the timing of the decision can establish why it was indeed the most rational choice at that moment.[33]

These observations can be very useful in the context of public policy decisions and their evolution. A dominant policy framework is something that is pulled together under difficult or crisis conditions. It is thus the 'fundamental' questions at stake that block a new revision of the framework: the high political investment, and the damaging wider costs to the national political system that would be incurred by a reheating of the extremist challenge to the mainstream. Path dependency then, in this context, is not sustained by the power of historical legacies or traditions, as some theorists using the term suggest.[34] It is not simply a question of habit, or an irrational reproduction of inherited conventions. It is, rather, a symptom of the contemporary political forces that are invested in the current status quo, and which need continually to reaffirm the current framework. Indeed, it is the identity provided by a mainstream consensus on the overarching frame and terms of political debate that enables the kind of positional bargaining and conflict of 'normal' political strategic calculations.[35] It is as much in the interests of the mainstream parties to maintain the identity of the existing policy framework, as it is for the extreme parties to try to challenge it.

In a normative perspective, it is no small achievement to have brought together a strong, ideas-led consensus on the national response to immigration and integration questions. These were quite literally the best responses that these two liberal democracies were able to produce – under strict political and institutional constraints – from the open and consensual democratic process of 'puzzling' sparked off by the crisis situation. It called on a co-operative instinct in the mainstream parties, and the need to combine the distinct influence of the three main institutional arenas within the state. These are the democratically elected executive and political representatives; the independent judiciary and the courts; and the bureaucratic technocracy of civil servants and government agencies. In other words, it brought together and combined the democratic rationale of public opinion and voting, the legal rationale of rights-based reasoning, and the technocratic rationale of implementing the best, most scientifically true, technical response. Moreover, the solution that came together has had to fulfil three steep conditions for success: firstly, it was able to solder a large and dominant social consensus; secondly, it defeated and dominated rival ideas or conceptions; and thirdly, it was able to establish itself over time as a self-reproducing and self-justifying public philosophy. I am therefore assuming here – in the tradition of most enlightenment-based political philosophy – that there is a direct normative connection between the nature of a liberal democratic political system and the epistemological effectiveness of its outcomes.[36] In other words, it is the effectiveness with which the outcome of the policy process maps on to the 'truth' and 'reality' of the social situation it addresses that in part explains its success.

Assuming that the democratic process that produced the 'solution' was a healthy one, it may well have produced a relatively 'truthful' and 'rational' public theory for the solving of integration problems. What progressive achievements are made are down to this. The new institutional framework may indeed facilitate the increasing participation of minorities in mainstream society, the reduction of ethnic conflict with the indigenous population, the reduction of racism and discrimination, the creation of a more harmonious, diverse, creative, or efficient multicultural society. Across different national cases, the pragmatic demands of applying ideas in practice may cause policy practices to converge over time, despite their rhetorical differences. Yet however well a public philosophy succeeds, the scale of the uncertainty and complexity it faced in responding originally to the 'fundamental' questions of social order will ensure that it is inadequate in many ways. Although it may shape 'reality' within its own terms, there are elements that will have been left out of policy formulation, others that are distorted to fit within it, and still others that will emerge as problems over time: because they either represent new information, or are unforeseen side-effects that can be traced to the original solution. These are what may generally be referred to as path dependent 'pathologies' (*effets pervers* in French).[37] Such consequences may be observed as a series of unexpected or bizarre developments. In my analysis, I will refer to these outcomes as symptomatic 'sore spots' in the politics of the country. I read them as 'absurdities' or 'blindspots'; or as 'contortions' and 'strange fruit'.

The problems discovered will be specific to the national institutional solution and framework that was set up, and need to be looked at through the empirical case material. Negative path dependency is significant to the extent that it prevents constructive or rational adaptation to these emerging problems over time. Adaptation is problematic because it cannot bring into question the overall framework without risking a renewed crisis. Yet it might be reform of the overall framework that is needed to address the problem. Certain adaptations of the given language and terms may well be possible, stretching concepts incrementally and matching existing institutions to new problems. Adopting the language of Lakatos' analysis, such adaptations can be read in effect as the creation of *ad hoc* 'epicycles', that are devised to produce a solution without touching the sacred core of the public philosophy that is needed to keep the overall framework firm. It is appropriate therefore to speak of the epicycle of immigration politics, or the epicyclical path along which it moves. Although positive and creative adaptation of public policies is always possible, the increasing disjunction between the original solution and later situations some years down the road will mean that the policy framework will always tend to be degenerate. There is, of course, the danger that the various sore spots identified

– and the new opportunities for debate expansion they create
– will provoke a new crisis, and spark new reform or fundamental change. Again, however, the balance of political forces
is strongly in favour of the existing path, and the costs of even
the most rational reform might be too much in terms of the
short-term crisis it might produce. Path dependency is thus
the source of ongoing problems within the framework, and
the theoretical device by which an observer may begin to evaluate institutional performance in critical terms.

The evaluation and criticism of national policy frameworks
is a comparative exercise, enabled by the juxtaposition of cases
and the possibility of counter-factual interpretation.[38] The distinct paths of institutional development found in other cases
make possible counter-factual readings of a particular framework. This can made in various ways: in terms of internal
changes that were made impossible by the configuration of
forces sustaining the existing framework; the external
example and different possibilities revealed in the mirror of
another nation's framework; or the potential benefits highlighted by a brand new 'ideal' solution for the new situation
faced. In my analysis, this counter-factual ideal is located at
a transnational level, in which different national solutions
converge in a European-level settlement of the question of immigration and integration. Such a settlement is strongly
demanded by common international problems now faced by
all European states: that is, new types of migration; the status
of non-nationals; a harmonised legal framework for anti-
discrimination laws; and the question of European citizenship.
Some of these developments indeed suggest the emergence of
what has been called 'post-national' citizenship, a form of citizenship in which rights and status are not dependent on membership in any particular nation-state.[39]

What is being evaluated in effect is the degree to which the
original settlement – at its most rational and effective at
the moment it was pulled together – continues to map on to the
'truth' and 'reality' of the new social situation it has to address at
later points in time. There are three dimensions to the epistemological effectiveness of a policy framework over time.

It depends, firstly, on the *coherency* in practice of the framework set up: how well the elements of the framework fit together when applied, across both different institutional arenas

and other public policy domains. Problems may follow if the public policy identifies the objects of policy in incoherent ways: calling them 'Blacks' in anti-discrimination law, and 'Muslims' in census collection. Such incoherencies can only be maintained by creating sharp institutional boundaries: between 'ethnic' issues and 'poverty' issues, for example. However, the constraining work that artificial institutional boundaries do has costs and can become strained if not secured by tenable justifications and concrete achievements over time.[40]

The second dimension is the *representativeness* of the policy framework. 'Facts' and 'events' exist outside of the narrower political 'reality' it constructs: the true numbers and origins of newcomers, or political developments taking place internationally. Faults in the representativeness of the policy construction can be diagnosed when an institutional structure has problems fitting the categories it imposes on the facts it seeks to shape. An example is 'race' legislation which tries to reduce other types of discrimination such as religious prejudice or xenophobia to the same existing categories for legislative purposes.

Thirdly, there is the question of *commitment* incurred by the establishment of a policy framework. If they are established and agreed to, the very use of abstract principles – for example, equality or liberty – in policy justification can have substantial feedback effects on society. These may be in the positive effect of universalisation and abstraction, when social and political behaviour is held up to a principled standard. Or they may be, in some cases, the kinds of problem caused when morally limited individuals fail to match up to the ideals set for them. If citizens are meant to be rational, publicly spirited, politically informed and ethically pure, then the public theory of integration will falter in practice if they are not in fact like that. One should think of there being stakes involved in the ordinary language use of certain words. Language contains within its meaning its own rules and prescriptions about its successful application to cases.

Chapters 5 and 6, then, will use these analytical tools and criteria to chart the evolution and performance of the dominant policy frameworks in France and Britain, and evaluate them critically against these standards by discussing the many examples of institutional pathologies that can be found. In my final chapter, I will go on to raise the European question and the comparison with other national cases in this connection. If internal pathologies and mutations do not break the path dependency and bring about a change in the policy frameworks, will the pressures at the co-operative European level force political actors to engage in a new process of puzzling and rethinking?

This question is an empirical one about how much negative path dependency a framework can sustain, or the degree to which adaptation is possible within a fixed framework. In the context of Western Europe – where national identity stakes were so much involved in the setting-up of initial immigration solutions – it is likely that fundamental change will come to these solutions via international exogenous factors rather than by internal transformation alone. The existence of post-national problems of immigration – in conflict with national politics of immigration – thus brings a new dimension into the picture. One of the central questions that a study of any national cases in Europe will raise, is the degree to which international factors were internalised within an original solution. Given the fact that national cases could be anywhere along the path of immigration politics I have set out, it is indeed possible that some cases have never even reached the stage where a 'national' crisis took place and a 'national' solution was found. These nations might opt immediately for a post-national solution. Furthermore, it can be predicted that, given the increasing internationalisation of the problem over the last twenty to thirty years, the earlier a country pulled together a national solution, the more difficulty it will have in adapting or responding to the new post-national politics. In these cases, it can be seen that one of the central 'sore spots' in the internal politics of immigration will be precisely the unrepresented international factors within the existing framework.

The cases of France and Britain – in comparison to others – indeed substantiate this observation. The French and British difficulties over Europe thus become the perfect metaphor of the self-damaging resistance these two old colonial nations have displayed in their problematic adaptation to new international political currents. Their behaviour over immigration and integration issues in coming years will therefore be a key test of their willingness to embrace political change now and in the future.

Notes

1. The only successful full-scale comparative work of this kind in English is the pathbreaking but now dated study by Gary Freeman, *Immigrant Labour and Racial Conflict in Industrial Societies: The French and British Experience 1945–1975* (Princeton NJ: Princeton University Press, 1979). In French, there are many poor comparative studies, a rare exception being Didier Lapeyronnie, *L'individu et les minorités: La France et la Grande Bretagne face à ses minorités* (Paris: Presses universitaires de France, 1993). One recent article, by Patrick Weil and John Crowley, 'Integration in theory and practice: a comparison of France and Britain', *West European Politics*, vol. 17, no. 2 (1994) lays out the distinctions successfully at a descriptive level, but does not dig much further. Gary Freeman revisits the cases in 1992, in 'The consequences of immigration politics for immigrant status: a British and French comparison' in A. Messina *et al.*, *Ethnic and Racial Minorities in Advanced Industrial Democracies* (London: Greenwood, 1992); see also the work of John Crowley, 'Paradoxes in the politicisation of race: a comparison of the UK and France', *New Community* vol. 19, no. 1 (1993); Cathie Lloyd 'Concepts, models and anti-racist strategies in Britain and France', *New Community*, vol. 18, no.1 (1991). There are also a number of interesting single-case studies written by nationals of the 'other' country: Catherine Neveu, *Communauté, nationalité et citoyenneté: De l'autre côté du miroir* (Paris: Karthala, 1993); Max Silverman, *Deconstructing the Nation: Immigration, Racism and Citizenship in Modern France* (London: Routledge, 1992); and Alec Hargreaves, *Immigration, 'Race' and Ethnicity in Contemporary France* (London: Routledge, 1995). I should also like to acknowledge the interesting doctoral work in progress by Elaine Thomas (UC Berkeley) and Erik Bleich (Harvard).

2. See Joseph Gusfield, *The Culture of Public Problems: Drinking-Driving and the Symbolic Order* (University of Chicago Press, 1981), for a study in a different policy domain.

3. For example, John Rawls, *Political Liberalism* (Princeton University Press, 1993); Charles Taylor/Amy Gutmann (ed.), *Multiculturalism and 'The Politics of Recognition'* (Princeton University Press, 1992); Amy Gutmann, 'Communitarian critics of liberalism', *Philosophy and Public Affairs*, vol. 14 (1993), and 'The challenge of multiculturalism in political ethics', *Philosophy and Public Affairs*, vol. 22, no. 3 (1993); Will Kymlicka, *Liberalism, Community and Culture* (Oxford: Clarendon, 1989); Will Kymlicka (ed.), *Minority Rights* (Oxford University Press, 1994); Will Kymlicka, *Multicultural Citizenship* (Oxford University Press, 1995); Joseph Raz, *The Morality of Freedom* (Oxford: Clarendon, 1986); Joseph Raz, 'Free expression and personal identification', *Oxford Journal of Legal Studies*, vol. 11, no. 3 (1991); Joseph Raz, 'Multiculturalism: a liberal perspective', *Dissent*, vol. 41, no.1 (1994);

William Galston, *Liberal Purposes: Goods, Virtue and Diversity in the Liberal State* (Cambridge University Press, 1991); Jeff Spinner, *Boundaries of Citizenship: Race, Ethnicity and Culture in the Liberal State* (Baltimore, Md: Johns Hopkins University Press, 1994). The best survey of these debates is Stephen Mulhall and Adam Swift, *Liberals and Communitarians*, 2nd edn (Oxford: Blackwell, 1996).

4. For example, Iris Marion Young, *Justice and the Politics of Difference* (Princeton University Press, 1991); Chantal Mouffe (ed.), *Dimensions of Radical Democracy: Pluralism, Citizenship, Community* (London: Verso, 1992); Anne Phillips, *Democracy and Difference* (Cambridge: Polity, 1993) and *The Politics of Presence* (Oxford University Press, 1995); David Held (ed.), *Prospects for Democracy: North South East West* (Cambridge: Polity, 1993); Andrew Arato and Jean Cohen, *Civil Society and Political Theory* (Cambridge, Mass.: MIT Press, 1992); Seyla Benhabib, *Situating the Self: Gender, Community and Postmodernism in Contemporary Ethics* (Cambridge: Polity, 1992); Jürgen Habermas, 'Struggles for recognition in the democratic constitutional state', in Amy Gutmann (ed.) *Examining the Politics of Recognition* (Princeton University Press, 1994).

5. See William Connelly, 'The dilemma of legitimacy', in William Connelly (ed.), *Legitimacy and the State* (Oxford: Blackwell, 1984). Connelly refers to this problem as 'the bifurcation of liberalism'. See also the series of essays about contemporary political theory on this theme by John Dunn, *Western Political Theory in the Face of the Future*, 2nd edn (Cambridge University Press, 1993); *Rethinking Modern Political Theory* (Cambridge University Press, 1985); *Interpreting Political Responsibility* (Oxford: Polity, 1990); and the introduction to *The Economic Limits to Modern Politics* (Cambridge University Press, 1993); and the caustic and often cutting voice of John Gray, *Liberalisms: Essays in Political Philosophy* (London: Routledge, 1989); *Post-Liberalism: Studies in Political Theory* (London: Routledge, 1993); and 'Why the owl flies late', *The Times Literary Supplement*, 4 Nov. 1993, his review of Robert Goodin and Philip Pettit (eds), *A Companion to Contemporary Political Philosophy* (Oxford: Blackwell, 1993), a comprehensive state-of-the-art survey which Gray likens to the encyclopaedia of Borges' imaginary land of Tlön, a book which describes 'a world in which causal connections are only associations of ideas'.

6. See the surveys in William Julius Wilson and Katherine O'Sullivan, 'Race and ethnicity', in Neil Smelser (ed.) *Handbook of Sociology* (New York: Sage, 1988); John Rex and David Mason (eds), *Theories of Race and Ethnic Relations* (Cambridge University Press, 1986); Will Kymlicka and Wayne Norman, 'Return of the citizen: a survey of recent work on citizenship theory', *Ethics*, vol. 104 (Jan. 1994); William Safran, 'Nations, ethnic groups, states and politics: a preface and an agenda', *Nationalism and Ethnic Politics*, vol. 1, no. 1 (1995).

7. For example, Centre for Contemporary Cultural Studies, *The Empire Strikes Back* (London: Hutchinson, 1982): Paul Gilroy, *There Aint No Black in the Union Jack* (London: Hutchinson, 1987); Robert Miles and A. Phizacklea, *White Man's Country: Racism in British Politics* (London: Pluto, 1984); Ambalavaner Sivanandan, *Communities of Resistance:*

Writings on Black Struggles for Socialism (London: Verso, 1990); Floya Anthias and Nira Yuval-Davis, *Racialized Boundaries: Race, Nation, Gender, Colour and Class and the Anti-Racist Struggle* (London: Routledge, 1993); J. Donald and Ali Rattansi (eds), *Race, Culture and Difference* (London: Sage, 1992). A French example is Etienne Balibar and Immanuel Wallerstein, *Races, nations, classes: les identités ambiguës* (Paris: La Découverte, 1988); an American example is Michael Omi and Howard Winant, *Racial Formation in the US from the 1960s to the 1990s*, 2nd edn (London: Routledge, 1994).

8.   See, for example, the unconvincing comparative frameworks in Robert Miles, *Racism After 'Race Relations'* (London: Routledge, 1993); John Solomos and John Wrench (eds), *Racism and Migration in Western Europe* (Oxford: Berg, 1993); and Robert Miles and Dietrich Thränhardt, *Migration and European Integration* (London: Pinter, 1995), where the accent is still on applying British anti-racist concepts to European concerns, for example to reveal the 'racist' dimensions of the so-called 'Fortress Europe'. Even technical comparative works reproduce this Anglocentric flaw: for example, Ian Forbes and Geoffrey Mead, *Measure For Measure: A Comparative Analysis of Measures to Combat Racial Discrimination in the Member Countries of the European Community* (Sheffield: Department of Employment, 1992).

9.   Rogers Brubaker (ed.), *Immigration and the Politics of Citizenship in Western Europe* (New York: University Press of America, 1989), and *Citizenship and Nationhood in France and Germany* (Cambridge, Mass.: Harvard University Press, 1992); Yasemin Soysal, 'Immigration and the emerging European polity' in S. S. Anderson and R. A. Eliassen (eds), *Making Policy in Europe: The Europification of National Policy* (London: Sage, 1993), and *Limits of Citizenship: Migrants and Postnational Membership in Europe* (University of Chicago Press, 1994); Gary Freeman, 'Migrant policy and politics in the receiving states', *International Migration Review*, vol. 26, no. 4 (1992), and 'Modes of immigration politics in liberal democratic societies', *International Migration Review*, vol. 29, no. 4 (1995); James Hollifield, *Immigrants, Markets and States: The Political Economy of Western Europe* (Cambridge, Mass.: Harvard University Press, 1992); Anthony Messina *et al.* (eds), *Ethnic and Racial Minorities in Advanced Industrial Democracies* (London: Greenwood Press, 1992); Wayne Cornelius *et al.* (eds), *Controlling Immigration* (Stanford University Press, 1994); Martin Baldwin-Edwards and Martin Schain (eds), *The Politics of Immigration in Western Europe* (London: Sage, 1994); Patrick Ireland, *The Policy Challenge of Ethnic Diversity: Immigrant Politics in Western Europe* (Cambridge, Mass.: Harvard University Press, 1994); Christian Joppke (ed.), *Challenge to the Nation State: Immigration in Western Europe and the United States* (Oxford University Press, 1998); Virginie Guiraudon, 'Citizenship rights for non-citizens: France, Germany and the Netherlands (1973–1994)' in Christian Joppke (ed.), *Challenge to the Nation State*.

10.   See the use of a models approach in Brubaker (ed.), *Immigration and the Politics of Citizenship*; Cornelius *et al.* (eds), *Controlling Immigration*; Baldwin-Edwards and Schain (eds), *The Politics of Immigration*; and the use of typologies in Soysal, *Limits of Citizenship*.

11. The most 'advanced' contributions in this sense are those by Soysal, *Limits of Citizenship*; Freeman, 'Migrant Policy and Politics' and 'Modes of immigration politics'; and work in progress by Guiraudon, 'Citizenship rights for non-citizens'.

12. See, respectively, Soysal, *Limits of Citizenship*; and Brubaker, *Citizenship and Nationhood in France and Germany*.

13. A rationale for this kind of enterprise is made by Michael Walzer in *Interpretation and Social Criticism* (Cambridge, Mass.: Harvard University Press, 1987).

14. My approach therefore shares some affinities with the early work of Brian Barry, *Political Argument* (Berkeley and Los Angeles: University of California Press, 1990 [1965]), and *Sociologists, Economists and Democracy* (New Haven, Cann.: Yale University Press, 1978 [1970]); William Connelly, *The Terms of Political Discourse* (Oxford: Robertson, 1983 [1974]); and Alan Hamlin and Philip Pettit, *The Good Polity: Normative Analyses of the State* (Oxford: Blackwell, 1989). I have been strongly influenced by Wittgensteinian approaches to the social sciences: see Hanna Pitkin, *Wittgenstein and Justice: On the Significance of Ludwig Wittgenstein for Social and Political Thought* (Berkeley, Calif.: University of California Press, 1972); Quentin Skinner, 'Language and political change', in Terence Ball *et al.* (eds), *Political Innovation and Conceptual Change* (Cambridge University Press, 1989; and Quentin Skinner (ed. James Tully) *Meaning and Context: Quentin Skinner and his Critics* (Cambridge: Polity, 1988). For examples of contemporary theoretical works, which consider the structural effects of ideas and arguments in a similar but purely theoretical way, see Stephen Holmes, *The Anatomy of Antiliberalism* (Cambridge, Mass.: Harvard University Press, 1993); and Albert O. Hirschman, *The Rhetoric of Reaction* (Cambridge, Mass.: Harvard University Press, 1991).

15. The classic reference being Peter Berger and Thomas Luckmann, *The Social Construction of Reality: A Treatise in the Sociology of Knowledge* (Harmondsworth: Penguin, 1966).

16. Here, I am adapting ideas from John Dunn, *The Politics of Socialism: An Essay in Political Theory* (Cambridge University Press, 1984), pp. 1–10; and 'Social theory, social understanding and political action' in *Rethinking Modern Political Theory*.

17. Robert Bellah *et al.*, *Habits of the Heart: Individualism and Commitment in America Life* (Berkeley and Los Angeles: University of California Press, 1985), and *The Good Society* (New York: Knopf, 1992), especially the appendix, 'Institutions in sociology and public philosophy'; Philip Selznick, *The Moral Commonwealth* (Berkeley, Calif.: University of California Press, 1992); Amitai Etzioni, *The Spirit of the Community: Rights, Responsibilities and the Communitarian Agenda* (New York: Crown, 1993); Michael Sandel, *Democracy's Discontent: America in Search of a Public Philosophy* (Cambridge, Mass.: Harverd University Press, 1995); Robert Putnam, 'Tuning in, tuning out. The strange disappearance of civic America', *Political Science Review*, vol. 28, no. 4.

18. John Rawls, *A Theory of Justice* (Oxford University Press, 1971); *Political Liberalism*.

19. For example, Will Kymlicka, *Minority Rights* and *Multicultural Citizenship*; Thomas Pogge, *Realizing Rawls* (Ithaca, NY: Cornell University Press, 1989); Joseph Carens, 'Aliens and citizens: the case for open borders', *Review of Politics*, vol. 49, no. 2 (1987) and other articles; Stephen Macedo, *Liberal Virtues: Citizenship, Virtue and Community in Liberal Constitutionalism* (Oxford: Clarendon, 1991); Rainer Bauböck, *Transnational Citizenship* (Aldershot: Edward Elgar, 1994).

20. See Jon Elster, *Nuts and Bolts for the Social Sciences* and *The Cement of Society* (both Cambridge University Press, 1989) for the basics. They are themes developed in the work of Russell Hardin, *Morality Within the Limits of Reason* (University of Chicago Press, 1988); Robert Goodin, *Political Theory and Public Policy* (University of Chicago Press, 1982) and *Utilitarianism as a Public Philosophy* (Cambridge University Press, 1995); Peter Ordeshook, 'The development of contemporary political theory', in William Barnett *et al.*, *Political Economy, Competition and Representation* (Cambridge University Press, 1993).

21. A critique developed theoretically by others. See Michael Walzer, *Spheres of Justice* (New York: Basic Books, 1983); 'Philosophy and democracy', *Political Theory*, vol. 9 (1981); Jon Elster, *Local Justice: How Institutions Allocate Scarce Goods and Necessary Burdens* (Cambridge University Press, 1992); Michael Taylor, 'Good government: On hierarchy, social capital and the limitations of rational choice theory', *Journal of Political Philosophy*, vol. 4, no. 1; Cass R. Sunstein, *After the Rights Revolution: Reconceiving the Regulatory State* (Cambridge, Mass.: Harvard University Press, 1990). For an example of an applied analysis in this vein which raises important normative questions, see Edward Laumann and David Knoke, *The Organizational State: Social Choice in National Policy Domains* (Madison: University of Wisconsin Press, 1987).

22. The best single theoretical statement is Douglass North, *Institutions, Institutional Change and Economic Performance*, (Cambridge University Press, 1990). For a comprehensive literature survey, see Peter Hall and Rosemary Taylor, 'Political science and the three new institution-alisms', *Political Studies*, vol. 44, no. 5 (1996). See also Kenneth Shepsle, 'Studying institutions: some lessons from the rational choice approach', *Journal of Theoretical Politics*, vol. 1, pp. 139–49 (1986).

23. Here, I follow the normative rationale for social and political theory developed by the late James Coleman: see parts 1 and 5 of *Foundations of Social Theory* (Cambridge, Mass.: Harvard University Press, 1990), and 'The rational reconstruction of society', *American Sociological Review*, vol. 58, no. 1. See also my discussion in Adrian Favell, 'James Coleman: Social theorist and moral philosopher?', *American Journal of Sociology*, vol. 99, no. 3, and 'Rational choice as grand theory: James Coleman's normative contribution to social theory', in Jon Clark (ed.) *James S. Coleman* (London: Falmer, 1996).

24. The ideas in policy-making literature. For example, Peter Hall (ed.), *The Political Power of Economic Ideas: Keynesianism Across Nations* (Princeton, NJ: Princeton University Press, 1989), and 'Policy paradigms, social learning and the state: The case of economic policymaking in Britain', *Comparative Politics*, vol. 25, no. 3 (1993); Giandomenico Majone,

Evidence, Argument and Persuasion in the Policy Process, (New Haven, Conn.: Yale University Press, 1989), and 'Public Policy: Ideas, interests and institutions', in Robert Goodin and Dieter Klingemann (eds), *New Handbook of Political Science* (Oxford University Press, 1996); Judith Goldstein and Bob Keohane (eds), *Ideas and Foreign Policy* (New York: Cornell University Press, 1993). See also the formal treatment of the role of ideology in Douglass North, *Structure and Change in Economic History* (New York: Norton, 1981). For an application of these theoretical concerns to the politics of immigration in the USA, see Peter Schuck, 'The politics of rapid legal change: Immigration policy in the 1980s', *Studies in American Political Development*, no. 6 (1992).

25.   See the introduction to Goldstein and Keohane (eds), *Ideas and Public Policy*.

26.   Peter Hall, 'Policy paradigms'.

27.   Thomas S. Kuhn, *The Structure of Scientific Revolutions* (University of Chicago Press, 1962); Imre Lakatos and Alan Musgrave (eds), *Criticism and the Growth of Knowledge* (Cambridge University Press, 1970). On the relation between Kuhn and Lakatos see Giandomenico Majone, 'Policies as theories', *Omega*, vol. 8. no. 2 (1980); and Shaun Hargreaves-Heap, *Rationality in Economics* (Oxford: Blackwell, 1989).

28.   James March and Johan Olsen, *Rediscovering Institutions: The Organizational Basis of Politics* (New York: Free Press, 1989); Walter Powell and Paul DiMaggio (eds), *The New Institutionalism in Organizational Analysis* (University of Chicago Press, 1991).

29.   See different models of this kind in Gary Freeman, 'Modes of immigration politics'; and Virginie Guiraudon, 'How did aliens acquire more rights?'.

30.   A model, adopted from E. E. Schattschneider, *The Semi-Sovereign People: A Realist's View of Democracy in America*, (New York: Free Press, 1961), that was reintroduced by Frank Baumgartner in *Conflict and Rhetoric in French Policy Making*, (University of Pittsburgh Press, 1989). Martin Schain, 'Immigration and changes in the French party system', *European Journal of Political Research*, vol. 16 (1988), and Guiraudon, 'Citizenship rights for non-citizens', also make use of this model.

31.   Stephen Krasmer, 'Westphalia and all that', in Judith Goldstein and Robert Keohane (eds), *Ideas and Public Policy*, discusses the role of the idea of 'sovereignty' in early modern Europe in these terms.

32.   Geoffrey Garrett and Barry Weingast offer a formal model of ideas as a focal point for policy-makers in 'Ideas, interests and institutions: Constructing the European Community's internal market' in Goldstein and Keohane (eds), *Ideas and Public Policy*.

33.   North, *Institutions*, pp. 92–104; Brian Arthur, 'Self-reinforcing mechanisms in economics', in Philip Anderson *et al.* (eds), *The Economy as an Evolving Complex System* (Reading, Mass.: Addison-Wesley, 1988).

34.   My formulation is thus significantly different than that found in Robert Putnam, *Making Democracy Work: Civic Traditions In Modern Italy* (Princeton, NJ: Princeton University Press, 1993). My criticism would also apply to other works of 'historical institutionalism' such as Rogers Brubaker, *Citizenship and Nationhood*; or the introduction to Sven

Steinmo *et al.* (eds), *Structuring Politics: Historical Institutionalism in Comparative Perspective* (New York: Cambridge University Press, 1992), which all tend to over-emphasise historical factors at the expense of contemporary political ones.

35. This echoes the novel solution to the Hobbesian dilemma developed by Alessandro Pizzorno in 'On the individualistic theory of social order'; and 'Some other kinds of otherness: a critique of rational choice theories' in A. Foxley *et al.* (eds), *Development, Democracy and the Art of Trespassing: Essays in Honour of Albert O. Hirschman* (Notre Dame, Ind.: Notre Dame University Press, 1991). See also Mark Granovetter, 'Economic action and social structure: the problem of embeddedness,' *American Journal of Sociology*, vol. 91, no. 3 (1985).

36. For example, in the grand theory of Jürgen Habermas, *Between Facts and Norms: Contributions to a Discourse Theory of Law and Democracy* (Cambridge, Mass.: MIT Press, 1996). For reflections in a different philosophical tradition on the relation between liberalism, democracy and truth, see also Joseph Raz, 'Facing diversity: the case of epistemic abstinence', *Philosophy and Public Affairs*, vol. 19 (1990), and Susan Hurley, *Natural Reasons: Personality and Polity* (Oxford University Press, 1989), especially the final chapter, 'Autonomy and democracy'. For a critique of this kind of 'enlightenment functionalism', see Roberto Unger, *Politics: A Work in Constructive Social Theory* (Cambridge University Press, 1987, 3 vols) especially the introduction, *False Necessity*; and even more disenchantedly, Alisdair MacIntyre, *After Virtue: A Study in Moral Theory* (London: Duckworth, 1981).

37. See Hirschman, *The Rhetoric of Reaction.*

38. A defence of this kind of work is made by Geoffrey Hawthorn, *Plausible Worlds: Possibility and Understanding in History and the Social Sciences* (Cambridge University Press, 1991).

39. See Yasemin Soysal, *Limits of Citizenship.*

40. See Michael Walzer, 'Liberalism and the art of separation', *Political Theory*, vol. 12 (1984).

3 France: The Republican Philosophy of *Intégration*. Ideas and Politics in the 1980s

Facing a set of political questions concerning policy towards ethnic minorities not dissimilar to those faced by other advanced western countries, France in the 1980s witnessed an outbreak of public reflection of a highly philosophical nature, extraordinary in its abstract and theoretical content, and wholly peculiar to the French political scene. Questions concerning the integration of these minorities became – in the formulation of politicians, policy-makers and policy intellectuals alike – explicitly couched in terms referring to the theoretical foundations of French political unity and cohesiveness: around grand themes of republican values, citizenship and the 'traditional' universal and cosmopolitan nature of French nationhood. From the mid-1980s through to the elections of 1993, debate about immigration and integration in these terms was arguably the most visible and salient issue in French politics.

   Certain conditions particular to France certainly made the policy-makers more receptive to the influence of an openly intellectual, ideas-based reformulation of immigration and integration policy. Parisian intellectuals traditionally have a higher visibility and social influence in France than intellectuals in many other states. This intellectual presence in policy debates has been a part of all the great political changes in France from the Revolution onwards. However, these background factors of French political life would not be sufficient by themselves to determine strongly the kind of policies chosen in this, or any other, policy domain. Policy-making in France, like anywhere, is usually determined by more obvious party political and institutional factors. The decisive entry of ideas into

40

the policy process, and the explicit and exclusive framing of questions of immigration and integration in terms of an idiom of republican citizenship, was a wholly contingent and puzzling political event that needs to be explained. The intercession on the political scene of an explicit debate about the national 'public philosophy' offers, then, the perfect venue for the kind of analysis and approach I have outlined in Chapter 2.

In the case of recent French political debate, it is not difficult to specify which arguments visibly mattered. The list of high-profile French books of the late 1980s, connecting classic themes of republicanism and citizenship with the particularities of the '*modèle français de l'intégration*' for dealing with ethnic and cultural differences, speaks for itself; as does the continual recurrence of these same media intellectuals, in both the central policy fora and highbrow media discussions.[1] Within this '*nouvelle synthèse républicaine*' (a new republican synthesis), as Patrick Weil calls it, the political parties and leading politicians spoke the same language: whether in the painful transformation of the Socialist line in the mid-1980s, the left–right jostling for position during the *cohabitation* of a Socialist president and conservative prime minister between 1986 and 1988, or the dilemmas of the right in fending off and distancing itself from the growing challenge of Le Pen.[2] To a remarkable degree, the language of educationalists, judiciary and police also used the same dominant idiom.[3] This interdisciplinary, cross-party and cross-institutional consensus among ruling elites on the terms and language of the debate came together to marginalise thoroughly the claims of other possible ideas about the nature and future of French political unity: principally, the nationalist and culturally exclusive rhetoric of the far right, and the multicultural and internationalist ideas of the radical left.

Spelling out the substance of these dominant ideas is made easier by centering the discussion on various official documents that represent the central crystallisation of these public discussions. I shall make reference to a variety of official reports and policy reflections on immigration, naturalisation, social policy and education. However, two particular sets of reflections stand out as the most important focus of official thinking. These were incidences of extraordinarily high-profile public reflection, continually referred to in the debates, scrutinised by the media, and used as the basic linguistic and conceptual blueprints for politicians and policy-makers in their attempts to revise and justify policy developments: the *rapports* of the *Commission de la Nationalité* (1987–8) and the *Haut Conseil à l'Intégration* (1990–3). Indeed, the public sessions of the *Commission* were broadcast daily on television, the first and only time this has ever happened in French politics.[4]

The first *Commission* came into being as a result of the heated arguments about reform of the *Code de la Nationalité* by the Chirac government (1986–8), and the all-party recognition that a thorough reflection on the nature of French political unity under the new social, cultural and demographic conditions of the 1980s was needed. The Commission, headed by Marceau Long, a well-known civil servant, was set up with the explicit remit of clarifying the law and its wider dimensions, and formulating proposals for reform. The task was given to a self-styled committee of *sages* ('wise men'), largely academics from elite Parisian backgrounds, in history, law, sociology and political science, including Alain Touraine and Dominique Schnapper. Their conclusions were based on the findings of an extraordinary public democratic forum. Almost a hundred prominent figures from all areas of French public life – leaders of immigrant associations, youth leaders, teachers, local politicians, religious representatives, ministers, journalists and other intellectual figures – were interviewed in public and broadcasted sessions about their technical knowledge, experiences and opinions on the immigration and integration issue. Each was asked his or her viewpoint on what it meant to be French now and in the future – '*être français, aujourd'hui et demain*' – the eventual title of the two-volume report. The report led to a number of concrete propositions for reform, together with a series of explicit philosophical statements about the nature of France, and the foundations of the dominant policy idea of *intégration.*

The follow-up to these findings was the setting-up in 1990 by Michel Rocard, the next prime minister, of a more long-term *Haut Conseil à l'Intégration*, again headed by Long. This time it was made up primarily of a select group of cross-party politicians, local *maires*, civil servants and judges, with one academic, Jacqueline Costa-Lascoux, as an advisor. The aims of this

Conseil were to explore the questions and framework set up by the first report, to establish a research programme to build knowledge and data about the actual progress of integration, and to confront a series of concrete institutional dilemmas with normative propositions for legal and political reform. The *Conseil* in all published six reports during the period 1990–3.

The documents can be read as the focal point of an extraordinary consensus in French public affairs, on the vocabulary, themes and theoretical frame they provided for more detailed political discussion and debate. In essence, it was a consensus which coincided with the emergence of *la République du centre* (the centrist republic), much discussed at the time: the recent surpassing of the historical divisions of left and right about the legacy of the French Revolution.[5] My analysis here, then, will concentrate on reading the consensus as a self-coherent public philosophy of integration – and distinct version of philosophical liberalism – that can be broken down to its essential theoretical claims, components and assumptions. Such an analysis will then enable a detailed comparison along the same lines with my second liberal case study, Britain, as the next step.

THE MYTH OF REPUBLICAN CITIZENSHIP

The public discussions have, in effect, set up a theoretical frame in France which not only purports to explain how their policies of immigration and integration can and should work, but also creates a comprehensive interpretative scheme that locates these policies as the 'natural' product of French cultural and historical particularisms. Actual policy changes and the novelty of some of the questions posed by recent post-war immigration have been elided from the picture, lost in the reaffirmation of a particular national myth which claims that questions of immigration and integration would always and self-evidently be dealt with in this way. In short, this is the myth of republican citizenship. As a starting point, it is worth spelling out the two essential normative and explanatory claims characteristic of this public philosophy; a theory so at pains to mask the recentness and artificiality of its construction and the incompleteness of the questions it focuses on.

The apparent rootedness of the public philosophy is testified by the fact that a number of recent American commentators, most notably Rogers Brubaker, have indeed 'corroborated' the official French self-perceptions by making what they call the 'historical cultural idiom' of republican citizenship the key variable in explaining French policy and politics in the 1980s.[6] These are American writers in the francophile vein of historian Eugen Weber, reflecting back to the French an even more classically 'French' version of themselves.[7]

The first claim is the historical one. This has, in effect, sought to wield the 'particularity' of France's political and culture heritage as the most important determining factor of the concerns and emphasis of present-day immigration policy. It argues that the rules of immigration and the process of integration can be set in strongly republican, citizenship-based terms, because they are a direct continuation of the decisive period of nation-building that took place during the Third Republic (1871–1914), itself a reworked inheritance of the Revolutionary and Napoleonic periods. During this period the various regional identities of France and a large wave of European immigrants were unified as a 'French' citizenry by a national *brassage* (intermixing) of all their diverse constitutive elements. It is argued that the classic civic idea of France put together during this period – of France as a universal nation of equal and free citizens – should be used to explain and understand the political dynamics of the present. The memory of a series of constitutive historical moments is typically evoked to confirm this: the French reaction to the Franco-Prussian conflict over Alsace–Lorraine, in which it was argued that French nationality was a question of voluntary adherence, not ethno-cultural belonging; the separation of Church and State that followed the Dreyfus affair, when a Jewish officer was wrongfully accused of betraying the nation; and the forging of universally inclusive nationality laws to establish boundaries and integrate regional peasants and new immigrants into the education system and military service. These events, it is said, not only cemented the idea of the French nation as it entered the twentieth century; they also created a formal institutional *legacy* that does and should determine the kind of policies adopted today on immigration and integration.

The second claim essential to the idea of republican citizenship is the formal, institutional imperative of framing questions in these terms. It identifies the legal and political definition of formal citizenship and naturalisation procedures as the root question at stake. Integration is said to hinge on formalising the idea of associative membership within the political space of the nation which, by defining boundaries and the lines of in/out between citizens and foreigners, establishes the shape and unity of a modern nation-state. It is this process of clarifying and applying formal rules to immigration that is assumed to be the key *enjeu* (stake) in solving the problem of social and political integration within a particular territory. The argument is taken to be equally applicable to the present day as to the nineteenth century; it thus lays a very heavy stress on exclusively *national* boundaries, belonging and identity in maintaining social and political order. The achieving of successful integration – a moral social order – is seen to be dependent on the nation-building process, rather than preceding it or being independent of it: this despite what one might expect in an increasingly interdependent, internationalised world.

These themes and arguments are common to nearly all the leading French theorists of the 1980s. They repeatedly affirm that France has a culturally particular idea of citizenship which sustains its own distinct idea of the nation; that the path of recent immigration politics and public reaffirmation of a classic idea of integration merely confirms the continued relevance and importance of assimilatory nation-building processes in solving the problem of integration; that the French nation is in some sense fundamentally resistant to the apparently inexorable progress of post-national forces; that there is a distinct French '*modèle*' of immigration and integration unaffected by other nation's practices and decisions. But is this myth or reality? All of these claims are made in the face of other developments which suggest the opposite: the convergence of policy practice and institutional forms in different countries; the breaking-down of culturally particular national models and idioms; the ineffectiveness of formal political and legal institutions in governing social life; the effects of transnational institutions and discourses. Does all the talk of republican citizenship truly reflect the 'classic' and 'inevitable' processes of nation-building said to be still taking place through the integration of post-war immigrants? Or is the talk merely a political symptom of a neo-nationalist backlash to forces beyond the nation-state's control? To answer this question, and assess the core theoretical claims of the public philosophy of republican citizenship, it is necessary to go back and retell the political story of immigration and integration in the 1980s and spell out the complex web of ideas that emerged from the official discussions of the decade.

FROM THE PRAGMATICS OF *INSERTION* TO THE HIGH PRINCIPLES OF *INTÉGRATION*

To account adequately for the role of ideas in debates on immigration and integration in the 1980s, it is necessary first of all to break out of the currently dominant ways of seeing the problem in France. So many of the leading French commentators were involved in the construction and naturalisation of the dominant public philosophy that it is impossible to separate the 'scientific' claims of their work from their normative and political intentions. They have to be read both with and against the grain, as it were, as symptoms of the very political problems they help identify and diagnose. The historical 'naturalness' of the focus on republican citizenship should thus immediately be brought into doubt by noting the fact that the underlying rationale of politics and practices towards the treatment of ethnic minorities was clearly different before the mid-1980s, and was transformed dramatically by the new republican concerns of recent years. Previously, there was no automatic connection of immigration with the ideas of republican citizenship; nor was the issue anything like as salient as it was to become in the late 1980s.[8] It would be wrong therefore to assume that these particular policy issues have always been so strongly framed – let alone determined in an explanatory sense – by ideas of a republican kind.

Up to the mid-1980s, the dominant logic of the state towards immigrants was centred on the idea of socio-economic *insertion*, located as a sub-set of general state social policy on welfare and political economy. *Insertion* is often presented as an *ad hoc*, unprincipled idea that focused too much on the im-

migrants' social specificities. This is done in order to highlight
the way the worked-out philosophy of *intégration* has formulated an inclusive, universal solution to the big cultural and
political issues raised by immigration.[9] Yet *insertion* functioned
precisely because it was not really a grand idea at all, but a
loose collection of narrowly targeted practices, which avoided
treating the big symbolic political questions that were to blow
up centre-stage in the 1980s: firstly, by tracking and responding to the presence of new immigrants through a concern for
their basic welfare and social needs; and secondly, by playing
down the issue, away from the centre of party political cleavages. The practices were pitched at a local level, at specific lo-
cations with a high concentration of new immigrants, and a
high risk of the social ills of poverty. Their goals were to assure
basic needs of housing, social security, and the registering of
new immigrants within local authorities. Such practices were
predicated on the official monitoring of key indices of income,
criminality, and educational achievement, criteria quantifiable
in strictly culture and colour blind terms, and measurable relative to certain statistically established norms. Insertion was a
nakedly instrumental strategy of the state for dealing with
a social issue it did not wish to see explode; however, it was
not without a 'progressive' dimension. Certain sites for the
optimal insertion of the new immigrants were privileged: participation in local self-help associations was encouraged, and
the trades unions facilitated the acceptance of immigrants into
the lower section of the workforce.[10] Where it helped, such
processes were also encouraged through the cultural groups
and representatives of the immigrants. A series of reports com-
missioned by the Socialists in the mid-1980s sought to explore
and extend the theory of insertion in these terms.[11]

The justification for this set of concerns – and the narrow
but specific compass of its ambitions – was a wholly pragmatic
one, formulated in technocratic 'elite management' terms. It
was an approach designed to avoid social disturbance, and to
ease and offset the potentially negative social side-effects of immigration, otherwise almost exclusively viewed in economic
terms as a strong benefit to the country. The rationale of the
state was thus focused on a quite different set of questions
from the new policy framework of the late 1980s, and remarkably unburdened with the kind of open public controversies

that were to become so central: that is, the big symbolic questions of 'belonging' and the cultural integrity of France; the moral 'otherness' of Islam and its threat to western values; the political obligations of citizenship as the necessary vehicle for civic incorporation; or the central abstract conception of nationhood, seen as so important to the maintenance of national identity in the face of cultural pluralism. The overall social and political integration of the nation was simply not thought to be upset by the new immigrants; nor was national identity seen to be in any way tested by the success of policies towards them.

In many ways, the lack of salience given to problems arising from *insertion* was assured by a relative innocence about the immigrant issue and the initially unproblematic numbers involved. Immigration was accepted as being driven by clear economic and demographic forces, pushing the recruitment of foreign labour to the French workforce. Immigration policy was determined by economic necessity, a translation of a simple utilitarian logic of justification that was essentially little different from elsewhere in Europe.[12] It was not necessarily thought that the immigrants would stay or need to be fully integrated into French culture; their presence was similar to that of the guest-workers that many other European countries had recruited during that period. When restrictions on further immigration came, forced in France as in other European countries by the economic downturn after the 1970s oil crisis, these too could also be unproblematically justified on the same utilitarian economic grounds: that France no longer needed the workers, and that an economic limit had been reached to the assured *insertion* of new immigrants. This indeed was the original instrumental sense of the expression '*seuil de tolérance*' (the threshold or limit to toleration), now often used by politicians as an exclusionary cultural or nationalist argument.[13]

Looking back, the question that needs to be asked, therefore, is how the issue of immigration blew up into the proportions it took during the 1980s. Why was it *this* issue that led to the return of a grand debate on the nature of French republicanism, with the integration of recent North African and African immigrants the epicenter of party political debate and positioning, and the key test-site for the continued validity of republican ideals? A number of the obvious potential explanations fail to do justice to the hugely symbolic nature that the question took. It is not that the politics of *insertion* could be said to have failed dramatically, or caused the kind of social breakdown that might have led to such a complete rethink in the state's rationale. The pragmatic practice had coped relatively well up until the early 1980s, and did not compare unfavorably – in terms of socio-economic welfare, legal rights and political participation – with the practices and social repercussions of immigrant policies in other comparable West European nations, while being on a broadly convergent path.[14] This was certainly no longer the case by the time the *rapports* came out in the late 1980s, with France taking a wholly particular national line in its new politics of *nationalité* and *intégration*. Nor could the crisis of the 1980s be accounted for solely in terms of the numbers of 'problematic' (that is, racially and culturally different) immigrants, or their offspring. Numbers had been dropping since the first immigration restrictions, begun in 1974, and the proportion of North and Central Africans in France, although it has grown, has always been less than that of immigrants of other origins.[15] In 1982, the total number of foreigners in France of Portuguese origin (764 860/21 per cent of the foreign population) was as large as the Algerians (785 920/22 per cent), with numbers of Moroccans (431 120/12 per cent), Tunisians (189 400/5 per cent) Turkish (110 000/3 per cent) and Central Africans (157 380/4 per cent) being rather smaller, and matched by immigrants from other European countries (Italians 9 per cent; Spanish 9 per cent; Others 8 per cent). In 1990, the same proportions broadly hold, except for a marked rise in Moroccan and Turkish immigrants: Portuguese (18 per cent), Algerians (17 per cent), Moroccans (16 per cent), Tunisians (6 per cent), Central Africans (5 per cent), Italians (7 per cent), Spanish (6 per cent) and Turkish (5.5 per cent). Of course, these figures do not include illegal immigrants, or indicate anything about the social class of immigrants arriving, or their concentration in poor urban areas. Finally, it would seem wrong to overstate the 'discovery' of Islam during the 1980s as a justification, and exaggerate the growing problem with its 'alien' cultural practices.[16] The immigrants had always been Muslim, and this had not been a problem until then: cooperation with religious representatives had in fact played a

key part in the rationale behind *insertion* through local political and union representation in the 1970s. And, while the
spread of religious fundamentalism has grabbed the spotlight
during the 1980s, the cultural clashes that took place and the
numbers of devout practitioners have always been overplayed,
usually with crude political purposes in mind.

To get at the wider context behind the emergence of these
particular concerns, the question of immigration needs to be
connected with other political issues that were growing in importance across all of Western Europe during the 1980s. That
is, the growing power of regionalism, the decline of the nation
as a source of social solidarity, and the decline in real terms of
both the state's powers of governance and its ability to fund
social welfare programmes. Seen this way, the question concerning the incorporation of North African and other immigrants into French life was but one in a class of questions
beginning to challenge the effectiveness of the dominantly
centralised French state in securing the social and political integration of the French nation *as a whole*. In this respect the
French experience was completely in line with the international evolution of liberal politics elsewhere from the 1970s to
the 1980s: towards deregulation, increased individualism, and
a more *laissez faire* relation between state and society. This tendency was indeed reinforced by the perceived failure of the
overtly state-socialist, centrally planned economic policies of
the first Mitterrand government (1981–3), which had attempted to go it alone in the face of dominant international
economic currents.[17]

In other ways, however, the same Mitterrand government
had openly sought to ride the wave of decentralisation. Public
solidarity was under threat because of the increased competition for welfare privileges and the growing corporatism of minority groups and regional interests, looking for some degree
of institutional autonomy from the centre. These developments were creating an increasing tendency towards clientel-
ism in the relation between welfare recipients and the state.[18]
One of the central responses to this by the new government of
1981 was the first attempt to decentralise business and administrative issues away from Paris.[19] A core element in this was
the place of cultural policies in a pro-active outlook towards
the regions. A new spirit was being articulated by the newly-

created Ministry of Culture headed by the popular and highly visible Jack Lang: a spirit focused on the idea of the *droit à la différence* (the right to be different), initially conceived as a vehicle for increasing institutional autonomy in the regions, symbolised around cultural issues.[20] Clearly, in practice, the new spirit would begin to pose serious organisational questions about how, in such a habitually elitist and centralised state as France, such a devolution might be possible.

However, although this was not the main intention of the policies, offering a 'right to culture' in these terms opened a wider set of questions than just regional autonomy. The *droit à la différence* was also quickly cited to characterise positively the treatment of North African immigrants in France. Their most popular organisational form had always been religious: Islam, a religion without an established institutional place in the secular public framework of France. The logic of expanding rights in this direction was leading to the obvious development of something very alien to the French political system: political pluralism, the sectarian bargaining for rights and resources by self-interested sub-groups of the polity. Although the natural development of a political pluralism of business and regional interests would seem inevitable and desirable in many ways, the critics of the decentralisation taking place focused their worries on the threat of ethnic, cultural and religious sectarianism and its challenge to centralised French unity.[21] These concerns were exacerbated by the claims sections of the Catholic church were again beginning to raise for more autonomy for church-organised education, a challenge to the historic separation of church and state.[22] Indeed, the huge public demonstrations which derailed Socialist plans to curb the religious education sector marked the first serious public defeat and crisis of the government in 1985.

Parallel to these internal developments, France's growing engagement in the European Community was also challenging the coherence of certain nationally-bounded state policies. Not only were economic policies increasingly slipping beyond the control of the nation-state into a new realm of international political economy, but the emergence of a European legal and welfare regime was also posing new questions about social rights and citizenship for non-nationals. With the need for harmonisation of the status of migrants and non-nationals across Europe – a process that would eventually lead to the 1985 and 1990 Schengen accords on border controls and other European agreements on the treatment of migrants – new issues were being raised about the access to welfare and social rights of non-citizens or denizens residing in France, and thus their *de facto* social incorporation in the nation.[23] One tendency was pulling France towards what might be called the 'United States of Europe' option: integrating France within a European framework for protecting socio-economic welfare as the basis for full incorporation. These are the kinds of practices found in Scandinavia or the Benelux countries. The pragmatic politics of the pre-1980s, in effect, fitted this kind of framework, because in their substance they did not clearly distinguish between the *insertion* of permanent new French citizens and other. Rights and benefits were attached to residence and locality, rather than membership in the nation. However, at the same time, in an atmosphere where social solidarity and welfare provision was seen to be more and more problematic and under threat, the generosity of these provisions could be used as an issue by politicians seeking to impose more restrictive conditions: that is, by making nationality and full French citizenship a basic condition of entitlement.

These series of challenges – regionalism, declining solidarity, Europe – amounted to a font of potential change to the idea of centralised state control and national polity unity. But the problems might not have been put together with the question of *les immigrés* in France, nor framed in terms of grand symbolic questions about the unity and integrity of the nation as a political and cultural entity, had it not been for the emergence centre-stage of Le Pen and his party, the *Front national*, at the heart of French politics in the mid-1980s. For sure, the conditions for the emergence of immigration as a public problem had already become evident in the late 1970s. Giscard d'Estaing, the president at the time, had made an unprecedented move to racialise the immigrant issue, as a justification for the forcible deportation of illegal immigrants to North Africa.[24] Moreover, working-class solidarity with the immigrants had in many places broken down. The trade unions were becoming increasingly less supportive of immigrant issues, and the ruling Communist Party in some cities had begun to pursue a new anti-immigrant line in local politics.[25] Into the

1980s, these currents had been picked up and used by the *Front national*, who were now taking votes from both the French Communist Party (PCF) and the right wing of the mainstream conservative parties, the RPR (*Rassemblement pour la République*) and UDF (*Union pour la Démocratie Français*). Their growing political presence was aided by Mitterrand's apparently deliberate playing off of Le Pen against the mainstream right. In 1985, he introduced proportional representation, an electoral move that allowed the *Front national* representation in the national parliament for the first time.

Le Pen's breakthrough was to take the issue of immigration, and focus the various strands of these many other political questions around one question: that of the integration of new immigrants and their place in France. His position was thus an articulation of both an anti-elitist, provincial and marginalised voice within the population, and of a particular, homogenous idea of France, built around its Catholic, anti-Semitic and anti-European poles. As such, it used the decline of the centralised state to propose a different basis for French national unity not so riven by the same kinds of tensions. It gave voice to 'legitimate' nationalist fears about the general extension of social rights and political pluralism, but framed them in terms of a centre-piece criticism of *les immigrés*: that they were the root cause of the debased nature of French citizenship and, in particular, the corrupting influence of North African and Islamic culture on the authentic French national culture.[26] Although an inversion and gross simplification of the wider political picture, it was a powerful and challenging line to the existing policies, in the way it used and played on fears about the underlying political developments connected with the decline of the nation-state, creating a new symbolic focus for the issue.

Some of the most skilful turning of the issues to his advantage centred around the dubious idea of the *droit à la différence*. In Le Pen's hands, this was interpreted as the bottom line of Muslim claims in France, and taken to mean: '*différence*' = 'not one of us', and therefore not truly French. Cultural difference and the sectarian demands by Muslims could thus be highlighted as the unwanted outcome of French society's past openness to newcomers. By emphasising their diverse cultural or religious background, and blurring the lines between new immigrants with full citizenship and those still foreign or illegal residents, the crudely identified *immigrés* were all thereby said to enjoy overly easy and unproblematic access to social rights and welfare. This was then argued to have debased the institution of French citizenship. Citizenship, it was said, should be based on loyalty to French territory, culture and history, and impose a strong cultural assimilation as a condition of political incorporation: '*être français, cela se mérite*', in the words of the extreme right think tank, *le club de l'horloge*.[27]

The political pay-off from this new rhetorical line was initially attractive enough to tempt the mainstream right into toying openly with Le Pen's rhetoric of nationalist exclusion. In 1986, the new prime minister, Jacques Chirac, announced proposals for exclusionary reform of French nationality laws that appeared to be supported by the current of public opinion. It was not to be: in reaction to his announcement and the simultaneous killing of a young immigrant by the police, waves of student demonstrators, already out in the streets to protest at educational reforms, were mobilised to protest against Chirac's proposals. This alliance between the students and immigrant and ethnic group interests was propelled by new youth-based 'social movements'-style organisations, among them *SOS Racisme* led by the telegenic Harlem Désir.[28] Despite the objective need for some kind of reform in the face of new migration pressures in the 1980s, the critics succeeded in framing the right's reforms as an attack on the classical universal idea of French citizenship, damning the tone of the proposals as a perversely 'un-French' nativist and reactionary line. In effect, what had happened was that Chirac had underestimated the stakes involved in supporting a conflictual, reformist line. In theoretical terms, Le Pen had succeeded in entering the mainstream political arena by expanding the public political debate. He thus raised 'fundamental' questions of national unity and cultural identity in place of the technical, policy-orientated issues of 'normal' political management of the immigrant question. His strategy was repeated by the marginal new left social movements, themselves looking for a political voice.[29] Chirac's initial attempts to ride this wave merely exacerbated the destabilising and conflictual politics newly aroused; threatening the stability of the *cohabitation* and the recent return of the right to power. Realising this, he rapidly changed tack to a centrist line: now emphasising the inclusionary aspects of a new nationality law, within the desire to control and regulate borders. Its introduction was also deferred. A new mandate was sought through the launching of an extraordinary *Commission de la Nationalité* to elaborate the reform proposals. The Commission would offer a solution to the 'fundamental' questions that had been raised: a comprehensive reflection on the basis of social integration and national unity in France, that would later lead on to the setting-up of a permanent *Haut Conseil à l'Intégration*. A propos of his change of plan, Chirac declared in September 1987: 'Any modification of nationality law depends on there first being a large national consensus'.

In the face of Le Pen's 'fundamental' challenge, and the popular concerns it played on, it was clear that a low-key justification of the integration of ethnic minorities along pragmatic lines was no longer sufficient. Once the issue became linked with wider concerns about French national integrity and the crisis in its institutional and constitutional structure, the mainstream political centre was forced to look for a new framework for its policies on immigration which might respond to Le Pen's claims. In other words, the political issue became the self-interrogation – the *self-theorisation* – of the state and its citizenry, with its eye specifically on those new members, thanks to Le Pen, now identified by everyone as the central problematic: in other words, the reconceptualisation of French community. It needed to know how these relations might be organised, if not by the kind of political pluralism and clientalist welfarism that was developing; and how the processes of devolution and decentralisation, that had developed in tandem with the pragmatic approach to immigrant *insertion*, could be reconciled with the old tradition of the centralised state in France.

One important factor in the thinking that this problem led to, was the degree of concern felt on both sides of the political spectrum for the drift of these questions. Both the left and centre-right felt a need not to be seen to give way to the nationalist exclusionary politics of the far right, while maintaining a strongly state-centred idea of the political maintenance of public culture and institutions. Here, then, were grounds for a potential consensus, something not difficult to envisage in a system where the French political elites of all colours share a strong common educational background. This is founded on an allegiance to the Parisian centre of an integrated and fiercely national meritocratic system, built around a hierarchical and concentric idea of public administration that is focused at its central points in the *grandes écoles* (elite specialist university colleges) and *L'Ecole nationale d'administration* (ENA), the national civil service college. In significant ways, the drift of the new developments was deep enough to challenge a number of the sacred core ideas of this concentric system: the interrelation of citizenship, civil service and the central administrative control of education, law, and political decision-making. Le Pen's challenge was a cry of *ressentiment* against all this: the voice of another, provincial France, far from the elite Parisian corridors of power. Drawing strength on the wider currents causing the French nation-state's decline, it questioned the automatic association of French national identity and political power with Paris and the cultural elite.

The elite faced a choice. They could give way to the currents drawing away its powers and seek a new decentralised rationale for the state in a new European context; or, rather, they could attempt a *surenchère* (a 'double or quits' inflation) of its central powers, however illusory: a reaffirmation of the idea of France as the centralised nation-state *par excellence*. The elite Parisian mandarins and politicians had no immediate interest in defining away their powers from the centre; the threatening vision of Le Pen's provincial legions helped make this line of development also appear an unpalatable one. In many ways, then, Le Pen's role was to cut down the potential options, and cut across potential differences that might have existed between the left and right without his presence. Given very little opening for an internationalist, Euro-centred approach to the problem, the potential solutions broke down into three revised visions of the French nation-state as a politically and socially bounded whole.

On one side, there was the cultural historicism of certain sections of the right, a sanitised backward-looking version of Le Pen's idea of the French 'gallic' people, associated most obviously with the aristocratic former president, Giscard d'Estaing. Its nation-sustaining idea draws on non-Republican sources: the centralised structures of the Catholic church in France, and a lingering sentimentalism about the distant royalist French past, recently revived again in the argument over Clovis, the alleged first king of France. For a variety of reasons, there is little of appeal to this position, except its clear chauvinist line on immigrants and the EC. It is a myth hard to sustain with the very strongly mixed ethnic make-up of the French population, and one that is strongly tainted by its anti-Semitic association with the Vichy years, and the hardline 'no surrender' defence of the *pieds noirs* (white French settlers) during the Algerian war of independence.

On the other side, there is the idea of France embracing a full cultural pluralism, that often draws on the post-structuralist and relativist anthropological thinking of the *soixantehuitards* (1968 intellectuals). Here the problem is not a *prima facie* incompatibility with the long cosmopolitan make-up of the French nation; the Socialists were clearly inclined to dabble in this kind of thinking in the early years of Mitterrand's presidency. Nor does such an idea have to be of a disenchanted anti-humanist kind, sceptical about the exercise of any political action. Rather, these policies, when implemented through the same top-down, centralised and paternalist political structures – as an abstract and formal *droit* rather than a new attitude of social tolerance – proved to be an inflexible disaster.[30] It was music to the far right's ears: stories of the segregation of Muslim children offered special language and cultural classes – ELCO (*enseignement de langues et de cultures d'origine*) – in French public schools; public money going directly to Muslim organisations with strong fundamentalist links in the Arab world; underhand negotiations with North African nations about national jurisdiction over family law, military service or the school curriculum.[31] It all amounted to a disastrous 'helping hand', quickly associated with declining standards: an unhappy symbol of the reality of *différence* at the level of immigrant achievement and social integration.[32]

Such failures bolstered the appeal of the middle option: the return to the idea of republican citizenship, and the defence of a universalist ideal of integration for immigrants through public virtues and civic incorporation in the old revolutionary tradition. Its primary advocates were a new 1980s generation of media-wise, self-promoting public intellectuals seeking to distinguish themselves from the dominant intellectual currents of the 1960s and 1970s, and keen to tender for direct political influence via all kinds of government-funded research projects, advisorships and commissions now available with the Socialists in power. As well as their fervent nationalist republicanism, what characterised the more successful and mediatised figures – for example Luc Ferry, Alain Finkielkraut, Pierre-André Taguieff – was that they were almost always *philosophes* in tendency, not empirical social scientists; they frequently came from Jewish backgrounds; and they had apparently easy access to the most influential organs of the intelligent liberal press, *Le Monde, Libération, Le Nouvel Observateur, L'Express*, and the widely-read academic journal *Esprit*. Other key interventions in a similar vein were made by Julia Kristeva and Tzvetan Todorov, East European *émigrés* of adopted French nationality. Their ritualistic, generational parricide of the post-structuralist and culturally relativist *soixante-huitards* – with Claude Lévi-Strauss, the man often cited as the most influential living intellectual in France, their *bête noir* – was accomplished by blaming, somewhat ingenuously, the influence of these ideas on the failure of anti-racism and cultural policies in the early 1980s.[33] Their positive philosophy was unanimous: a return to classic French republican ideas of integration through citizenship (*citoyenneté*), securalism (*laïcité*), and an end to the differential treatment of ethnic immigrant groups (their idea of *égalité*).

This was clearly a very easy set of clothes for the elite *énargues* (graduates of ENA) to slip into. With the search for a new statement of nationalist political identity to supplant the uncomfortable *dérapage* of pragmatic and piecemeal policies, something was needed with a sufficiently broad and abstract application across all the aspects of the question; a new 'old' currency was the perfect solution. Across the spectrum of policy and political intellectuals, a very clear new vision was thus articulated, a vision of France claiming a long and noble heritage, but which said more about French political elites in the 1980s than the long tradition to which it referred. Adopted by the court, and annointed by all the leading intellectual press, the new generation of intellectuals could thus announce publicly the coming of *la République du centre* – the overcoming of traditional left–right political schisms – to coincide with the coming *bicentenaire* of the French Revolution.[34]

Such was the mysterious reinvention of the republican tradition, by a process of 'laughter and forgetting' worthy of Milan Kundera's Czechoslovakia: trumpeting the grand moments of modern French self-definition in 1789 (the universal declaration of the rights of man), 1805 (the Code Civil), 1870 (the Franco-Prussian war), 1905 (the separation of church and state and the creation of the Third Republic model of public education); and forgetting the rest. Of themselves, these are not dates that a large section of the French population would remember with any great affection: connected as they are with the institutional subjugation of Catholicism, the harsh repression of regional languages and identities, and the external ambitions of war and colonialism to impose the French code across the globe. Moreover, a number of equally integral and relevant components of the republican treatment of national unity and cultural difference had to be simultaneously airbrushed out of the national 'story': the Vichy years, the left's naive infatuation with communism, the post-colonial débâcle in Algeria. Yet, renarrated in a certain teleological way – as the establishment of a particular French idea of the modern democratic state, the unity of the nation, and the continued successful transformation of wave after wave of different immigrants into *citoyens* – the republican tradition sets itself up as the fundamental deep theory on which the continued social integrity of the nation is dependent.[35] In this light, the integration of North African Muslims thus becomes the great contemporary test of the theory as a valid story of French political nationhood and democracy; hence its elevation to centre-stage in the politics of 1980s.

It may well be asked why, when such a diverse set of cultural components is seen to constitute the idea of the modern French nation, do North African immigrants in particular come to be identified as the central *problématique* challenging the 'one and indivisible' constitutional idea of France? After all, the original idea of the global republican model that fuelled French colonial ambitions had not hesitated about the viability of the secular conversion of natives on grounds of cultural or racial difference.[36] Here, the source of the problem is much more recent and specific: the open scar of the Algerian

War and the brutal shock this experience gave to the normative logic underlying France's attitude towards colonialism and
post-colonial withdrawal. Up to 1962, Algeria was not an overseas colony or settlement, like other countries in the French
and British empires. It was rather an integral *département* (a
county or region) of the French state, distinguished only in
administrative terms by its physical separation from *la France
métropole* (mainland France) on the other side of the
Mediterranean. With the forced amputation of this idea, and
the separation of Algerians into French who left and Algerians
who stayed, the idea of universality inherent in the colonial
picture was ruptured. The re-emergence of a republican ideal
in the newly shrunken France reinvents the colonial universality within the strict bounds of the post-colonial European
nation-state, with the Algerians who came to settle the clear
symbolic centre-piece of these claims. In a way, they have to be
exemplary, be more French than the French, to prove the republican case. The pragmatic universality of treating them as
narrowly economic actors or welfare recipients clearly does
not fulfil the claim; it is only their successful acculturation as
'Frenchmen' that can prove the universality of the political
cultural mission.

The challenge of post-colonialism is the threat of relativism,
celebrated by post-colonial writers as the revolt of the op-
pressed Other to establish its own independence and self-rule
away from the dominant power.[37] The universalist response to
this slide towards cultural relativism in the justification of political practices, is to try to rebuild universality in one nation;
redoubling the effort of anti-relativism, and tying this stance
even more closely to the identity and unity of the nation.[38] It is
this kind of logic that has been played out recently in France,
looking to renew its republican tradition in the new context of
the 1980s. One needs to add that the universalism envisaged is
not only universal in the way it prescribes the good for each
and every individual – the virtue of the good republican
citizen – but universal in that it is 'open to all' races, cultures
and ethnies: providing there is a wish of the *de facto* resident to
become French in a substantive sense. Cultural pluralism in
France, openly at least, is never denied; what cannot be admit-
ted is the disunity of political interests and goals within the
central political institution of citizenship: the divisions caused

by political pluralism, and the centrifugal separation of institutions. Furthermore, the justification of this conception is not only driven by the internal need to achieve and assure national unity and membership closure. In important ways, it is for others too, the eyes of the international community, in order to guarantee the superior *distinction* of the French conception.[39] Hence, the building-up of this paradoxically nationalist French universalism is enacted through the continual self-comparison with what are read as other liberal nations' '*modèles*' of nation-building and social integration, portraits of others so often stereotypical as to be silly.[40]

Firstly, there is the time-honoured 'classical' comparison with Germany as primordial ethno-cultural nation, where the idea of political citizenship is said to be dangerously subordinated to the exclusionary blood ties of '*das Volk*' (the German people). Harking back to Third Republic philosopher Renan's clarion call – itself a response to the German romantics' criticisms of French cosmopolitanism in post-revolutionary France – contemporary intellectuals have derived from this a clear accent on ethno-cultural openness to newcomers who wish to become French, and a belief in the abstract individualism of the relation between citizen and state.[41] Then there is the bad example of Britain, France's colonial competitor, and her divisive differentialist treatment of the natives. Britain gets it all wrong because of the persistence of an idea of sovereignty rooted in the *ancien régime* (the old royalist regime) and not the people, its fatalist attitude to political progress, and the lack of constitution and rights; from this, a lesson is drawn about integration having to pass through active political participation and the conscious constructed will of individuals, not any kind of *laissez faire*.[42] Finally, there is the bad example of the United States – France's sister constitutional republic – heading rapidly down a road towards the ethnic nightmare of racial segregation and breakdown, *à la* South Central, LA, 1992. This is put down to its laxity towards ethnic and cultural particularism, the all-pervasive power of political correctness (a veritable French obsession), and the social destructiveness of free market inequalities; from this a lesson is drawn about the need for universal social welfare, and the absolute need to avoid the reduction of politics to the self-interested pursuit of non-integrated racial and ethnic interests within a system of political pluralism.[43] Because of their alleged common reliance on '*communautarisme*' rather than '*individualisme*' to integrate ethnic minorities, Britain and the USA are indeed often conflated meaninglessly as the '*modèle anglo-saxon*'.

Pulling together these various ideas, and pushed by the configuration of political forces in the mid to late 1980s, the dominant elites in France thus built a policy consensus on foundations provided by a new generation of policy intellectuals. It represented a new improved and modernised version of republicanism, with the integration of North African Muslims the key problematic at the heart of the matter. This consensus, substantially, is the one spelt out in the *rapports* of the *Commission de la Nationalité* and the *Haut Conseil à l'Integration*. A reading of these *rapports* and other prominent documents from the period will thus help spell out the fine print and deep structure of the distinctive theory of social integration that has developed within French politics in the 1980s. The theory hinges around the concept of *citoyenneté* – a particular working-out of the idea of 'strong citizenship' – whose content and force as a political argument is particular to France and the contingent circumstances of the 1980s. This will become obvious as I spell out the architecture of the French public philosophy in the following pages. The republican philosophy of *citoyenneté* is a political theory of integration that goes well beyond the determining of boundaries and membership, and goes to the heart of theorising moral and social order and the political transformation of individuals into constitutive elements of the democratic nation-state. As I have indicated, the reinvention of this philosophy has transformed the pragmatic theory of social insertion through socio-economic enablement and welfare security, into one now overlain with a whole new set of moral and cultural preconditions about turning culture-bound individuals with divergent interests into a unified citizenry.

CITIZENSHIP AND NATIONALITY

The starting point of all public reflection in France about immigration and integration is always the connection between the idea of citizenship and the formal status of membership in

the nation, spelt out in nationality law. Other political phe-
nomena or social processes may also be recognised as part of
the process of successful integration; however, it is axiomatic
that whatever happens within the nation is first said to be dependent on the successful definition by nationality law of the
line that decides who is a citizen and who is not. The spelling-
out of the full French public philosophy of integration should
therefore rightly begin where the French public reflection of
the 1980s itself began: with the text of the *Commission de la
Nationalité* report, *Être français aujourd'hui et demain*. How does
this text theorise the criteria by which the status of someone's
nationality is determined, and how does it theorise why this
might be politically relevant to their treatment? Further, how
does it set out why this status might be a precondition for the
possibility of their full social integration into French society?[44]

The report's conclusions set themselves up as a self-styled
philosophical reflection on the foundational relation of *intégration, identité nationale*, and *nation*, said to be expressed by
nationality law (*le Code de la Nationalité*). It immediately puts
the emphasis on the intellectual necessity of 'coherence'
between 'two distinct notions, one a fundamental political
principle, the other instrumental and legal: the idea of the
nation and the law of nationality'. This raises the question of
coherence between 'the political idea of the first notion, and
the juridical mechanisms of the second' (EFAD, p. 82). It thus
sets out to define both the 'human, political and social objectives embodied in our idea of national membership' and the
mechanisms by which nationality law is a 'tool in the service of
these objectives'. To do this, 'we need to define its principle
rules and functions, which must harmonise with a long-term
vision of the future [*du devenir*] of France's (EFAD, p. 81).
Clearly, such a starting point presupposes the *normative* nature
of such reflection, both as set of legal norms and as a grander
vision of the goals of France and French society: 'a country in
which the very highest ethical and spiritual values are offered
to its members for their conscious approval and adhesion'.
That is, that the attraction of France as a nation 'was due to its
place in the history of liberty and rights, and to the permanent incarnation there of a political project of universal scope
and ambition [*de portée universelle*]' (EFAD, p. 90). This normative dimension is, from the outset, predominant in any of

the factual or explanatory discussions of the workings of the law, the nature of French national identity, or the mechanisms of integration.

From the outset, the report makes it clear that it is proposing and defending a certain abstract idea of nationhood bonding as the preliminary underlying condition for French national identity, without which social integration and moral order is not possible. The report announces itself with Renan's ringing idea that nationality is 'a plebiscite which takes place every day' (EFAD, p. 87): immediately putting the emphasis on the self-constituting and self-conscious individualist idea of French nationality. This is a conception of the nation where people choose to belong ('*la conception élective*'), in contrast with the supposedly 'determinist' or 'organic' ethno-cultural adhesion of Germans to their nation (EFAD, pp. 89–90). The French nation is thus conceived as a self-elective membership association. Moreover, membership in these terms is to be strictly disassociated not only from blood, racial and cultural restrictiveness – the clearest concession to the new status of North African and other immigrants in post-colonial France – but also from historical accident, geography, or unquestioned convention.

Much of the background to this assertion is found in the busy work of rather whiggish French historians concerned with establishing the continuity of *le creuset français* (the French melting pot) and its track record of assimilating people of diverse national and religious backgrounds in the last century. The most influential of these, Gérard Noiriel – another staunch neo-republican – builds his thesis in opposition to his *soixante-huitard* master, Fernand Braudel. Noiriel offers a rewriting of Braudel's French history that seeks to negate the non-conscious, non-political aspects of the process of nation-building, and rediscover its 'forgotten' immigrant roots.[45] Again the mythical throwback is to the period of the Third Republic, and the moral victory won by the republicans over anti-Semitism in this period (the Dreyfus affair): a story that appeals very well to the strongly self-assimilatory allegiances of Jewish French immigrants, who fill the ranks of the French intellectual class.[46] The teleology of this continuity is, of course, less than wholly convincing. The problematic status of recent, coloured immigrants, has a lot more to do with the painful process of post-colonialism, and a coming to terms with the relative cultural distance of Islamic and African culture, perhaps most vividly played out in the final years of the French–Algerian separation. Moreover, in recent years the French Jewish intellectual community has been increasingly split in its attitude towards French cultural assimilation: the dominantly secular Ashkenazim Jewry often upholding the most fervent republicanism, the less-westernised Sephardic Jews turning back to a mild defence of cultural separatism and identity. The logic of the teleological line on nationality is that no special class of immigrants is to be created out of post-colonial guilt and responsibility: in deep contrast with Britain. Here the dominant logic is one of continuity, with the grand universal ideas of nineteenth-century colonial France, brought back within her European borders. Those immigrant French, who for one reason or another find themselves legitimate members within those bounds – regardless of race, culture or origin – are notionally and formally French, a constitutive identity that encompasses any others.

This thought lays the ground for the first essential precondition for integration to take place: that integration is not, indeed *cannot* (for the self-consistent meaning of *être français*) be possible without the full membership of all residents. This, it is argued, must entail the political identity of full *citoyenneté*. The new terms of nationality law then, are clearly stated to be not a set of regulations controlling immigration, but a set of preconditions for successful integration. However, the spelling-out of nationality law cannot by itself assure integration, and is secondary in importance to it (EFAD, p. 83). Whatever criteria are used to generate the nationality of a French citizen – 'blood line, place of birth, residence or individual choice' (EFAD, p. 92) – they do not of themselves determine the success of integration, which, therefore, must be the predominant focus of political action. This is not a document that primarily aims to build boundaries or exclusion, but rather one that is aimed at questions of inclusion and the potential effect a clarified Nationality Act can have on improving the moral order of the nation. It is a document which sets out very firmly not to follow the line of debate dictated by the far right; although, as I shall argue later, this has proven to be an unavoidable consequence of the obsession with nationality status. Furthermore, it should also be noted that illegal immigration and increased international migration is here not an issue, and is not addressed in any of the normative directives of the report. Rather, it seeks to stabilise the normative status of legal immigration, as the primary mode of access to full citizenship and successful integration. This immediately delimits the scope of the reflections to the idea of full national belonging: incredibly, there is nothing in the report about political refugees, resident 'denizens' (non-nationals residing permanently in the country with some social rights) or the potentials of EC policy harmonisation.[47] Since integration is premised on full membership, there is simply no space in the official theory for these cases.

As the report rightly points out, the French combination of *ius soli* (or *droit du sol*, citizenship by birth in the territory) and *ius sanguinis* (or *droit du sang*, citizenship by blood line) is 'a dispute without any grounding' (EFAD, p. 92), because there are in fact four different, mixed ways of acquiring nationality. However, the stance is laden with a symbolic valency, much more than just a set of formal rules for distinguishing between members and other subjects under the territorial jurisdiction of a nation-state. French nationality, whether obtained by one or the other means, is an endowment with political and moral dimensions, that imposes a normative burden on its recipients. A French national, once a member, cannot escape the constitutive French identity that such membership imposes. It is for this reason that membership cannot be seen as an act of charity to stateless people, or a merely instrumental act of the state to classify newcomers, but is always 'connected to a much larger project' (EFAD, p. 83): integration and the moral order of French national identity.

This perhaps helps explain the stakes riding on the fairly technical changes to the *Code de la Nationalité* proposed by the Commission. Nationality is automatically granted at birth to children with at least one French parent. This is tempered by a strong requirement of physical presence; one can lose one's citizenship if absent over a long period of time. Moreover, there is a strong, and well-protected idea of *ius soli*, which is automatic to third-generation children born on the territory (*double droit du sol*), and easily accessible to second-generation children at majority, providing they have five years' residence and a clean criminal record. The situation is complicated by the anomalous rule that any Algerian parents born before 1962 (the year of independence) are also considered French, and that their children, although nominally second-generation *immigrés*, are in fact considered French at birth. The defence of these old traditions in the report is based on the thought that time and presence in the country supposes 'a true growing of roots (*un enracinement réel*)', particularly when these immigrants have undergone the process of integration inherent in the process of French education (EFAD, p. 93). Inclusion is the accent of the report, not social closure: precisely because the report recognises the need to normalise the status of recent settled immigrants in France. It accepts that a place must be found for them in the national identity, in order to regain political jurisdiction and obligation over such residents, often caught between nationalities and identity allegiances. As such, the main proposals of the report focus essentially on the requirement of voluntarism for a second-generation child, who must between the ages of sixteen and twenty make an individual declaration to want to become French; and of clarifying and improving the procedure and administrative set-up that this requires (EFAD, pp. 213–36). These seemingly innocuous changes were the focal point of a huge and contentious debate that monopolised much of the legislative politics about immigration/integration policy in the late 1980s and was not resolved until new laws (the Pasqua laws) were finally passed in July 1993 by the new right-wing government, implementing many of the substantive recommendations of the report. I will go on in Chapter 5 to discuss these debates and their pathological consequences. Here, I wish first to set out the philosophical claims and assumptions involved in this strong introduction of *volonté* (individual free will or choice) into the process of accession to French nationality.

I have already noted how one of the key strategies of the far right in raising the immigration problem concerned the alleged devaluation of French citizenship in the existing nationality laws. French status was said by them to be something that should be 'deserved', not automatic: a line taken in response to the automatic nature of the third-generation *double droit du sol*, and, more pertinently, the automatic French status of children of Algerian parents born prior to 1962. The right wing also jumped on the fact that, for many North African immigrants, opting for French nationality was merely an instrumental question of avoiding problems with the police or military service in Algeria: a decision which did not implicate their deeper identifications and cultural allegiances, which often remained with Islam or their country of origin.[48] The report's line on *volonté* was a response to these arguments. Citing the weakening of the French nation's traditional sites of *le creuset français* – the school, the military, the trade unions, political militancy, even the family – the report states a lack of confidence in 'automatic social and cultural processes' leading to integration, and the corresponding need to make the conscious individual affirmation of French national identity the foundation of the integrative process (EFAD, p. 86). The Commission thus proposes that the *Code de la Nationalité* become a symbolic reference point for this affirmation.

Here, the issue is far more than the relatively small and specific numbers of cases where individuals have to make a voluntary application to become French; elsewhere, the report rejects the American idea of an oath of allegiance. Rather, the question runs deeper, connecting with the talk in the report of the contractual nature of French citizenship. In fact, the report wants to use the question of the nationality status of new immigrants who become French, as a symbolic issue which can help highlight a more society-wide shift in the conception of the nation: 'a conscious and organised passage from one conception of membership in the nation to another' (EFAD, p. 87). This would be a France in which 'a new mode of organising French society must be found to fit with the idea of individuals expressing a free will to be French' (EFAD, p. 90). The symbolic accent on the *volonté* of immigrants to embrace French nationality is thus the first step towards establishing a new, individualist conception of the *contrat social* in France: the social contract that guarantees the political and social order of France as a political entity. In stating their voluntary adhesion to the nation, new members engage in a new moral relation to their adopted nation, which puts the accent on their individual rights and responsibilities. In this way, the report recognises the diminished role of the state's power over individual citizens as a 'new given' of the 1980s, and that there must be 'a new drawing of lines between the power of the state and the rights of individuals' (EFAD, p. 98). It then justifies the restrictions on automatic acquisition, and the clarification of legal procedures that block acquisition on these grounds. Although this line has an air of anti-centralism and deregulation about it, in is in fact a self-defensive response by the central national powers to the growing individualism of the 1980s. The argument seeks to preserve the privileged line between citizen, state and nation in the republican philosophy, by making the demands of citizenship – and being French – rest even more firmly on individual moral responsibility and political agency.

The framing of the new nationality law in this way, then, indicates how in the 1980s the accession to French nationality is no longer a question, as in the past, of the state's need to conscript members for its armies or get instrumental social control over the residents in its territory; but is rather a symbolic moral theory of the ideal-type bonds of individual rights and obligations that link diverse French citizens as a common citizenry. This rationale thus amounts to a new 'explanatory' thesis of the source of French political unity: one both dependent on the philosophically idealist nature of the proposed new social contract in France, and with its eye on the self-justification of the moral superiority of the French *modèle*, untainted by relativist compromise.

In sum, the first keystone of this thesis is the presumption about an individual's nationality. To become French, it has to be the case that an individual's identity is not definitively determined by their racial or cultural origins, or indeed any other national identity that might clash with their new adopted French identity. The 'autonomy' to choose and become one's (French) nationality is thus the first precondition to the possibility of integration, since it is only through this act of individual *volonté* that the moral requirements of political and social integration can become possible. Of course, the existence of other social processes effecting the transformation of individuals is not denied; but by themselves they would not be *morally* significant – as they must be for the sake of the 'political project of universal scope and ambition' – unless this first condition about autonomy and nationality is taken as a premise. This is ultimately a theory about the nature of an individual's national identity (a pro-active, not passive, form of belonging), which reveals a concern with the preconditions for the achievement of moral social order – the conditions of democratic citizenship – that goes far beyond the theme of assuring boundaries and social closure. Hence, the discussions of nationality law naturally presuppose and carry over into the more detailed discussion of *intégration* that were to follow in the reports of the *Haut Conseil à l'Intégration*. It is here that we will find a more detailed account of the republican theory's underpinning ideas and assumptions.[49]

CITIZENSHIP AND CULTURE

The new philosophy of republicanism in the 1980s is very specific about the openness it wishes to promote: the *diversité* of cultural pluralism is recognised openly as integral and beneficial to the vision of France it promotes. This is both a new and enlarged vision for the 1980s, and a confirmation of the nation's integratory powers in the past. But this acceptance in itself immediately defines a particular problematic for the political unity of the nation: to achieve 'cultural integration' there must be both 'diversity and cohesion', a balance, that is, compatible with the maintenance and renewal of a strong idea of French national identity. The politics of *intégration*, therefore, must combine two things: on the one hand,

> the legitimate desire of individuals or groups, whatever their geographical, religious, linguistic, ethnic or cultural specificities, to have the full freedom to preserve and develop their means of expression, worship, communication and lifestyles – whether in the private, personal or associative spheres – and by this contribute to the richness and diversity of French society;

on the other, the classic '*modèle français*' of political unity, which is based on rejecting 'the logic of there being distinct ethnic or cultural minorities, and instead looking for a logic based on the equality of individual persons' (CJCI, p. 7).

As I have shown, a belief in the *volonté* of nationality is the first condition of the possibility of integration. The reports of the *Haut Conseil à l'Intégration* spell out the other conditions, together with the detailed theory of how such a model of integration can in practice be possible. They are concerned with two central things. Firstly, identifying certain public spaces – '*lieux priviligiés*' – where the integratory process is particularly likely to happen: 'schools, associations, the media ... where the coming together of cultures takes place, or ought to take place' (CJCI, p. 8), areas for which it argues the state has an interventory or legislative role. Secondly, establishing a normative ideal-type conceptualisation of the relation of individuals to their culture, which will enable the reconciliation of cultural diversity with political unity.

The individualist accent of the new *modèle français* is here, again, an ever-present current. Rejecting the former policies of *insertion*, the report sets up a distinction between the old idea of assimilation, driven by a nation-building logic imposed by the centralised state, and the new one of integration, in which *intégration* is an active process, driven by 'the choice and participation of new members' (PMFI, p. 8). Here, it publicly endorses the arguments of Jacqueline Costa-Lascoux, the academic advisor to the *Conseil*, citing her well-known formula for integration in France: 'from immigrant to citizen (*de l'immigré au citoyen*)'. Although an innocuous-looking slogan, this phrase in fact encapsulates the enormous *qualitative* change of moral and cultural identity that the ideal-type integration of an immigrant is supposed to imply. This transformation is to be enabled by equality in front of the law, but not an equality that might lead to the '*logique de minorités*'. It is a line dependent on an official public and political definition of the individual *vis-à-vis* her culture, that imposes a strong definition of the subordinate place of culture in the eyes of the state. It refuses any kind of official recognition of minorities as such, where individuals are identified with a minority group – be it racial, confessional, cultural, and so on – for the purposes of state action (whether redistributive or affirmative). This goes as far as to eliminate even the collection of census data based on any kind of ethnic classification, other than distinguishing whether the person had any grandparent of non-French origin. This of course frames the positive intent of any politics towards the promotion of integration in a very strong way: members of ethnic minorities can only claim rights in virtue of their being individuals, not in virtue of their being members of any particular cultural sub-group of the polity.[50] In the French mind, of course, this stands in deep contrast with Britain, and, above all, the USA.

The equality of individuals is at once an institutional, political and moral equality. Very significantly, the definition of equality proposed in the reports is a substantively new one, particular to the mid-1980s picture. Prior to 1980, under policies of *insertion*, equality was something defined and measured in strictly socio-economic terms: in terms of relative poverty, access to work and housing, and opportunity for achievement in education. The politics stuck to narrowly definable, quantifiable terms. With the new accent on social integration, and its strongly normative concerns, the definition of equality has been given further dimensions. It is indicative of a quality of the person as a political being, before a law that embodies French national identity. Equality of this kind entails a political obligation that individuals develop a different relation as *citoyens* towards their culture and its place within the polity. Further, as I shall show, this is a *moral* obligation as well.

The reports are very much concerned with the practical implementation of these goals. To facilitate this, one of the central aims of the *Haut Conseil* was to enable the collection of a far more systematic set of data, experience and knowledge about the facts of immigration and the practice of integration across France. As part of the research for the reports, an extraordinary survey questionnaire was sent out to the town halls of seventy-three city authorities (*communes*) across France, which led to the formulation of a set of criteria for the measurement of *intégration* as a social process (PMFI, pp. 152–82). These criteria are an excellent indication of how the official concerns, even at their most empirical, are structured and dominated by the normative restrictions on classification, and the ideal-type definition of an individual's relation to culture. The criteria are grouped around four key sections: nationality, family, social advancement, and social involvement. While some of the questions in the third and fourth sections are clearly quantifiable, and culturally neutral – the measurement of social advancement, achievement, unemployment, poverty, health, delinquency, housing, household expenditure and so on – the first two sections ask a series of questions that are based on distinctions of a cultural nature. Firstly, they ask about the degree of attachment to the home country, degree of family regroupment, money going out of France, voluntary demands for nationality, the use of the French language; secondly, and more strongly, they ask questions concerning the number of polygamous families, and the rate of pregnancies.

Despite the supposed fluidity of the French conception of diversity, such official criteria are in fact dependent on a fixed opposition between the behaviour of 'normal' French and the *groupe cible*: the object group, defined as 'made up of immigrants and their second-generation children, whether they are foreigners or French nationals ... or at least ... foreigners or immigrants of different origins'. This definition indicates very well that any interpretation of the data would perpetuate an opposition between 'real' French and the 'different' *immigrés* – what is often discussed as the pervasive logic of '*altérité*' (otherness) – which suggests the commitment to diversity is in fact subordinate to a strong substantive idea of what culturally being French should be. Another influential *rapport* of the *cohabitation* period, right-wing deputy Michel Hannoun's *L'autre cohabitation: Français et immigrés* (1986), employed exactly the same insidiously binary framework for its 'progressive'-minded intervention. Moreover, the definition of the 'object group' also indicates the inability of such an official enquiry to transcend the all-powerful normative frame, which prevents seeing the objects of integratory policies as anything except *immigrés*: that is, fundamentally, outsiders and newcomers who must be transformed into citizens in some way. This clearly becomes a senseless categorisation over two or three generations of settled French nationals, but the normative injunction prevents any other classification of a distinct group based on skin colour or cultural origin. Such classifications, sociologically speaking, might be far more revealing of how distinct groups actually behave. Moreover, it would open up an understanding of something these criteria completely fail to address: how persons of a different culture are received by the host nation, and how the behaviour of the indigenous population might be changed by this. But this would be to assume, as the *rapports* rarely do, that integration might be a two-way process. Instead, all such a frame allows is the positing of a fixed ideal at the positive end of the *intégration* process – the *citoyen* – who presumably embodies all the norms from which differences can be measured. Inevitably, of course, reality will fall short of this ideal.

In the second phase of the *Haut Conseil* reports, the emphasis shifts to the legal and institutional problems of dealing with cultural diversity. Here, the guiding idea is a reinvention of the idea of *laïcité* (secularism) as the centre of French public policy (CJCI, pp. 35–50). They go so far as to retrieve the very texts and fine print of the 1905 legislation, and the guiding hand of its founding figure, Jules Ferry.[51] Two main institutional spheres are focused on: education, and the institutional place of Islam in French society. Regarding education, the report restates a set of ideas about the secular foundations of civic education, and its integral role in the facilitating of integration. Two other important educational reports were produced during this period, with rather different emphases that indicate how ideas had been changing. Jacques Berque's 1985 report *L'immigration à l'école de la République*, pleaded for a recognition of cultural difference, and the '*islamo-méditerranéan*' dimension of French national identity. By the time André Hussenet's widely-cited report *Une politique scolaire de l'intégration* was published in 1990, however, a 'classic' republican vision was back in its place. The following passage from the latter report is a good example of the flavour of the stridently reaffirmed French educational ethos:

> To integrate is to establish a stricter interdependence between the members of society, something which implies that the *Ecole de la République* must impart to all its pupils a common knowledge [*un savoir commun*], humanist values of equality, liberty, solidarity, and enable their access to rational thinking, while at the same time underlining the opening of French culture to the world ... In order to achieve these objectives, we propose a single principle: the same ambition for everyone and two main orientations: the removal [*correction*] of inequalities and the opening of French culture to the world.

What is novel in both this and the *Haut Conseil*'s ideas on education, is the opening of French education towards the world, and the idea of it being a 'secular intermixing [*brassage séculaire*]' which covers a diversity of religions, cultures and international perspectives. The accent here, then, is on reconciling the universal extent of world cultures with the universality of the republican ideal: international culture might be embraced, but it is to be institutionalised within a nationally-bounded system that embodies strong ideas about the positive need for secularity and particular political values in civic life. The real problems involved in the strongly secular line – which had already manifested themselves spectacularly by this point in *l'affaire du foulard* of autumn 1989 – are not discussed explicitly in the section on education.

Regarding the institutional place of Islam in French society, the reference to 1905 lays down a clear injunction. The French political system is founded on the separation of political and religious spheres, which entails that *la République* should not fund any '*cultes*' (religions), should ensure all its public institutions are entirely independent of any religious interests, and should practice a strict neutrality among the various transcendental claims made by religions about the true foundations of a good society. The state takes upon itself the role of fixing the legislation within which religions operate. But it also guarantees the private sphere and the conditions for the fundamental exercise of the right to religious practice – 'a freedom which is affirmed, protected and organised' by the reports (CJCI, p. 36) – and the defence from defamation. It reads these commitments as following from the articles about religion in the UN declaration of human rights. The report argues that this is a return to the original sense of *laïcité* in opposition to the militant secularism often associated with the word, and is thus compatible with a commitment to cultural pluralism, public debate about religion and the encouragement of individual responsibility (CJCI, p. 39).[52]

The report is clearly reaching for a compromise position that will reconcile the fact of Islam with the *modèle français* of political unity. In places, the report takes on a rare sociological aspect as it discusses the actual phenomenon of Islam in France, the numbers involved, and what counts as a practising Muslim (since it is both a religious and a cultural allegiance). It recognises that the religious can be an important refuge and source of solidarity – an *identity* – for immigrants in very difficult social circumstances. But the basic line is not to give way to this as an excuse for deviating from the secular principles. The real problem under discussion is the submission of

Islam to the rules of the public game. Hence, the main focus of the report is on those practices that can be interpreted as possible violations of international private law – particularly practices towards women and children – and the need for the practice of the religion to recognise the precepts of French public political order as a pre-condition of its being allowed religious freedoms. The report thus speaks of the value of religious belief, not for its value as an identity or moral resource in its own terms, but as a potential vehicle for a more profound participation in public civic life. To this end, the report introduces the role of public associations as the bridge between the two, recommending that the idea of *laïcité* be focused around the law of associations (1901) which is more supple about the organisation of '*cultes*' as organisations in the public sphere, rather than the harder line taken in the 1905 law about the separation of church and state (CJCI, pp. 39–45).

The report thus proposes the idea of associations as the model for the adaption of religion to the republican ideal, in which the individual's cultural practice is structured – one might say 'disciplined' – by the need to pursue the practice via an official engagement in the public space. Religion is thus to be organised on rule-following associational lines – that cover finance, membership, rules of entry and exit, and so on – which endow this public engagement with a moral significance as a step towards *intégration*:

> Public association is a fundamentally ambiguous thing: it represents at the same time the affirmation of identity founded on certain cultural values *and* the wish to adapt oneself to the rules of French society by dealing with day-to-day problems through legitimate channels. Even the affirmation of a particular identity does not usually represent a turning in on one's culture [*un repli sur soi-même*], but a means of finding the path to a better insertion into the wider society.

It is argued that the relation of associational life with the process of integration is a particularly rich one, and that the 'fact alone of belonging to an association changes the perspective held by the member about their social environment and about themselves' (CJCI, p. 58). Underlying this then, is a heavily normative causal theory of how the rules of the public space, and the process of publicly affirmed *recognition*, generates a positive process of integration. It pictures a process of moral learning in which the culturally backward individual is socialised (integrated) via the participation in a rule-guided association. This is a suspicious echo of the model of the moral socialisation of children, proposed by French Swiss psychologist Jean Piaget, in which the child follows a step-by-step socialisation through the discipline of authority, rules and then principled public association. But are Muslim immigrants to be thought of as children in this sense?

The discussions about associations naturally raise the greater question of the problem of the official recognition of Islam as a public religion in France, on a par with Catholicism, other Christian denominations and Judaism. This is something that has hitherto been refused. The report here follows the line of certain figures who have long been arguing for an adaption of the laws of religion in France to make room for Islam within *la République*. The most important public voice in this respect has been Bruno Etienne, whose work is a provocative and idiosyncratic upturning of many of France's sacred secular ideas about itself. Etienne made a key intervention in the *Commission de la Nationalité* debates, and it is significant that among the significant intellectual players his voice is the *only* non-Parisian voice: a voice from *le midi*, much better tuned in to the Mediterranean world-view.[53] One other important voice in favour of the 'special relationship' between France and *les peuples méditerranéens* is Mohammed Arkoun of the Sorbonne, Paris, one of the very rare public intellectuals of Arab or Muslim origin.[54] In political terms, this position was spectacularly affirmed by the then defence minister, Jean-Pierre Chevènement, during the Gulf war, when he stormed out of the cabinet on exactly this issue: claiming that France had betrayed its special relationship with the Arab world through its involvement. The report endorses the formation of the CORIF (*Conseil de réflexion sur l'Islam en France*), a group of senior representatives of Islam in France that was put together at around this time to discuss ways of institutionalising the religion as a means of promoting integration (CJCI, p. 45).[55] Through this, it was possible to lay down some guidelines about small but symbolically significant questions such as the provision of Islamic sections within public cemeteries, the recognition of certain Islamic festivals and food requirements. It also systematised the public recognition and assistance for mosques and local Muslim organisations which had been going on in reality at the local level, despite the restrictions in the 1905 laws.

The key note in this spirit of compromise is, however, the way in which it ensures the strict *encadrement* (framing, fixing) of any cultural manifestation within the institutional frame of the French polity. Indeed, even the language and formalities of French public institutions impose a strong format on the way in which claims might be made by a religious or cultural group. The culture held by those who make claims within this frame *must* be subordinate to the rules of public life. It is only by way of the strict adherence to the organisational structure of public participation that is imposed, that the manifestation of culture can have any value as the exercising of an individual freedom. 'When organisation is deficient, freedom is likely to suffer' (CJCI, p. 49). It is perhaps this that spells out most clearly why these concessions to Islamic organisations in the public sphere are emphatically not a step towards political pluralism as far as the official line is concerned. '*Les intéressés*' (individuals with private or particular interests) are not to be allowed to pursue or gain the intrinsic value of their culture for their own benefit alone, since particularistic interests that have not been 'organised' will impair the liberty of others. Thus the interests have to be structured to coincide with the interests of the collective. When there is a conflict, the political structure naturally imposes its priority over cultural interests. Individuals have to be able to distance themselves from their cultural perspective when the situation rationally demands it. Here, the intellectual echo is the belated arrival on French shores of the American philosopher, John Rawls. His famous treatise, *A Theory of Justice*, was only translated into French in 1987, and it arrived at just the right moment to be picked up by the new current of individualist republicanism and neo-Kantianism, sweeping a generation of French intellectuals in search of something *after* Marxism. Particularly important was the interest in Rawls shown by leading philosophical figures Paul Ricoeur and Claude Lefort.[56] Although frequently misunderstood, this vogue for Anglo-

American political philosophy has grown immensely in recent years, at the expense of home-grown French social and political theory.

It is here, therefore, that a second fundamental dimension of the meaning of 'autonomy' in the French contractual picture becomes clear: the 'autonomy' of the individual from his or her own culture, proven by the fact that, when structured by the rules of public participation, the individual is always able to step back from his or her cultural perspective and affirm the primacy of the public sphere. There can, therefore, be no room for manœuvre outside the political frame, which seeks to be an all-encompassing definer and guarantor of the sphere of rights and liberty: this is, in effect, the French 'overlapping consensus'. However, this form of republican participation is rather different from the public democratic competition of diverse interests in search of the best pragmatic outcome, which too leaves a certain private realm untouched: the American 'model'. Rather, in France, the diverse interests of *each* become the unified collective interests of *all*, through their equal participation in the public sphere. Its rules are the *Code de la Nationalité*; its symbol the *carte d'identité*. Together they express the idea of *citoyenneté* as full *intégration*, and hence, *nationalité réussie* (proven and successful national membership). This represents the ideal-type end-goal, in which the new immigrant, now fully French, pursues his or her *organised* freedom and cultural interests entirely integrally to the French national identity, and without any externalities not captured within the overall *cadre* of the nation-state.

CITIZENSHIP AND MORALITY

The components of the official public theory discussed so far spell out the basic theoretical conditions and institutional requirements that are necessary for individuals of diverse and divergent cultural backgrounds to be integrated as full, participant *citoyens* in the French nation state. As is now clear, the passage '*de l'immigré au citoyen*' pictured by the reports is founded on something rather more than a set of (relatively) tenable sociological and political propositions about individuals and social and political life. The role of the state is defined as imposing a structure of *normative* preconditions about individuals and their relation to culture and nationality, that overrides the testability or empirical validity of any of the reports' other claims. And, in so far as it has a historical justification, it is a history pulled by the ideal-type end-point defined as the predestined '*devenir de la France*': The public philosophy is thus both a functionalist explanatory theory, and a perfectionist normative one. Clearly, for such a theory to be valid, there is more to the explanation and justification it proposes than empirical proofs. Hence, beneath the factual arguments, a deeper set of conditions for the possibility of integration and the political rightness of the *modèle français* can be found: a 'metaphysics', as it were.

This should come as no surprise, since the structure and intellectual movement of the *rapports* are clearly those of a metaphysical philosophical enterprise: spelling out the *fondements* (foundations) – the conceptual fixed points and values – of the ideas, and hence the transcendental conditions for the universal model to be possible. Once these are identified, it specifies a normative *telos* that becomes both the justification and explanation of the political programme. Any other factual, historical or sociological facts or events are read to conform with this direction. The distinction between this and a social scientific enterprise is underlined by the idea of making a philosophical search the source of policy-making. Political and legal mechanisms are thought only to be able to shape and intervene in the course of events when armed with such normative foundational principles. Indeed, in the hearings and the public debates that followed, the main sociological opposition was drowned out by the slick polemics of the media-friendly *philosophes*, Alain Finkielkraut, Pierre-André Taguieff and the ever-present Bernard Henri-Lévi. What makes it peculiar as a philosophical enterprise, however, is the fact it is so bounded by the idea of the nation as the context in which all these principles have their expression. In this respect, the debates in France make the relation of principles to boundaries and membership clear – in the old Aristotelian way – unlike the rather vague, uncontextualised cosmopolitanism of much contemporary political philosophy.[57] Ideally, of course, the nation and its principled politics coincides with the universal: the philosophical premise explored most insistently by Raymond Aron's daughter, Dominique Schnapper, in her widely-read post-*Commission* writings.[58]

La France de l'intégration, as Schnapper calls it, is thus an ideal theoretical construct populated by voluntaristic and self-conscious, yet exclusively bounded and defined individuals. What makes this possible is the fact their liberty, unity and cohesion all coincide in a national political identity, which allows them freedom of culture (it is not an all-encompassing cultural identity) but unites them as a political citizenry. This gives a clue to the deeper metaphysical nature of the *contrat social* that the individuals enter into: their liberty is in fact conditional on embracing the obligations and rights of the political sphere as their own. Autonomy, then, which is presumed to be possible as a condition of the theory, is not a pre-existent property of individuals as such. It is in fact constituted by the *act* of entering into the social contract in which particular interests are subordinated to those of the all-encompassing collective. What is more, it is this transformation of interests, from self-interests to collective interests, that enables the nation-state to constitute itself and be the democratic *République* of philosophical lore. Thus, the reports speak of this foundational idea within the *modèle français* as a

> fusion within the individual … [in which] the true attachment of the majority of individuals to the society in which they live … are the possibilities that a society offers to its members to invest in themselves, to realise themselves, to be recognised, in short to find reasons for living and to defend the world in which they live. (PMFI, p. 12)

Moreover,

> integration in effect cannot work in the long run, and society will not find its dynamic equilibrium, if all individuals with their different interests, French people as well as foreigners, do not, by seizing the very mechanisms of society, its potentials and constraints, and – rising above passion driven reactions to turn in on themselves or reject others [*l'autre*] – put their energy and civic commitment in the service of these goals. (CJCI, p. 8)

The reports are thus said to outline the 'preservation of the social bond [*lien social*] through the analysis of problems linked to the most intimate springs of action of the individual'. This is the private realm of individual free will, guaranteed by the granting of individual rights by the state. Only the individual who chooses to act within the political structure offered can be moral, since acting outside of it is by definition to act in a selfish, particularistic or anti-national way; to fail to do so is to fail to be truly French.

The other distinctly philosophical and prescriptive dimension of the *rapports* is their concern with picturing the question of *intégration* as an intellectual problematic, to which the *Haut Conseil* can provide solutions. Since they visualise the problem of Islam as the vital test case for the new improved *modèle français*, they treat the question as one which requires the specification of the limits of diversity as a trade-off with political cohesion: hence, they are a philosophical line-drawing exercise. Here, the focus becomes the specification of the 'juridicial conditions for integration': how French law should approach the concrete questions that are thrown up by the integration of Islamic practices in France, and the justification for this approach. In this vision, the law is not considered merely in positivist terms. It is itself fully expressive of the ideal of the good society spelt out by the end-goal of successful integration, and thereby directly expressive of the very moral order that holds together the political unity of the French nation.

To set this up, the *rapport* introduces its reflections with a deep revision of a second fundamental normative political principle, to match its revised conception of equality: that of 'public order'. This is defined, not in terms of order, discipline or social control, as might be supposed, but as 'the totality of values to which French society is profoundly attached and which found its cohesion' (CJCI, p. 11). In connection with this, the dilemmas of *intégration* are said to relate principally to the question of personal statute. This represents an individualisation of the rationale for treating the problem, in line with the emphasis throughout the reports on the individual as the focus of normative concern: the individual as the morally autonomous agent of choice and responsibility. These two definitions are said to be grounded in the definitions laid out in international private law, and the universal declaration of human rights (CJCI, pp. 15–16). The state then takes it upon itself to defend these rights of the individual within the national sphere, when certain cultural practices infringe the public order as defined.

These definitions amount to an extraordinary combination of ideas. Firstly, the definition of public order as a moralised definition of the public good – as a normative goal rather than an instrumental value or a pragmatic outcome – interprets the concept as a set of 'French' values, again deeply particular to, and constitutive of, French national identity. And then, by grounding the defence of individuals, not in virtue of their nationality or as the cultural responsibility of the French state, but as universal individual rights-holders, the *rapport* takes it that the profound values particular to France are in fact entirely convergent with those expressed by international human rights. That is, France, as a political entity, is the constitutional *paragon* of a nation-state entirely conforming to the universal idealist model inscribed in international law. In particular, this entails that the restrictive laws it proposes are justified entirely by their being an embodiment of human rights: it denies that they are justified in reference to any instrumental *raison d'état* or national or cultural interests.

The substance of this definition is directed with a very particular target in mind – the exclusion of Islamic fundamentalism from France – but the justification of its acceptability is presented in the most abstract philosophical terms. The legislators have in mind the symbolically sensitive area of practices towards women and children in Islamic culture that violate western norms – particularly *excision* (female circumcision) and polygamy – although numerically these are rather 'freak' cases, compared to the rather more mundane task of deciding which nation has jurisdiction over ex-nationals residing in French territory in less spectacular cases in family law. The report clearly uses the moral unpleasantness of the symbolic cases to bolster its line that France should seek jurisdiction as far as possible over *all* cases in family law, in the name of international private law and human rights. No compromises are allowed to interfere with the absolute deontological right of the Law, as embodied by the French state, to pass judgment on those cases that it seems as infringing human rights: compromises of a long-term utilitarian kind (for example, that it would be better overall not to make a fuss over such symbolic line-drawing because it fuels fundamentalism), or of a sociological kind (for example, that the maintenance of certain practices aids integration by combating *anomie*; or that the good of the child within her community needs to be considered). This line enables the report to defend a position that overrides the practical difficulties experienced by many lawyers in recent years, of making the personal statute of foreigners in France compatible with the French law.[59] As such, it allows the principal that the *loi du domicile* (law of residence) may override considerations of the national origin of the subjects. A proof of durable residence in France is enough, something which gives a strong interpretative role to French judges as to who in fact is counted as subject to French law (CJCI, pp. 27–30).

It might seem extraordinary that the legislators should go to such lengths to impose a moral justification on a technical legal question more ordinarily left to pragmatic bargaining between nations. But it has to be recognised that the effort is driven by the perceived threat of Islamic fundamentalism, that smoulders forever in the French mind, as it worries about the ongoing troubles in Algeria. From this, the politics of dealing with Islam in France are forever turned into a symbolical struggle between the universal political virtue of the French public system, and its heavily legislated public/private distinctions in opposition to the threat of Islamic '*intégrisme*' (a state in which church and politics are not separate). This is the term which is always used in France to refer to religious fundamentalism, perhaps since the French principals of *intégration* are themselves so clearly 'fundamentalist' in spirit. It expresses well the dominant image of Islam, and the way in which its precepts about the relation of the spiritual and the temporal break the cardinal law of the French polity: the separation of church and state, and the state's monopoly on moral judgement.

The sum of these two classic philosophical dimensions – the search for transcendental foundations and the drawing of moral limits – combine to justify the exclusion of any particularist communal, cultural or spiritual claims in politics on moral grounds, since the political morality of public action is exhaustively defined and bounded by the individual/state relation. Moreover, as I have shown, they cannot be defended on the grounds of their being particular cultural or collective interests – that is, sociological 'special' cases – since these too only have validity when convergent with the collective interests of the 'universal' state. These conditions dramatically up the stakes that the philosophy lays down about the individual as a member of the political nation, heavily moralising the relation between the individual and the state. Indeed, as moral behaviour cannot be conceived outside of the political sphere, and must necessarily embody the universal rules of the national political morality, one might say there is something inherently *sacred* about the relation of the individual – as moral actor and *citoyen* – and the national collective. It should come as no surprise to find this echo of Durkheim's idea of organic social morality at the heart of the *prima facie* individualist political morality of French political unity. It is this logic which underlies the deeper constitutive strand in the French *contrat social*: that the individual's identity as an individual is expressive of the political morality of the state, and his or her individuality is indeed constituted by the adhesion to the collective. This, then, is how the selfish interests of the individual can be transcended in the unified political morality of the state: a state which expresses the institutional frame of an organic, ordered society built around secular symbols, in which the religious urge has been replaced with a predominantly civic faith.[60]

Here, finally, is the bedrock of the theory of *intégration*, the neo-republican squaring of the circle between individual and collective, which is the ultimate guarantee that the resolution of the two objectives of integration – diversity and cohesion – is and can be a possibility. It is conveyed in the particular metaphysical idea of individual autonomy the reports build upon: that the individual, in order to undergo the transformation *de l'immigré au citoyen*, has to break with the contingency of particular culture, interests and self-understandings, into the necessary realm of giving the law unto oneself, reconstituting oneself as the individual embodiment of the law and the deepest values of the nation. It is a conception whose grounding has been sought in the 1980s return of French philosophers and political theorists to reading Rousseau in the light of Kant and not Marx. That is, interpreting the abstract ideal of citizenship in the universal nation – *la République* – as the prosaic embodiment of 'the kingdom of ends' on earth, the full and true embodiment of the universal rights of man.[61] This indeed was the philosophical agenda for the neo-republicanism in France set principally by Luc Ferry and Alain Renaut's essential text *Des droits de l'homme à l'idée républicaine.*

Clearly, this is a conception of political liberalism thoroughly at odds with political pluralism and democracy as it is understood in the Anglo-American world. It is also a conception thoroughly and irrevocably bounded by the idea of its setting within the nation-state. What is missing is any kind of meaningful way of bridging the national and the international spheres: although the latter does exist and must surely intersect and impinge on the former in some way. The objects of normative action are citizens of France first, and only very vaguely the world next; it is their status as French that determines their moral status. What is more, the reaffirmation of such a centralised philosophy of the state palpably also lacks any serious thought to converting theory into practice at local, devolved levels. Yet without doubt, there are benefits to such an up-front declaration of philosophical intent. When the political circumstances, as they did in the 1980s, raised immigration as a 'fundamental' question of national integrity and the threat to unity, the philosophy can prove to be a powerful and dominant discourse; not least in the way the self-styled fate of the nation is so intimately connected with proving the practical viability of the abstract philosophy. Being a theory that deliberately puts metaphysical assertions above any realistic explanatory or empirical considerations, it is a philosophy that demands a leap of faith. Perhaps it is this sacred dimension that has enabled it so successfully to reproduce itself as the ideal at the heart of the institutional creed that the French Parisian administrative elites have been brought up on and cannot afford to relinquish.

The very philosophical French defence of the nation-state as a normative universal and national political entity makes a heroic stand in its exclusive privileging of the political sphere as the site of cultural integration. Moreover, its refusal to see politics as an affair of pragmatic management or *laissez faire* is profoundly anti-conservative, and in the best traditions of modernism. At the same time, I have begun to suggest the kinds of problem that can arise consistently from this way of framing the core theoretical question of achieving moral social order from cultural pluralism. These are several: the threats to true moral, cultural and political autonomy when morality is monopolised by the high church of the state; the moralisation of cultural behaviour on a scale of 'us and them'; the turning of political bargaining into a grand test of moral integrity and political piety; and the tendency for all the high-minded ideals and universal aims of *la République* to dissolve into exclusionary French cultural and historical particularism. The universal French mission is bound to run up against the harsh difficulties of accommodating different cultures and – internationally speaking – different institutional practices towards the problems. One thing however is clear: the triumph of philosophy in the rapports of the *Commission* and *Haut Conseil* does at least confirm, once again, that if philosophers were ever likely to rule the world, they would without doubt be French.

In this chapter, I have sought to identify the political forces and philosophical foundations behind the deep consensus on immigration and citizenship that emerged in France during the 1980s, and indicate the stakes it involves. Before I go on to the next step and explore the consequences of this official theory, a comparative dimension is required. This is important to avoid assuming that the particular version of philosophical liberalism established in France is the only form that a public philosophy, faced with the dilemmas of cultural pluralism, may take in one nation. For this, I must now turn to the case of Britain, which will be found to have a completely different philosophy of integration.

Notes

1.   Among the most prominent works across a variety of disciplines were: Claude Nicolet, *L'idée républicaine en France 1798–1924 essai d'histoire critique* (Paris: Gallimard, 1982); Luc Ferry and Alain Renaut, *Des droits de l'homme à l'idée républicaine* (Paris: Presses universitaires de France, 1985): Gérard Noiriel, *Le creuset français: histoire de l'immigration XIXe–XXe siècle* (Paris: Seuil, 1988); Jacqueline Costa-Lascoux, *De l'immigré au citoyen* (Paris: la documentation française, 1989); Dominique Schnapper, *La France de l'intégration* (Paris: Gallimard, 1991); Cathérine Wihtol de Wenden, *Les immigrés et la politique* (Paris: Presses de la Fondation Nationale de la Science Politique, 1988); Gilles Kepel, *Les banlieues de l'Islam* (Paris: Seuil, 1987); Tzvetan Todorov,

Nous et les autres: la reflexion française sur la diversité humaine (Paris: Seuil, 1989); Pierre-André Taguieff, *La force du préjugé; essai sur le racisme et ses doubles* (Paris: La Découverte, 1988); and the collection he edits, Pierre-André Taguieff, *Face au racisme* (Paris: La Découverte, 1991, 2 vols). A useful survey of these works in English is John Crowley, '*Immigration, racisme et intégration*: Recent French Writing on Immigration and Race Relations', *New Community*, vol. 19, no. 4 (1992).

2.   Patrick Weil, *La France et ses étrangers: l'aventure d'une politique de l'immigration* (Paris: Calmann-Lévy, 1991), pp. 187–207; Pierre-André Taguieff and Patrick Weil, 'Immigration, fait national et citoyenneté', *Esprit* (May 1990).

3.   See, respectively: on the juridical sphere, Costa-Lascoux, *De l'immigré au citoyen*; on education, Françoise Lorcerie, 'La République à l'école de l'immigration', *Revue Française de pédagogie*, no. 117 (Nov–Dec. 1996); and, on the police, Michel Wieviorka *et al.*, *La France raciste* (Paris: Seuil, 1992) pp. 225–76.

4.   See the account in Sami Naïr, *Le regard des vainqueurs: les enjeux français de l'immigration* (Paris: Grasset, 1992).

5.   François Furet, Jacques Juillard and Pierre Rosanvallon, *La République du centre* (Paris: Calmann-Lény, 1989).

6.   For example, Rogers Brubaker, *Citizenship and Nationhood in France and Germany* (Cambridge, Mass.: Harvard University Press, 1992); James Hollifield, 'Immigration and republicanism in France: The hidden consensus', in W. Cornelius *et al.* (eds), *Controlling Immigration* (Stanford University Press, 1994); and William Safran, 'The French and their national identity: The quest for an elusive substance', *French Politics and Society*, vol. 8, no. 1 (1990). Two more recent studies, Miriam Feldblum, *Reconstructing Citizenship: The Politics of Nationality Reform and Immigration in Contemporary France* (State University of New York Press, 1999): and Virginie Guiraudon, 'The reaffirmation of the republican model of integration: Ten years of identity politics in France', *French Politics and Society*, vol. 14, no. 2 (1996) offer accounts closer to mine.

7.   Eugen Weber, *Peasants into Frenchmen: The Modernization of Modern France* (Cambridge, Mass.: Harvard University Press, 1977) and *My France: Politics, Culture, Myth* (Harvard University Press, 1991).

8.   For an idea of just how different these concerns were throughout the period prior to the new republican synthesis, see the collection of articles from *L'Express* in 1992, 'Dossier: Immigrations' (Hors série no. 3). See also the best American comparative study of the 1970s mentioned already, Gary Freeman, *Immigrant Labour and Racial Conflict in Industrial Societies: The French and British experience, 1945–1975* (Princeton NJ: Princeton University Press, 1979), where there is little or no trace of the highbrow republican concerns in the portrait he makes of French policy-making during this period.

9.   Costa-Lascoux, *De l'immigré au citoyen*, does a convincing job of presenting the main ideas of *insertion* in a negative manner, in order to sustain her contrast with the positive ideal of *intégration*. See also Weil's history of the policies, *La France et ses étrangers*.

10. See Michel Wieviorka, *L'espace du racisme* (Paris: Seuil, 1991); Kepel, *Les banlieues de l'Islam.*
11. For example, the report for Georgina Dufoix, the Ministère des Affaires Sociales et de la Solidarité Nationale, *1981–1986: Une nouvelle politique de l'immigration* (1986); Commissariat Géneral au Plan, *Immigrations: Le devoir d'insertion* (1988).
12. See James Hollifield, *Immigrants, Markets and States: The Political Economy of Western Europe* (Cambridge, Mass.: Harvard, University Press, 1992); Rogers Brubaker (ed.), *Immigration and the Politics of Citizenship in Europe and North America* (New York: University Press of America, 1989); Tomas Hammar (ed.), *European Immigration Policy: A Comparative Study* (Cambridge University Press, 1985).
13. Max Silverman (ed.), *Race, Discourse and Power in France* (Aldershot: Avebury, 1991).
14. See the comparative evidence in Hammar, *European Immigration Policy*; Stephen Castles *et al.* (eds), *Here for Good: Western Europe's New Ethnic Minorities* (London: Pluto, 1984); and the more recent report by Didier Lapeyronnie (ed.), *Immigrés en Europe: politiques locales d'intégration* (Paris: La documentation française, 1992).
15. See the figures quoted in Weil, *La France et ses étrangers*, pp. 367–84; Costa-Lascoux, *De l'immigré au citogen*, pp. 31–52; Paul Champsaur (ed.), *Les étrangers en France: contours et caractères* (Paris: INSEE). François Dubet, *Immigrations: qu'en savons-nous?* (Paris: La documentation française, 1989), offers an overview and partial demystification of the official knowledge of the subject in France.
16. See Kepel's somewhat alarmist study, *Les banlieues de l'Islam*, which had a significant impact on the public debate; or Tomas Gerholm and Yngve George Lithman (eds) *The New Islamic Presence in Western Europe* (London: Mansell, 1988). In contrast, see the perspectives offered by Jean Leca, 'L'Islam, l'état et la société en France: de la difficulté de construire un object de recherche et d'argumentation', in Bruno Etienne, *L'Islam en France* (Paris: CNRS, 1991); and the work of Michel Oriol, especially 'Sur la transposabilité des cultures populaires en situations d'émigration', in *L'immigration en France: le choc des cultures* (L'Arbresle Centre: Documentations Thomas More, 1987), and 'Islam and Catholicism in French immigration', in Donald Horowitz and Gérard Noiriel (eds), *Immigration in Two Democracies: French and American Experiences* (New York University Press, 1992).
17. Peter Hall, *Governing the Economy: The Politics of State Intervention in Britain and France* (Cambridge: Polity, 1986), pp. 192–226.
18. See the historical treatment of these questions in François Ewald, *L' Etat Providence* (Paris: Grasset, 1986).
19. Pierre Sadran, *Le système administratif français* (Paris: Montechrestien, 1992).
20. See the ministerial report for Jack Lang, by Henri Giordan, *Démocratie culturelle et droit à la différence* (Paris: La documentation française, 1983); and the collection by Réné Gallisot *et al.*, *La France au Pluriel* (Paris: l'Harmattan, 1983). The politics of this is discussed in William

Safran, 'The Mitterrand regime and its policies of ethno-cultural acco-modation', *Comparative Politics*, vol. 18, no. 1 (1985).

21. A graphic illustration of these concerns is the special dossier 'La France éclatée', in *Le Nouvel Observateur*, 22–8 Oct. 1992; see also Claude Nicolet, *La République en France: état de lieux* (Paris: Seuil, 1992); and Guy Sorman, *En attendant les barbares* (Paris: Fayard, 1992).

22. See the anxious treatment of this in Gilles Kepel, *La revanche de Dieu: Chrétiens, Juifs, Musulmans à la reconquête du monde* (Paris: Seuil, 1991).

23. Tomas Hammar, *Democracy and the Nation State: Aliens, Denizens and Citizens in a World of International Migration* (Aldershot: Avebury, 1990); Yasemin Soysal, *Limits of Citizenship: Migrants and Postnational Membership in Europe* (University of Chicago Press, 1994).

24. Patrick Weil, 'Racisme et discrimination dans la politique française de l'immigration 1938–1945, 1974–1995', *Vingtième siècle*, no. 47 (Jul.–Sep. 1995); Martin Schain, 'Policy and policy making in France and the US: Models of incorporation and the dynamics of change', *Modern and Contemporary France*, vol. 3, no. 4(1995).

25. Wieviorka, *L'espace du racisme*; Martin Schain, 'Immigration and changes in the French party system', *Journal of Political Research*, vol. 16 (1988).

26. Guy Birenbaum, *Le Front National en politique* (Paris: Editions Balland, 1992); Pierre-André Taguieff, 'Les métamorphoses idéologiques du racisme et al crise de l'anti-racisme', in Taguieff (ed.), *Face au racisme* (Paris: La Découverte, 1991, 2 vols); Nonna Mayer and Pascal Perrineau (eds) *Le Front National à découverte*, 2nd edn (Paris: Presses de la fondation nationale des science politiques, 1996).

27. Club de l'horloge, *L'identité de la France* (Paris: Albin Michel, 1985); Jean-Yves Le Gallou and Jean-François Jalkh, *La préférence nationale: réponse à l'immigration* (Paris: Albin Michel, 1985), and *Etre français: cela se mérite* (Paris: Albatross, 1985).

28. Sarah Wayland, 'Mobilising to defend nationality law in France', *New Community*, vol. 20, no. 11 (1993).

29. Jan Willem Duyvendak, *The Power of Politics: New Social Movements in an Old Polity 1965–1989* (Boulder, Colo.: Westview, 1995); David Blatt, 'Towards a multicultural political model in France: The limits of im-migrant collective action 1968–1994', *Nationalism and Ethnic Politics*, vol. 1, no. 2 (1995).

30. See especially the work of Françoise Lorcerie for nuanced discussion of this: 'L'Islam au programme', in Bruno Etienne (ed.), *L'Islam en France* (Paris: CNRS, 1991), and 'La République à l'école de l'im-migration'.

31. Documented in Kepel, *Les banlieues de l'Islam*.

32. Taguieff, 'Les métamorphoses idéologiques du racisme et la crise de l'anti-racisme', in Taguieff, *Face au racisme* (Paris: La Décoverte, 1991) makes much of this in his analysis.

33. See, for example, Claude Lévi-Strauss, *Le regard éloigné* (Paris: Plon, 1983). A very influential critique of these thinkers is Luc Ferry and Alain Renaut, *Le pensée 68: essai sur l'anti-humanisme contemporain* (Paris: Gallimard, 1985); a line followed by Todorov, *Nous et les autres*; Taguieff, *La force du préjugé*; and Alain Finkielkraut, *La défaite de la*

pensée (Paris: Gallimard, 1987). See also Julia Kristeva, *Lettre ouverte à Harlem Désir* (Paris: Rivages, 1990). See Eric Fassin, 'Two cultures? French intellectuals and the politics of culture in the 1980s, *French Politics and Society*, vol. 14, no. 2 (1996).

34.   Furet *et al.*, *La République du centre.*

35.   The most important books developing this line have been Nicolet, *L'idée républicaine*; Noiriel, *Le creuset français*; Yves Lequin (ed.), *La mosaique française: histoire de ses immigrés et l'immigration* (Paris: Larousse, 1988).

36.   See Raoul Girardet, *L'idée coloniale en France de 1871 à 1962* (Paris: Pluriel, 1979); Todorov, *Nous et les autres.*

37.   The bible of this is Frantz Fanon, *Les damnés de la terre* (Paris: Gallimard, 1961).

38.   See especially the polemic by Finkielkraut, *La défaite de la pénsee*; the discussion in Taguieff, *La force du préjugé*, pp. 428–95; and, in critique of the paradoxes of French universalism, Etienne Balibar and Immanuel Wallerstein, *Races, nations, classes: les identités ambiguës* (Paris: La Découverte, 1988).

39.   Taguieff, *La Force du préjugé*, reads this in a positive republican light. A less enthusiastic analyst of the French obsession with national *distinction* is Abdelmalek Sayad, 'Etat, Nation et immigration: l'ordre national à l'épreuve de l'immigration', *Peuples Mediterrannéens* (Apr. – Sep. 1984) and essays collected in *L'immigration ou les paradoxes de l'altérité* (Paris: Boeck, 1991). A critical perpective of the binary oppositions in recent French politics – strongly influenced by the work of Sayad and Balibar – is at the heart of Max Silverman, *Deconstructing the Nation: Immigration, Racism and Citizenship in Modern France* (London: Routledge, 1992).

40.   A good example of this is Dominique Schnapper, *L'Europe des immigrés: essais sur les politiques de l'immigration* (Paris: Bonnin, 1992), or, even better, Emmanuel Todd, *Le destin des immigés: assimilation et ségrégation dans les démocraties occidentales* (Paris: Seuil, 1994), a compendium of pseudo-anthropological stereotypes that falsely characterises Germany, Britain and the USA in order to build its vision of French republicanism. The book won an important national prize, and is prescribed in pedagogical courses as the state-of-the-art comparative study on the subject. Compare the much more sober – but much less widely read – attempt to understand the complexities of other nation's policies in Jacqueline Costa-Lascoux and Patrick Weil (eds) *Logiques d'Etats et immigrations* (Paris: Editions Kimé, 1992).

41.   Ernest Renan (ed. Joel Roman), *Qu'est-ce qu'une nation et autres essais politiques* (Paris: Presses poches, 1992). For the classic French view of Germany, still going strong, see Louis Dumont, *L'idéologie allemande: France–Allemage et retour* (Paris: Gallimard, 1991), and *Essais sur l'individualisme* (Paris: Seuil, 1983); Alain Renaut, 'Logiques de la nation', in Gil Délannoi and Pierre-André Taguieff (eds), *Théories du nationalisme* (Paris: Editions Kimé, 1991); Patrick Weil, 'Nationalities and citizenships: The lessons of the French experience for Germany and Europe', in David Cesarini and Mary Fulbrook (eds), *Citizenship, Nationality and Migration in Europe* (London: Routledge, 1996).

42. See the discussions in Costa-Lascoux, *De l'immigré au citoyen*; Gilles Kepel, *A l'ouest d'Allah* (Paris: Seuil, 1994); Todd, *Le destin des immigrés*; and the marvellously silly franco-français article by Todd, 'France–Angleterre: le tournoi raciste', in *Le Nouvel Observateur* (26 Mar.–1 Apr. 1992). in which he claims: 'A Londres on se sent blanc, à Paris non…'.

43. D. Pinto, 'Immigration: l'ambiguité de la référence américaine' *Pouvoirs*, no. 47(1988); Kepel, *À l'ouest d'Allah*; Todd, *Le destin des immigrés*. Loïc Wacquant, 'De l'Amérique comme utopie à l'inverse', in Pierre Bourdieu (ed.), *La misère du monde* (Paris: Seuil, 1993) is an acute observer of these transatlatlantic paradoxes.

44. The text of the report, *Etre français aujourd'hui et demain*, was published in two volumes: the first, a verbatim transcript of the public sessions; the second, a synthesis and presentation of the propositions. The references here to EFAD are to the second volume.

45. Noiriel, *Le creuset français*, pp. 50–69. This important historical contestation is alluded to in the text of the Haut Conseil à l'Intégration report, *Pour un modèle français de l'intégration*, p. 12.

46. See Pierre Birnbaum, *Les fous de la République: histoires politiques des Juifs d'état de Gambetta à Vichy* (Paris: Seuil, 1994).

47. Hammar, *Democracy and the Nation State*; and Daniel Cohn-Bendit *et al.*, *Towards a European Immigration Policy* (Brussels: Philip Morris Institute).

48. Bernard Lorreyte (ed.), *Les politiques d'intégration des jeunes issus de l'immigration* (Paris: L'Harmattan, 1989); and H. Malewska and G. Cachon, *Le travail social et les enfants des migrants* (Paris: L'Harmattan, 1988).

49. In all, five texts were published, collected in 1993 as *L'intégration à la française*. In order they were: *Pour un modéle français d'intégration* (PMFI, Mar. 1991); *Conditions juridiques et culturels d'intégration* (CJCI, Mar. 1992); *Les étrangers et l'emploi* (Mar. 1993); *La connaissance de l'immigration et de l'inteégration* (Nov. 1991, Mar. 1993). The references here are to the first two reports listed, and page references to the original reports.

50. The issue of *how* to collect statistics in France has of late been an enormously controversial one. See, for example, the problems concerning the funding and reception of the recent study by Michèle Tribalat *et al.*, *De l'immigration à l'assimilation: enquête sur la population d'origine étrangère en France*, a report for INED that differed from the standard statistics collected by INSEE, presented in Champsaur, *Les étrangers en France*. See also the discussion in Martin Schain, 'Policy making and defining ethnic minorities: the case of immigration in France', *New Community*, vol. 20, no. 1.

51. See Yves Déloye, *Ecole et citoyenneté: l'individualism républicain de Jules Ferry à Vichy* (Paris: Presses de la fondation des science politiques, 1994).

52. See the collection of essays in: 'Islam, France et laïcité: une nouvelle donne?', *Panoramiques* (1991).

53. Bruno Etienne, *La France et l'Islam* (Paris: Hachette, 1989), and (ed.), *L'Islam en France* (Paris: CNRS, 1991).

54. Mohammed Arkoun, *Ouvertures sur l'Islam* (Paris: Grancher, 1992).

55. See the report and interview with ministre de l'intérieur, Pierre Joxe, in *Le Monde*, 17 Mar. 1990.

56. See Catherine Audard (ed.), *Individu et justice sociale: autour de Rawls* (Paris: Seuil, 1988); and the article in *Libération*, 31 May 1988: 'John Rawls roule pour la justice'. Highly interesting francophone uses of Rawls have been made by Philippe van Parijs, *Qu'est-ce qu'une société juste? Introduction à la pratique de la philosophie politique* (Paris: Seuil, 1991); and the Kantian feminism in Véronique Munoz-Dardé, *La fraternité: un concept politique. Essai sur une notion de justice sociale et politique* (Florence: EUI PhD thesis).

57. Frederick Whelan, 'Democratic theory and the boundary problem', in J. Roland Pennock and John W. Chapman (eds), *Nomos 25: Liberal Democracy* (New York University Press, 1983). Michael Walzer, *Spheres of Justice* (New York: Basic Books, 1983) ch. 3, 'Membership', was one of the rare contemporary works that addressed the problem, until the recent post-1989 fashion for studying nationalism again in philosophical terms: for example, Yael Tamir, *Liberal Nationalism* (Princeton University Press, 1993); David Miller, *On Nationality* (Oxford University Press, 1995); Will Kymlicka, *Multicultural Citizenship* (Oxford University Press, 1995).

58. Dominique Schnapper, *La France de l'intégration.*; and *La communauté des citoyens: moderne de nation* (Paris: Gallimard, 1944). See also Julia Kristeva, *Nations without Nationalism* (New York: Columbia University Press, 1993).

59. Ferruccio Pastore, 'Familles entre les droits. Pour un encadrement de la problematique du statut personnel des familles immigrés des pays musulmans en Europe' (1994, unpublished).

60. Durkheim's 'Third Republic' republicanism is a very strong influence in the work of Gérard Noiriel, *Le creuset français*, and Dominique Schnapper, *La France de l'intégration* and *La communauté des citoyens*. See also Pierre Rosanvallon, *Le sacré du citoyen: histoire du suffrage universel en France* (Paris: Gallimard, 1992).

61. On this turn in contemporary currents of political thought – which was very symptomatic of the 1980s – see Steven Lukes, *Marxism and Morality* (Oxford University Press, 1985).

4 Britain: The Paradoxical Triumph of Multicultural Race Relations

In many ways, Britain's policies towards immigration and integration provide the perfect complement and contrast to France. From the outset, the difference in concepts and institutional set-up is obvious: the focus on 'race relations', 'ethnic minorities' and 'cultural toleration', concepts anathema to the French way of seeing things. Yet it is equally clear that these are two nations with parallel colonial pasts, demographic conditions, and social problems very similar to one another. They are close cousins, two paradigmatically 'old' nations, with perhaps the closest family resemblance in Europe, even if they do spend much of the time denying it in the name of national distinctiveness.

The timing of Britain's institutional solution to the social problems and consequences of post-colonial immigration predates France's by some time, and it is fair to say that many of the convulsions that France has experienced during the 1980s have their clearest echo in the politics of the 1960s and 1970s in Britain. As in France, these politics led to the emergence of a clear cross-party consensus that founded a range of legislative institutions designed to deal with the problems of cultural pluralism, and ease Britain's path towards integration. The difference is primarily in the shape and justification these institutions took; based on a set of ideas and reworked 'British' political practices very distinct, indeed alien, to anything in the French post-revolutionary idiom.

The view from France helps us get an idea of what these forms look like, but only in the crudest, most stereotypical way. From the highbrow perspective of republican *citoyenneté* and *intégration*, the British way of dealing with things fails on many French philosophical counts. It is 'minoritarian', perpetuating distinctions – and hence *inégalités* – between the

94

dominant majority and the persons of distant origin it marks
out and identifies as 'ethnic minorities'. It is 'differentialist',
allowing minority cultures to marginalise themselves through
state-promoted multiculturalism that imposes no strict public
political identity or obligations on the newcomers. It is 'race
obsessed', perpetuating racism and a kind of soft apartheid
through its classificatory legislation and social insistence on
preserving the marker of colour in individuals' self-descrip-
tion. And, finally, it is 'unprincipled', allowing the pragmatism
of *laissez faire* and paternalist race relations management to
override the prescriptive lines that should be laid down by
droit and *constitution*.

Like many stereotypes, this is a picture that has at least a
germ of truth in it. From a critic's point of view, many of these
first impressions do indeed sketch out some of the problems
with the British approach to its ethnic dilemmas. It is certainly
also the perspective any unprepared reader would get from
most of the home-grown sociology of race and ethnicity, dominated as it is by the disaffected Marxist and post-Marxist
agenda of a generation of 1960s and 1970s radicals. The rise
of cultural studies in the 1980s has done nothing to change
this: only now the all-pervasive racism and oppression of
British social and political institutions found by these writers is
dressed in the theoretical language of postmodern cynicism.[1]
The perspective is even abetted by the academic publications
of the liberal mainstream: unreflective and descriptive in
nature, these works – whether associated with the government
agency, the Commission for Racial Equality (CRE), the
influential NGO, the Runnymede Trust, or the Centre for
Research on Ethnic Relations (Warwick) – maintain a strictly
instrumental and pragmatic self-conception of the mainstream
institutions, producing mainly technical legislative and demographic work to help engineer them. Yet it is a very superficial
perspective. Stereotypes can cut both ways, and the British are
no less prone to mischaracterise the French conception as
crudely assimilationist, intolerant and culturally exclusionary.
Very little comparative work that escapes these traps has been
done, because so little of it takes the trouble to translate concepts and ideas out of the context which gives them sense and
meaning. Such work is impossible without first recognising
Britain's institutional and legislative frame as the expression

of a coherent official public philosophy of its own, on a par with the French philosophy of *intégration*. It represents a distinct and complex version of philosophical liberalism, that responds in its own fashion to the dilemmas of cultural pluralism.

The problem with this is that the theory and its principles need to be drawn out and reconstructed from what is a very fragmented set of ideas and public justifications found in the diverse pieces of British legislation about nationality, citizenship, race relations and multiculturalism. There have been no policy reflections as centrally powerful as the *Commission de la Nationalité* and *Haut Conseil à l'Intégration* – and certainly no comparably influential public intellectuals – from which the British legislative consensus can be directly read out. But the fact the subject is rarely reflected on in explicitly philosophical terms does not mean that there is not an underlying justification to be found. Indeed, this *apparent* void is perfectly characteristic of the kind of justification that in fact exists: the 'Great' British art of calculated, piecemeal, evolutionary, 'anti-philosophical' pragmatism. This marries a concern with the practical implementation of a paternalist utilitarianism, with a theory of moral social order built on rather different premises than the French philosophy. That is, a quasi-sociological thesis about the origin of social civility rather than transcendental conditions, and a distinct traditionalism hostile to the artifice of French republican thought and its rationalist, constitutional formalisation. The two institutional frames thus have quite distinct logics and precepts. The British conception of the relation of state to individual – with its canonical accent on negatively protecting the individual from the state rather than positively forming the political citizen through political participation – reverses the primacy of polity to society, thus allowing a wide sphere of culture untouched or unstructured by the public political sphere; hence, the flourishing of multiculturalism and the concept of race relations as the 'management' of public order, rather than the principled laying down of rules on an *a priori* basis.

Here, I will trace the story of how these institutions came into place, and reconstruct the foundational ideas, theoretical assumptions and goals they seek to achieve. These hinge around two different sets of legislation: on the one hand, the development of nationality law, and the changing justifications for very harsh and restrictive controls on immigration; on the other, the creation of relatively enlightened and progressive race relations legislation, that has evolved through the courts and regulatory practice, and extended in the 1980s into a broader conception of Britain as a multi-racial and multicultural society. As well as the legislation itself, a number of key reports and documents spell out the basic terms and ideas of the British conception. I will thus look at the jurisprudence of the race relations legislation; technical literature on census gathering and demographic change; reports on immigration procedures and policy implementation in the city; the Scarman report on inner city disturbances in 1981; the Swann report on multicultural education in 1985; and the report of Britain's own Commission on Citizenship, that appeared in 1990. Unlike the French *rapports*, these are documents that rarely seek to dig down to their own theoretical and philosophical foundations; a fairly free, interpretative reading is required. But underneath, the clear outline of a distinctly British political and social philosophy is unmistakable.

The curious fact in all this is that the conception of Britain as a multi-racial and multicultural society, tightly bounded by very strict immigration controls, is one clearly accepted as a wide consensus by both sides of the political spectrum, that over the last twenty-five years has isolated and largely silenced the aggressively nationalist and xenophobic voices of the extreme right who once set the agenda. Moreover, only very rarely since the Second World War has there been any marked political conflict between the mainstream left and right about the politics of race and immigration. These are developments which clearly need to be explained, even if this harmonious picture may now be changing. The answer lies in the ideas peculiar to the British liberal tradition that have been picked up and put together as a core theory and solution for dealing with the dilemmas of cultural pluralism. And, as in the French case, reconstructing this philosophy helps explain both the kinds of positive social integration it has enabled, as well as the institutional and social dilemmas into which it has led the country.

THE MYTH OF CITIZENSHIP AND SOCIAL PROGRESS

Like France, Britain has its own myth of citizenship sustaining
national unity and national boundedness. In its own way, it
offers a comforting frame for making sense of British politics,
grounding it in the self-styled particularity of a peculiar national political culture and naturalising political change and
innovation in a long-term historical *telos*. Ironically enough,
one of the inspirations for this myth is its being a negative
anti-model of the French rationalist, revolutionary, republican
tradition. Ever since Edmund Burke's famous *Reflections on the
Revolution in France*, British political self-interpretation has
made a virtue of the nation's *ad hoc*, pragmatic, evolutionary
method of dealing with social and political dilemmas. The
secret of Britain's success, and thereby the true source of
social progress, lies – it is said – in the accumulated wisdom of
its political and legal institutions, and their fabled flexibility
in shadowing the course of slow, tempered social change.

This myth is often presumed to be a classically conservative
line of thought: associated most famously in recent times with
the work of Michael Oakeshott.[2] However, the myth is in fact
no less present in much left-leaning political thought in
Britain. The most famous work of modern times in this vein
is, of course, T. H. Marshall's *Citizenship and Social Class*.
Representing the more whiggish end of the social progress argument, his story charts the progressive expansion of rights
and membership in nineteenth and twentieth-century Britain
– from civil and political rights through to full social and
welfare rights – to ever more marginal parts of the population;
culminating in the post-war welfare state and the full
identification of the working class with an inclusive British national identity.[3] It is a comforting narrative of incremental
social progress, and as such offers what would appear to be
the perfect normative and explanatory frame for charting the
progressive integration of ethnic minorities in Britain,
through a similar logic of expanding rights and membership.
This indeed has frequently been the interpretation of 'progressive' advocates of the British legislative frame of multicultural race relations.

At its very inception, the agenda-setting Rose report of
1969, *Colour and Citizenship: A Report on British Race Relations*,

cited Marshall as its guiding logic in the proposing of new legislative powers to protect and integrate British ethnic minorities. This report, which represented the high-water point of
the so-called 'liberal hour' of progressive intentions in policy
on ethnic and racial matters, set itself up explicitly as the
'Myrdal' for Britain. That is, it was a report in the model of the
famous post-war study on racial inequality in the USA, *An
American Dilemma*, which was ultimately so instrumental in the
creation of civil rights in the 1960s.[4] Over twenty years on, and
Marshall's story is still the blueprint for national unity and
progressive change. Once again, the report of the Commission
on Citizenship of 1990, *Encouraging Citizenship* – an extraordinary all-party consultative study in the French manner on
the social bases of political life in Britain – prominently used
his framework to give foundations to the idiosyncratic British
conception of citizenship. The report argues, among other
things, that it is this conception of citizenship which has
enabled the flourishing of ethnic minorities and assures the
certain sense of community and social order that represents
the 'best' of the British way of life in a rapidly changing
world.[5] In the softer, kinder British political scene that followed the end of the harsh Thatcherite 'divide and rule' days,
both the right and left scrambled to claim this idiom of
citizenship as their own, at a time when the new – if somewhat
different – citizenship idiom was also sweeping politics in
France, indeed the rest of the western world.[6]

There are thus two key elements in the self-styled particularity of the British idea of citizenship and social progress, as read
through Marshall. One is the way it reads history, looking back
from the present and arranging the past as a progressive, evolutionary continuum passing up to and through the present
day. Change is thus read as internal and organic; it is never
the product of a rupture or the intercession of unexpected
new or external factors. The Marshall framework thus reads
the expansion of membership to ethnic minorities as the
'natural' partisan response of the enlightened political and institutional framework to ethnic minorities' protests for inclusion and representation: the same old 'success' story,
repeating the inclusion of women or of the working classes.
The theory as a historical blueprint is thus read as a benign,
one-way, and thoroughly functionalist teleology, which, like

the reinvention of republicanism in France, offers the perfect self-justification for the untroubled continuity of the legislative institutional framework; the perfect self-contained national 'cultural idiom', in fact, for the British way.

Secondly, there is the idea of citizenship itself. As in the idea of republican citizenship, the goal is to achieve full social integration and membership in the nation. British citizenship is equally a conception of an inclusive, bounded national community; an idea of belonging. However, this is an ideal end-goal of citizenship that is not particularly dependent on the formal political definition of naturalisation procedures, or of the rights and duties of the political citizen. The good citizen is not necessarily the fully participative, morally autonomous, individual political actor. Citizenship is, rather, something else: a certain quality of communal social life, of civilised behaviour. The rights and entitlements granted are but a means to this end; and they are no guarantee of its success. Political and legal intervention thus only sets the context in which social integration – the civilising process of becoming and being accepted as British – takes place. It is still nation-building; but nation-building by another means.

Like all myths, the British idea of citizenship and social progress, crystallised in Marshall, is both enlightening and mystificatory. It points the way to certain genuinely particular features of the British case and the conception of integration that is embedded in the British institutional solution of multicultural race relations. But it also falsifies parts of the story by which these institutions emerged, and obscures shared elements which might help show what the two cases of Britain and France have in common. Most importantly, it leaves out or denies parts of the picture which might be used to challenge the naturalness and smooth continuity of the way these policy problems are dealt with in Britain. Like France, Britain may well be hiding its own inadequacies and inability to evolve, behind a self-narrating, self-sufficient facade that denies the novelty and threat of changes that are going on around it internationally. To answer this, then, a closer look needs to be taken at the story by which the multicultural race relations framework emerged, and the ideas and arguments that sustain it in practice.

RETELLING THE TRIUMPH OF MULTICULTURAL RACE
RELATIONS

Looking back over the progress of policy and legislation concerning racial and ethnic questions since the war, it is remarkable, as I have noted, how little political disagreement has
marked its course. Britain's own writers on racial and ethnic
politics – who naturally enough put race and their own ideological struggles within the race relations lobby at the centre
of their accounts – often fail to appreciate how consistently
low the salience of these issues has been in British politics
when viewed comparatively.[7] This current quietness is certainly a startling exception in European terms. The underlying
consensus that has evolved into the current set of institutions
has been unique in British politics, so often divided along
sharp class or regional lines; it is a consensus that has even
escaped the collapse of the post-war consensus about the
welfare state. Part of its success must surely be the way the legislation and institutions combine and make sense of a number
of widely held ideas about the nature and aims of politics in
Britain. There is certainly a distinct and surprisingly coherent
British philosophy embodied in the institutions, although the
way the ideas fit together across the political spectrum and
have been applied to the specific problem of ethnic minorities, is rather idiosyncratic to this particular political issue and
the timing of its solution.[8] As in France, then, it is the contingent, political way these ideas have been used in consensus-
building that is interesting; they should not be read as proof of
there being some kind of immutable historical 'cultural
idiom'. But it is true that the duration and continuity of these
ideas in the last twenty-five years is beginning to give them the
air of a deeply rooted institutional 'culture' in the Marshallian
teleological vein.

The story begins in the immediate post-war period.[9]
Britain's peculiar relation to the post-colonial Commonwealth
ensured that, in this period, Britain maintained an open door
relation to members of the Commonwealth who, as sovereign
subjects, were effectively like British citizens with rights of
entry and abode. This expansive policy was confirmed in the
1948 Nationality Act. Both left and right were happy with the
situation, if sometimes for different reasons: to the left it was

the appropriate response of Britain to its international responsibilities to the ex-colonies; to the right, it was the inevitable expression of the fact that any Commonwealth subject could say '*civis Britannicus sum*', the fulfilment of Britain's role as empire leader, and the preservation of sovereign rule. Essentially, then, both sides supported an open 'universalism' towards the Commonwealth, and a national self-conception unsullied (in this part of the public philosophy at least) by any racial or cultural specifics.

There were important differences in the colonial heritage of France and Britain. For sure, both nations sought to remake the rest of the world in the image of themselves. France, where nation, national (universal) culture and polity coincided in the idealist notion of the colonial nation, tried to civilise the natives by turning them into true French *citoyens* (although this did not apply to Algerian Muslims until after 1959). Britain, however, ruled by letting the natives be as they were, civilising them through the order and reasoned institutions they enforced, that were often modifications of the ones they found in the native culture. French colonies were thus an integral and physical part of *la Grande France*; Britain meanwhile saw its Empire as a dominion of generic British civilisation, in which all the cultures of the world could flourish under the never-setting sun. This idea behind 'her' special obligation to the Commonwealth, was universal in virtue of its sovereign power, not in virtue of any global humanist mission, and was made possible by the fact that, unlike in colonial France, the British state and a 'British' national culture did not coincide as one and the same thing. Britain is not and never has been a monocultural nation-state, but is rather a sometimes precarious (and imposed) union of four nations. Its political institutions of colonial rule were not necessarily dependent on a unitary idea of national culture, even if in practice 'English' culture has always had the upper hand.[10] Indeed, maintaining the boundaries of the nation-state – such a problem in the formation of other continental European nations – was never really such a decisive factor in the British case, as a natural territorial island state. The boundaries of membership – thereby essentially geographical and physical in nature and not strictly bound to any cultural 'imagined community' – have until recent times remained unproblematic, and no great barrier to foreign settlers: an invisible boundary, as it were.

Large-scale immigration from what was to become the New Commonwealth began in the late 1940s and continued throughout the 1950s. The immigrants were recruited and encouraged to come over as a replenishing source of labour in the post-war boom, coming first in great numbers from the West Indies and later the Asian sub-continent. Many of these first immigrants, particularly those from the West Indies, had been brought up on British education and culture, and saw Britain as a natural second home from home. Only in 1958, with the outbreak of the first race riots in Notting Hill, London, and Nottingham, orchestrated by white extremists against the black population, did the issue of immigration – and the inevitable integration it foresaw – first become a central political concern. The first government reaction was hard and populist: the 1962 Commonwealth Immigrants Act, which put in place the first restrictions on immigration, cutting open immigration from the New Commonwealth, and thus clearly demarking and limiting future coloured immigrants from others of (white) origin. For the first and only time, the passing of the act was marked by deep political dissensus: the Labour leader, Hugh Gaitskell, mobilising his beleaguered party with a series of hard-hitting ethical criticisms of legislation on its racist criteria about restricted access to work permits. But what might have become a significant and permanent rift in the ideas of the two parties about immigration and racial politics, was in fact quickly sealed by a deeper consensual logic, a logic that was to emerge clearly through a series of political developments over the next decade and a half.

Despite closing the doors on immigration, racial tension was not lessening. Racial discrimination by the majority white population – who had been initially tolerant in the early days of immigration – was getting worse; and the black community itself was showing more signs of discontent and willingness to provoke disorder. When Labour came to power in 1964, it sought to alleviate these problems with forward-looking legislation that might manage and defuse the emerging problem. It quickly left behind its promises to repeal or reform the immigration controls put in place; indeed, it reinforced them with amendments of its own. These conservative measures

were henceforth unanimously accepted as part of any 'progressive' solution. The rationale behind this is summed up
well in a now classic statement made in 1965 by Roy Hattersley,
then a junior Home Office minister: 'Integration without
control is impossible, but control without integration is inde-
fensible'. Plans were mooted for what were to become the first
Race Relations Acts of 1965 and 1968.

These years are often read as the halcyon days of the 'liberal
hour' in British race relations innovation and legislation. With
an energetic, liberal minister, Roy Jenkins, in the Home
Office, the 1960s in full swing and the civil rights movements
at its peak in the USA, the later triumph of many of his policy
ideas are often put down to a rare and enlightened, *zeitgeist*-
inspired swing towards progressive ideas in a generally conservative population, and the pressure of the minorities and their
representatives themselves. For sure, Jenkins, vision of pluralist integration was remarkably prescient and forward-looking.
For example, his often-quoted speech of 1966:

> Integration is perhaps rather a loose word. I do not regard it
> as meaning the loss, by immigrants, of their own national
> characteristics and culture. I do not think we need in this
> country a 'melting pot', which will turn everyone out in a
> common mould, as one of a series of carbon copies of
> someone's misplaced vision of the stereotyped Englishman
> ... I define integration, therefore, not as a flattening process
> of uniformity, but cultural diversity, coupled with equality of
> opportunity in an atmosphere of mutual tolerance ... If we
> are to maintain any sort of world reputation for civilised
> living and social cohesion, we must get far nearer to its
> achievement than is the case today.

However, these ideas by themselves would have been
insufficient to pull through any kind of reform had it not been
for the political dimension behind their development. The
actual mechanisms of this demonstrate a very unwhiggish sort
of story, very different from the Marshallian myth of left-wing
partisanship and civil rights-style campaigning from below.

In fact, there was a good deal of resistance in the Labour
Party and the Trades Unions in particular to progressive-style
legislation. The working-class population was generally hostile

to the minorities' cause, and the minorities had no real political voice of their own besides the remote intellectual arguments of white liberal progressives.[11] The real focusing point of change over the issue was an unexpected event: the explosion into open debate of the ideas articulated by Enoch Powell, a prominent right-wing Conservative, in his famous 'rivers of blood' speech of 1968.[12] It was a classic instance of debate expansion: raising the fundamental issue of nation and the stability of the 'British' Union. Powell was clearly speaking for a sizeable part of the population, when he called on a mythical discourse of dominantly English cultural unity and distinctiveness. This distinctiveness was embodied for him in the long historical tradition of constitution and sovereignty and spilt over into cultural exclusionism. Immigrants were thus pictured as invading hordes who, with their peculiar practices and origins and predilection for crime and moral turpitude, would never be able to assimilate. In the speech he speaks of the terrified white working-class family reduced to a racial minority in their own street; and predicts the bloody outcome that will ensue if measures are not taken to repatriate the new immigrants. It was an argument addressed primarily to a fundamental British concern with public order, rather than hinging on any arguments of moral superiority (even if latent in his arguments). For Powell, the danger of allowing a multi-racial society to be born in Britain is that it will undo the delicately balanced and historically time-worn fabric of the British way of life; since, he argues, it is a social and cultural fact that different races cannot and never will be able to live together in peaceable harmony.

Significantly, the response – and silencing – of Powell was effected in defence of the very public order he claimed was under threat. Mindful of the kind of anti-immigrant violence and reactions such inflammatory speech could stir up, both the Labour and Conservative parties were forced to work to distinguish their own positions from his. Behind this was a series of bigger fears: that Powell's anglocentric unionist nationalism against immigrants might ignite far bigger conflicts in the British 'nation', between English nationalism and the periphery nations of the so-called 'United Kingdom'. With this threat in mind, the mainstream was moved to get race off the political agenda, and distance it as far as possible from any other issues of 'national' unity. A chorus of liberal condemnation – and affirmation of the progressive toleration of ethnic minorities – followed. Powell was sacked from the shadow cabinet, and marginalised within his own party. The 2nd Race Relations Act of 1968 – which outlawed direct discrimination in employment or other public places, and incitement of race hatred – was consolidated.

Powell in this way served as the British Le Pen, to solder across the two parties a central consensus that now could not go back on a commitment to at least assuring enlightened race relations for those immigrants already established in Britain. His influence in aligning the Conservative Party – an organ hardly famous for its progressive social thinking – in favour of the liberal centre on this issue cannot be underestimated. While Powell's ideas were also an important source of the rise during the 1970s of the neo-Nazi National Front (later the British National Party) – which traded on an intellectually cheapened version of his central thesis – in the long run this liberal alignment has stood firm because of the underlying stakes recognised by all. The 1970s was a decade of British politics torn by fundamental conflicts over devolution, Northern Ireland and open class warfare; nobody in the mainstream really wanted to add race and immigration to the boiling pot. It was in this atmosphere that all the progressive legislation went through; a core set of legislation that has provided the basis for all further progressive social developments, and which despite occasional voices of dissent from the right, has never been in danger of being rescinded.

The logic of the dualistic development of further legislation through the 1970s should be understood in the light of this: on the one hand, ever-tightening immigration control; on the other, ever more inclusive integration policies. The Conservative government added to the immigration control side of the legislative scales in 1971, passing a further Immigration Act, which fixed the restrictive rules that had been practised during the 1960s, and introduced certain new quota systems for Commonwealth entrants. By this stage, in reality, the doors had been shut to allow only the most limited of numbers. Only immediate relatives of those already established in Britain had any kind of privilege, with immigration control strictly monitoring the legitimacy of marriages and other attempts seen to pervert what were seen as generously conciliatory clauses about family reunion.

Within this tightly controlled frame came the culmination of the progressive legislation begun in the 1960s: the Race Relations Act of 1976. Much dissatisfaction had been expressed about the extent of the initial legislation, especially in the fact that it only addressed direct discrimination that could be proven in specific cases to be harmful. The existing agencies and legal support for alleged victims were poor and deterred cases, and there was little co-ordinated promotion of the wider aims of the legislation. The new Act thus sought to extend the principle of 'racial buffers', the agencies co-ordinated by the original Race Relations Board, set up to channel racial issues at local levels. New provisions were put through that extended the legislation to cover indirect discrimination, where cases could also be brought against organisations which unintentionally used discriminatory grounds, or impersonal ones which in practice had a discriminatory effect. Moreover, a new organisation, the Commission for Racial Equality, was created to oversee the pursuit of anti-discrimination cases and provide legal aid and assistance. The Commission was also empowered to instigate investigations into organisations or practices thought to be discriminatory, and publish public codes of conduct.[13]

What can be said looking back is that the legislation has been more symbolic than proactive: the CRE deals with a large number of individual cases, but it is only empowered to deal with discrimination reactively. As a piece of open-ended British law, the legislation has, however, been open to evolution through the interpretative judgment of cases extending the law to a wider variety of cases. It remains a highly centrist, only mildly progressive institution. By a similar mechanism to that which marginalised Powell and aligned the Conservatives with the centre, the often very vociferous radical lobby of race activists have always succeeded in alienating the liberal centre – and any reformist influence they might have – by their extremism and tendency to split themselves into distinct, squabbling sub-groups. This has been the fate of all such groupings, from the CARD (Campaign Against Racial Discrimination) organisation of the 1960s, the 'race and class' activists of the 1970s, to the 'loony left' local politicians of the 1980s.[14]

Clearly, as a channel for race relations 'management', the legislation is mechanically limited, and – where racial discrimination has coincided with urban social deprivation and a declining economy – its powers weak. The end of the 1970s saw an increase again in racial tensions, and – temporarily – the return of the issue to a more prominent place in the agenda. The new Thatcher government promised tougher immigration controls and played on a right-wing line somewhat hostile to the liberal flavour of the recent race relations legislation. But it was the streets of the cities that blew the issue back onto centre-stage: the devastating urban riots of Toxteth, Brixton and Southall during the long hot summer of 1981. For once, here, the causes were actually identified as urban deprivation and poverty, and some token measures were taken for the inner city. Moreover, the widely read and accepted report of the unrest, by the liberal Law Lord, Leslie Scarman, recognised the deep challenge to public order posed by the riots, and sought to impose new, liberal, community-friendly policing methods – adopted slowly during the decade, after some initial resistance – together with amendments to the Riot Act and recommendations about preserving inter-racial peace. Britain's inner cities remain volatile: riots returned in 1985, on the streets of Handsworth, Birmingham, and remain an ever-present possibility in many places.

One set of more tough measures did mark the early Thatcher years: the new Nationality Act of 1981, which came into force in January 1983. With ever tighter turning of the screw, it now extended new controls to British overseas dependencies; closed loopholes for certain types of New Commonwealth family reunification; and, most significantly, ended the thousand-year-old practice of automatic *ius soli* for children born on British soil of non-British parents (persons not full citizens or 'settled' in terms of the Act). Moreover, it created a confusing tripartite category of distinct national citizens – some of whom, such as Hong Kong citizens, had British passports but were now no longer allowed in. As might be expected, the law was bent for the Falklands islanders after some protest. The most important consequences of the brief Conservative enthusiasm for a bolder nationalist rhetoric was the elimination of the extreme right as a force in British politics. On the whole, though, against the grain of the decade, the existing consensus over race and ethnic relations has held firm. For sure, there have been periodical attacks from the new right on the 'race relations industry'. These were fuelled particularly by the rise within many inner city councils of radical anti-racist movements – an extreme left minority unable to get into national politics – who have always been dismissive of the multicultural liberal centre. The new right took as its motif scandals such as the one surrounding the 'Honeyford affair' in 1987, for example, in which a headmaster suggested that white children suffered from being educated in a majority Asian school. These symmetrical extremes, however, are loud, over-represented voices which have not been able to puncture the consensus or effect any significant policy or legislative change.[15]

By the mid-1980s the consensus position has evolved towards a fairly open *de facto* acceptance of the 'reality' of multicultural Britain on all sides. The Swann report of 1985, an educational report on ethnic disadvantage which was switched away from Caribbean anti-racist concerns towards a more Asian multicultural agenda, represents the high statement of this vision. Although the report was not accepted with enthusiasm by the government – and has certainly not been implemented in anything except local and piecemeal ways – its rather bland vision holds the centre ground as the one to which most parties in the debate adhere. It is the outcome of a long, pragmatic process of trade-off and balancing that has rarely had the ethnic minorities' direct best interests as its central guiding logic. This process was always driven by a paternalistic and somewhat avant-garde progressive logic, designed to forestall future problems that it was thought might arise. This is not to say that it was always a benign progress. Rather, the course of the legislation was very sharply calculated in instrumental terms – with externalities of benefit to the ethnic minorities themselves – designed to manage and minimise the chances of race and ethnicity arising as a divisive and socially damaging 'hot' issue; as it has in France during the 1980s. This has not always been achieved, and there have been spectacular outbreaks of just such moments of social tension. But on the whole, the aims of the legislation have succeeded in minimising and pacifying the issue. It has thereby facilitated the long social process of integration that enabled Britain, and particularly its major cities, to become a genuinely multicultural society – at least by European standards – by the 1980s.

This, then, is the picture of the consensus that had been established prior to the late 1980s, and a series of more recent developments I will go on to discuss later. Having retold the story, and sketched a little of the underlying logic, I will now take a closer look at the key legislation, reports and surrounding documents that articulate the consensus and spell out the distinctive British way of dealing with ethnic dilemmas.

BORDER CONTROL, PUBLIC ORDER AND INTER-RACIAL EQUILIBRIUM

The distinctiveness of the British solution to these problems rests first of all in the relation between the two sides of the legislative framework put in place: on the one hand, nationality law and the border controls it institutes; on the other, the subsequent provisions to promote social harmony and create conditions for ethnic minority integration within these borders. Whereas in France the questions raised by nationality law are also taken to be a constitutive part of the general problem of integration, in Britain the two sets of legislation are taken to be wholly separate questions, with distinct logics and justifications.

Border controls are thus seen to set strictly the context within which the progressive aims of multicultural race relations can be pursued. The justification of strict controls is essentially a negative one. The following is a quote from the general instructions issued to immigration service staff:

> The function of immigration control is broadly to ensure that people ... are admitted only in such numbers and for such purposes as are consistent with the national interest. The objectives of the control are to prevent the entry of people who are personally unacceptable, for example because of a criminal record, to protect the resident labour force and to keep the rate of immigration within limits at which it will not give rise to serious social problems.[16]

The balance of ordered race relations is dependent on satisfy-ing these conditions. To move from the negative logic of border control to the progressive one of race relations is thus a move with a lexicographic kind of ordering: first one set of rules is established and applied; when these have been satisfied, a different set of rules may come into play. Immigration controls, for example, are not subject to the pro-visions of the Race Relations Act. Openly discriminatory crite-ria among different classes of immigrants can, and have, been applied; their justification is separate and prior to the equality of opportunity instituted by the race relations legislation.

The effort of border control is highly geographical and linked to the entity of Britain as a fixed island territory. It is a decision on membership access that has its focus on the point of entry of immigrants to the country; this, of course, is what characterises the practice of the controls, and their vulnera-bility to unjust application. The strictness is proportionate to the consequences of letting someone in: once in, and recog-nised as a legitimate resident, there is little – in the absence of the kind of population monitoring made possible with identity cards and so on – to prevent full freedom of abode, movement and, in most cases, full citizenship. Officially, the discrimina-tory nature of immigration policy – and the control criteria and verification which is applied much more strictly to coloured immigrants from the New Commonwealth – is justified on the 'pressure to emigrate' argument. That is, these immigrants are coming from countries where there is a greater economic and political incentive to leave, and there-fore they are more likely to seek ways of circumventing or cheating the entry rules. Little or no statistical evidence has ever been produced to justify this; it is an assumption, and one largely responsible for immigration control's racist reputa-tion.[17] However, coupled with the order criterion about the conditions for maintaining good race relations, the logic of the rules cannot be said to be arbitrary as such. They are, rather, calculated, predicated on their results and the achieve-ment of certain integration-directed goals.

Clearly, there is a conservative bias in the criteria used, a kind of '*seuil de tolérance*' (limit of toleration) argument, which has also been used on occasion in France. It is prey to exagger-ation and capture by populist concerns, if the issue becomes public and is fanned by a certain section of the main political parties. However, it is not necessarily a conservative argument if the conditions it creates do in fact enable the issue not to become a 'hot' one. It is here that the lexicographic logic of the relation between the two sets of legislation becomes apparent. On pragmatic terms, border controls are justified if they do in fact maintain a balanced control on immigrant numbers, prevent the majority population from becoming intolerant about existing immigrants (feeling 'swamped', as Mrs Thatcher once infamously put it), and instil in the immigrant population a demographic stability which enables them to settle. This has been an essential element in the relative success of race relations and multiculturalism over the years. After the first major groups of immigrants were allowed in, the influx was, at a certain point, sharply reduced. From this point on, two changes in the status of these original immigrants were effected: first, they became settled and permanent 'ethnic minorities', distinct from the category of 'immigrants', which must be reserved for the class of newcomers after the controls were put in place; second, they have had a clear period of twenty to thirty years to establish themselves and a place for their culture and ethnicity within the British nation. Their relatively stable demographic profile – particularly their youth, the fact there are far fewer of them beyond retirement age than in the majority population, and their geographical concentration – has facilitated this process.[18] The overall process, then, has had benefits for the ethnic minorities themselves, even though the initial instrumental calculation was based on reasons very far from humanistic or rights-based grounds.

This kind of argument spells out a familiar utilitarian pattern in British political thinking, which emphasises the consequential rather than the *a priori* deontological aspects of ethical and political reasoning. What these provisions make little or no place for is the thought that human rights or international responsibilities might impose on the British nation a duty to respond to the demands of new kinds of immigrants and migration. Only the original Commonwealth immigrants were ever identified as the 'responsibility' – a very special one at that – of the British state. Others more recently, such as the Hong Kong Chinese, new political refugees and poor white migrants from Eastern Europe, have not been so fortunate.

Leaving aside these recent aberrations, the general border control argument has worked and invariably been accepted as an unavoidable part of the political consensus; even if some easy rhetorical points can always be scored against it. Openly, spokespersons from the right or left would doubtless be critical of it; tacitly, the compromise position has remained strong. Its strength has in fact been the neutrality of its instrumental criteria: the fact that its logic is not primarily driven by culturally nationalist criteria, as is often falsely argued by radical critics keen to brand the British state 'racist'.

The lack of any real deontological substance to the thinking also indicates why formal citizenship – the status and rights given to immigrants who do manage to get in – fails to carry any significant moral or political weight in the public philosophy of integration. The burden of justification for these institutions falls on the aggregate effects of this or that policy, not on there being any substantive moral and political conditions attached to becoming 'British'; the opposite is true in France. In effect, this amounts to a trivialisation of the idea of *citoyenneté* – the idea of 'strong citizenship' – as the French would understand and defend the concept. Accordingly, and given the different nature of Britain as a national state, the kind of legislation that emerged in Britain differs along very distinct lines from those in France. Being British 'culturally', being a British national (with a right of abode), and being a British citizen (a subject of the sovereign) are distinct forms of 'citizenship', whereas they are all sacredly bound together in the French conception. In Britain, as I shall show, citizenship only takes on a strong sense when it signifies the quality of full, participative social membership in civil society.

The new categories put into place by the Nationality Act of 1981 should be seen in this light.[19] 'Citizenship' here, indeed, becomes a concept with which all kinds of licence is taken. The 'open' citizenship of 1948, predicated on members of the Commonwealth being subjects of the sovereign, was replaced by a three-tier citizenship: for citizens with direct UK connections and residency; citizens of British dependent territories (dependencies such as Hong Kong and the Falklands); and British Overseas citizens (other Commonwealth citizens who were formerly British subjects). The first, 'full' citizenship, gave a right of abode. The other two categories were essentially a device for excluding from this right those that still fell in some sense under British sovereign nationality while keeping them under the wider sovereign umbrella. As a set of categories, it certainly renders meaningless the idea of citizenship in any substantive formal sense: as, for example, a mark of moral equality, membership, or social entitlement. Yet, it is also interesting to note that the categories were defended against an amendment which called for all three classes of subjects to be called 'nationals', to bring Britain in line with international law. This too was resisted on the grounds that it implied too much about the British state's responsibilities towards its subjects. The logic underlying this concept of formal citizenship is in fact precisely its almost empty nature. It entails nothing except the minimal right of abode, thus making it an easily accessible transition category to shift the object of policy from a logic of external boundary maintenance to a logic of internal race relations. Assuming immigrants can legitimately get in, the lowest possible conditions are put on their 'being British' for official purposes. It is, in other words, the most efficient way of marking them as under British control, and subjecting them to British law. Thus it is as territorially present political *subjects* that the deeper obligations of political and social membership will be felt.

The other key symbolic redefinition of the 1981 Nationality Act – the abrogation of the traditionally automatic *ius soli* – also needs to be read in a careful way. It cannot be put on a par with France, where the maintenance of such a right carries much greater political and constitutional significance, as well as severe practical consequences, given the high numbers of non-citizenship-holding foreign residents. In Britain, the numbers affected by the change were relatively small, and – despite some popular fears – it did not affect the immigrant population already settled. The actual rationale for what was indeed a break with a long tradition – the tradition of the land, connecting membership of the nation with physical birth in the territory – conforms more with the contingent exigencies of the new citizenship categories, than with the kind of neo-nationalist ambitions its left-wing critics have claimed. With British citizenship conferring as little in rights as it demanded in obligations, the Government were concerned not to create a pool of people with no permanent connection in Britain, whose children would have automatic and costless entitlement to immigrate in the future. France has sought to solve this problem, by upping the content of what it means to become a citizen. Britain simply closed off the loophole, because to set any higher conditions to citizenship would entail defining it in a substantive political and constitutional way.

That the government were prepared to make such a break with history, and completely redefine citizenship in such an idiosyncratic way – entirely dictated by the recent conditions and instrumental concerns of post-war, post-colonial immigration – indicates an interesting characteristic of the pragmatic British approach. For such an 'old country', with such historically proud traditions, British politics has been remarkably willing to play openly cavalier games with its national myths in the service of short-term instrumental ends. With no written constitution or higher legislature to force successive governments to be consistent with the rules of the game, it has been easy and costless for politicians to use and trade on invented conceptions of the nation, both of a traditional or radical nature. It was as easy for post-Suez Britain to relive its Empire glories during the Falklands War, as it was for everyone to proclaim and accept Britain as a profoundly transformed multiracial and multicultural society, with ethnic minorities totalling around 6 per cent of the population (compared to over 50 per cent in some states of the USA). Many radical commentaries that speak of the new racism and new nationalism of the Thatcher decade in Britain do not make the essential distinction needed: between the form of nationalism clearly being built through the inward-looking, island-based legislative framework of multicultural race relations – assented to in practice by both main political parties – and the culturally pure nationalism they argue the Tories were building.[20] What in fact was being built was multiculturalism in one nation, multicultural nationalism: something as distinct from ethnic nationalism as from an internationalist multiculturalism.[21]

It is important to keep in mind these points about the borders of race relations and multiculturalism in Britain, because once the lexicographic shift has been made to the progressive logic of the internal legislation, the boundary question, for the most part, becomes invisible. In its own terms, race relations works on two basic premises: first, that it is the best way to avoid public order problems; and hence, second, that avoiding racially-based public order problems is the necessary condition for ethnic groups to be integrated into the moral order of British society. Membership is by this stage taken for granted: there is no sense of the process of integration actually being the way in which membership is confirmed, as *nationalité réussie* (proven nationality), as in France.

Border control is the precondition of this order, the bounds within which it can be achieved. Then there is the internal structure of the order itself. It is in this light that the famous formula of Roy Jenkins should be understood: as a balance or equilibrium between the three elements – equality of opportunity, cultural diversity, and mutual tolerance – that taken together can achieve the fully moral social order desired. The key point is that they are interdependent. This is important, since it is often claimed by commentators on the left that a justice-based equality of opportunity is the core value around which the legislative frame of multicultural race relations is built. These interpretations tend to be over-formalised rationalisations of something that is based on a much more sociological and utilitarian reasoning. They are rationalisations, for example, that see equality of opportunity as a set of formalised rights spelt out in constitutional terms, defending classes of persons (women or blacks, and so on) from discrimination in the American civil rights way.[22] Or they read it as the clear dividing line between public and private spheres, with equality of opportunity the ruling logic in the public sphere, and a private moral multiculturalism ruling in the private sphere.[23]

Rather, the dominant logic of the concept of equality of opportunity is negatively defined in relation to a counter-factual sociological claim; there would be equality of opportunity, and hence inter-racial harmony, if the one factor that most provokes inter-racial distrust and conflict could be eliminated: racial discrimination. The concept thus relies on a sociological thesis about the origin of public disorder and strife in an inter-racial society; together with a normative ideal or end-point – public order – which the removal of these problems would assure. Time and time again, in the development of race relations legislation during the 1960s, the fear of public disorder built up by cycles of discrimination, and the social deprivation it caused, was cited as a justification.[24] The five functions of race relations law identified by the Race Relations Board in its first annual report in 1967 cite consequentialist reasons rather than deontological criteria of fairness or justice as reasons:

> 1. A law is an unequivocal declaration of public policy. 2. A law gives support to those who do not wish to discriminate, but who feel compelled to do so by social pressure. 3. A law gives protection and redress to minority groups. 4. A law thus provides for the peaceful and orderly adjustment of grievances and the release of tensions. 5. A law reduces prejudice by discouraging the behaviour in which prejudice finds expression.[25]

The justification this expresses is that equality of opportunity is the right or just legislation to follow because it is the best way to achieve a certain end; not because it expresses some deeper constitutive or moral equality of persons. Similarly, arguments in the early days which put an accent on ensuring welfare levels for ethnic minorities did so for consequentialist, not rights-based, reasons; one of the reasons why, as time has gone on, it has been easy to drop or overlook this aspect of the philosophy of integration in policy practices.

In pure philosophical terms, this kind of argument for fairness is of course highly contestable; most Anglo-American political philosophy in a Rawlsian vein has spent the last thirty years trying to show why equality should be based on rights and justice. However, in British politics, consequentialism is always the preferred mode of justification found in the legislation and public reflection. A good illustration of how this thinking is applied practically is the Scarman report of 1981, one of the central defining moments of the British philosophy towards these problems.[26] It is a report which seeks to draw empirical and moral lessons from what were the worst inner city riots in modern British history. Scarman's strategy is twofold: first, to set up a normative ideal as the central aim of legislation and policing, reading the riots as 'aberrations' from this standard; second, to identify the reasons and conditions for the riots breaking out, and hence the best way to re-establish the ideal state.

The dilemma posed by the riots is thus read as a problem of public order, with its main recommendations put forward (as was the Race Relations Act of 1976) as revisions of the Public

Order Act of 1934. As a report essentially addressed to the question of how to police and maintain this order, it sets up its recommendations in terms of what the police are trying to defend: 'the Queen's peace', described as the 'normal state of society ... in a civilised society, normality is a state of public tranquillity' (BD, p. 62). Crucially, police methods are identified as part of the problem: without the 'consent' of the community and the 'balance' of discretion in applying the law, they will make matters worse.

> Law enforcement, involving as it must, the possibility that force may have to be used, can cause acute friction and division in a community – particularly if the community is tense and the cause of the law-breaker not without support. *Fiat justitia ruat caelum* (let justice be done, though the heavens collapse) may be apt for a judge: but it can lead a policeman into tactics disruptive of the very fabric of society. (BD, pp. 62–3)

Law enforcement thus must be driven by a calculation of the effects it will have. The police are exhorted to seek the consent of the local community in achieving these aims; and the building-up of better and more independent means of accounting for police action as integral to the harmony of the local community itself (BD, pp. 62–4).

The report's account of 'racial disadvantage' can be read in the same light. Scarman sees nothing wrong as such with the existing liberal frame of institutions that have been set up to deal with the problem of race relations. He denies the existence of institutional racism – something often discussed in the anti-racist literature as inherent in the official universalist policies of equality of opportunity, and so forth – arguing that the institutions are guided by the right values, since they do intend to work in an unprejudiced way to eliminate 'discrimination'. Racial disadvantage, rather, has been caused by the deprivation of the inner city in the areas of housing, education and unemployment, and the failure to co-ordinate ways of tackling these problems. The involvement and participation of the community is sought in the problem of putting into practice the basic ideals of good race relations; it has been this practical problem that has been the main failure

(BD, pp. 131–3). Policy must be guided by the pragmatic 'elimination of the unsettling factor of racial disadvantage from the social fabric of the United Kingdom' (BD, p. 135): the object of liberal reform and intervention is therefore clearly conceived as a safety valve for tensions that otherwise will burst out in violence and disturbance on the streets.[27]

Scarman's report, significantly, did not seek to alter the framework of the Race Relations Act (1976), which sets out the rationale for attacking the problem of racial discrimination.[28] As I have argued, this framework is dependent on a social theory about racial discrimination as the central root of disorder and disharmony. As a normative set of standards, its main role as a piece of law and statement of public policy has thus been to identify and define what counts as 'discrimination' on the one hand, and what counts as 'racial' on the other. The legislation is dependent therefore on making any of the kinds of discrimination it wishes to eliminate conform with the essentially racial logic of the Act. It defines the target of the legislation as 'discrimination which involves less favourable treatment' made 'on racial grounds', which are defined as 'any of the following grounds, namely colour, race, nationality or ethnic or national origins'. 'Racial', extraordinarily, is thus defined in a way that is distinct from any of its possible common or scientific meanings; any one of these criteria or a combination of them can in theory be applied, except – as Muslims have found out in recent years – in the grey area of religious discrimination. To be effective, the legislation relies on the evolution and adaptation of the criteria to the kinds of cases that arise. It is part of the curiosity of British legislation that it makes the normative goal of fighting discrimination dependent on such floating criteria.

The 'objective' racial classifications have their obscure root in the colonial practices of British administrators in far-flung parts of the empire: the practice of classification following the paternalist utilitarian logic of discovering and using the best management techniques for controlling the natives.[29] Translated back home, the racial classificatory scheme has helped engineer the Act through the progressive evolution of official statistical means to identify and classify the actual population in accordance with the legal criteria set down, and measure the progress of the legislation. While the 1971 census still amassed information about the ethnic minorities according to origin of the grandparents, by the 1991 census a new ethnic question had been introduced which asked the respondent to identify with one of nine particular ethnic groups (or the tenth, 'White'). In 1991, ethnic minorities accounted for 3 015 100 of Britain's total population of 54 888 800. These figures break down into the following pattern: Black-Caribbean 500 000; Black-African 212 400; Black-Other 178 400; Indian 840 300; Pakistani 476 600; Bangladeshi 162 800; Chinese 156 900; Other-Asian 197 500; Other 290 200. Labour data surveys have provided a good picture of ethnic minority demography through the 1990s. The data collection itself and the relativisation of what it means to be 'British' certainly contributes to the elimination of seeing ethnic minorities as foreigners, and of promoting the idea that Britain is a multi-ethnic entity. Though there are certainly disadvantages with the collection of racialised data, particularly in the prolongation of fairly arbitrary racial distinctions, it has in fact provided the institutional framework with a particularly effective empirical resource for promoting balanced and effective discussion of the size, nature and needs of ethnic groups, and their geographical concentrations, and working towards eliminating false beliefs and prejudices about them.[30]

Despite the extension of its powers in 1976, the main agent of the legislation, the Commission for Racial Equality, still depends more on its symbolic role to promote its ends, rather than its direct powers of monitoring, investigation or censure. Cases are often chosen by the CRE as a way of pushing the scope of the legislation expressed through the racial categories into particular grey areas, as a way of indirectly bolstering its powers. The interpretative incrementalism of the peculiar institution of British (case) law and precedent is thus another important factor in the promotion of progressive aims: what on paper looks like fairly unprincipled or limited guarantees against discrimination, can over time allow for a much more extensive liberal application to develop. For example, the legislation has proven sufficiently adaptable to extend to the case of Sikhs wearing turbans or Asian women wearing trousers at work, even if Sikhs are a religious group and wearing trousers at work does little to protect public order or promote equality of opportunity.[31] Indeed, it can be fairly argued that this has been an effective way for such groups to gain public recognition and distinction for their cultures and particular needs. As my interpretation later will suggest, however, such flexibility can also have negative side-effects.

In other ways, moreover, the familiar institutional structures of British political life limit the scope and range of the legislation.[32] The fanfared extension of the Act to cover indirect discrimination may at first glance seem to extend beyond the classic liberal criteria of proven personal 'harm' as the principle of legislative intervention, into a more 'redistributory' kind of protection, that protects persons in virtue of their membership of a class of people discriminated against. The American Civil Rights Bill of 1964 is often cited as a model in this respect. In fact, this is a classic example of an inspired idea being warped in its translation by the new institutional context. Victims of discrimination still have to bring cases as private individuals against named organisations. And, while the decisions have symbolic meaning in so far as they reinterpret the categories covered under the law, short of a Bill of Rights, the judgments do not represent Supreme Court-type judgments about the moral wrongness of discrimination, the basic rights of a citizen, or the constitutional basis of the defence of particular groups. Discrimination is still a private affair, to be punished retributively after the fact: it is not a question of public morality, or constitutional ethics. The legislation, then, is inherently resistant to its becoming a form of positive discrimination for society as a whole. The wider social function of the law thus mitigates its innovative formal aspects, which introduced the notion of equity into a legal framework built around the supremacy of contract.

The extent of positive action actually achieved by the legislation is unclear. The CRE has been instrumental in trying to push more extensive equal opportunities policies through local education authorities, for example, and has been proactive in trying to push better ethnic monitoring through public and private organisations. Again, the benefits of this kind of concern are perceived to be justified on a more sociological basis, rather than a constitutional rights-based foundation of principle. Paradoxically, the promotion of official equal opportunities has probably progressed way ahead of the attitudes of the general public, which can still be seen to contain strong elements of racism or xenophobia. It is commonplace for public organisations and large firms to have in place well-developed model ethnic monitoring procedures, along the lines suggested by the CRE.[33] These have largely been implemented without legislation pushing them from behind; rather, they have presumably been put there because they are in the perceived public (race) relations interest of the companies, perhaps even in terms of efficiency.[34] This kind of development has been made possible by the very British belief in the hands-off role of government in promoting progressive aims in public life; that some kind of 'social capital' has been generated through the opening-up and allowing of progressive social developments in society, that are guided but not explicitly enforced by the legislation. Again, this fits well with the general utilitarian logic of the British conception, even if it resists formalisation or rationalisation on rights-based or constitutional grounds.

I have tried to read the lexicographic combination of strict border controls and progressive but idiosyncratic race relations legislation as an exemplary translation of a characteristically British political philosophy into a set of legislative institutions. As has to be granted, at least part of the normative force of these institutions is dependent on the consequential effect over time of the framework on the well-being or interests of the public at large – defined collectively in the normative standard of public order – and the side-effects and benefits this has on the place of ethnic minorities within the dominant majority population. The most important developmental aspect of the legislation and the social progress it has enabled in Britain, has been the emergence of a self-conception beyond the idea of the multi-racial society, of Britain being a multicultural society. It is to this that I now turn.

CULTURE AND PLURALISM: THE MAKING OF GOOD CITIZENS

From any constitutional or rights-based perspective, the consequentialist philosophy and social theory that the British approach to race relations embodies would immediately raise objections. It is, it would be argued, an approach that on prin-

ciple allows nothing to be fixed in advance – as politically untouchable rights – and therefore that any protection the minority populations receives is always at the mercy of the
majority's wishes. This is the standard deontological critique
of utilitarianism – associated with the work of John Rawls and
his followers – and it is worth considering here.[35] Is the British
system of selective, targeted legislation, and *laissez faire* driven
by a logic of maintaining public order – and thus the rule of
law – a kind of amoral *modus vivendi* between ethnic groups, in
which the powerful (the majority white population) are always
likely to get the better?

This question can be pursued by distinguishing Britain from
the United States, a country which can be fairly described as
having a self-conception of ethnic pluralism in politics, in
which the outcome amounts to a competitive *modus vivendi*
between groups.[36] This is a simplified picture of the USA, in
which all that matters in the American context are the constitutional and political rules of the game; within these, ethnic
groups are free to associate and bargain for their own 'selfish'
interests, without considering any higher universal or society-
wide common ends. In this version of pluralism, the more
powerful and better-organised groups are always likely to win
in the political process: especially with the difficulties of mobilising collective action to pursue communal group ends.[37] In
recent years, there has been much political concern among
traditional liberals in the USA – some of it rather hysterical in
tone – about the apparent effectiveness of ethnic groups,
under the banner of multiculturalism, in capturing political
and social resources and power in the service of their own particularistic ethnic ends. These are ends, it is claimed, which
contravene the supposedly civic ideals of American political
citizenship.[38]

Whatever the case in America, it is clear that the British
theory and practice of race relations and multiculturalism is
very far from being a form of *modus vivendi* ethnic pluralism.
The British legislative and institutional framework is clearly a
calculated, paternalistic attempt to engineer a kind of social
harmony and multicultural equilibrium well in advance of the
preferences of the general public, and without the relatively
small ethnic minorities ever really lobbying for the measures,
beyond the crudest kind of public demonstrations and revolt.

Again, this overturns the smooth evolution envisaged in the Marshall myth. Moreover, the legislation does not really empower or enable the ethnic minorities to bargain for political power as a collective interest group in the way the civil rights legislation and multicultural movement in the USA has.[39] Britain is certainly not waiting for its first Black or Asian prime minister. The logic of enlightened legislation, rather, is dominated by the liberal centre's attempt to balance majority–minority relations, and to do so by removing the issue as far as possible from the centre of public political discussion. Race and ethnicity, unlike in the United States, are very far from being politicised as issues in mainstream politics; and the conventional wisdom all along, on all sides, is that the ethnic communities are better off – and the general public more tolerant – if things are kept that way.

In its own way, though, Britain does have an idea about how to encourage the making of good citizens: that is, the structuring of individual behaviour so that it contributes and enhances the overall social order. What is this idea of citizenship? Here, the report of the Commission on Citizenship is a useful reference point.[40]

> Citizenship, whatever it means, is a cultural achievement, a gift of history, which can be lost or destroyed. The Commission's purpose in publishing this Report is to propose practical ways in which our participatory arrangements can be strengthened so that they remain efficient rather than simply dignified, or ceremonial, parts of the constitution. (EC p. xv)

Citizenship is thus a virtue of a certain cultural heritage and way of life, which may happen to conform with formal expressions of international human rights and so forth, but is not underpinned by them. And, most significantly, the report lays out the defence of the concept of 'active' citizenship that most clearly marks this as a wholly different set of ideas from the French concept of *citoyenneté*. Indeed, British politicians are more likely to imagine the citizens they speak of as consumers than as political participants of a classical Greek or Roman public forum. One need only think of the way John Major's government translated the citizenship rhetoric into all their proactive talk of the Citizen's (singular) Charter, which lay out the basic rights of consumers of public services.[41]

In a positive sense, it is the practice and purpose of active citizenship that is the most essential element of the idea of citizenship as a binding that holds together the good society Britain aspires to be. It is defined as behaviour in which individuals respond to the civic duties that extend beyond their own selfish interests, and which is not necessarily expressed through the formal political sphere.

> The challenge to our society in the late twentieth century is to create conditions where all who wish can become actively involved, can understand and participate, can influence, persuade, campaign and whistleblow, and in the making of decisions can work together for the mutual good. We deliberately did not, therefore, confine our attention to formal structures alone, for civil, political and social entitlements are not delivered solely through official institutions. We considered the numerous forms of independent and voluntary contribution to society and its citizens, for they too play an important part. (EC, pp. xv–xvi)

The good citizen is the one who, by his or her own volition, gets involved in local and voluntary organisations for the benefit of the wider public. Hence the good citizen is not something really predicated on any impersonal public political role; but on the fulfilling of a particular involvement in the local community, a magnanimous service to 'thy neighbours'. It is, as Marshall might have said, the mark of a true gentleman. Given such a definition, there is much in the report which fits perfectly with the habitually benevolent vision of the model British ethnic minorities, including those most involved in the service of their own ethnic interests, who, as participants and representatives, are the epitome of active citizens.

Here, then, citizenship is based on the promotion of voluntary involvement at local levels, and the fulfilling of commitment to local communities; so unlike France, where this is meant to happen through the public political identity of *citoyenneté*; or America, where it has always been through the public pursuit of power or money through the political or economic system.[42] It is Britain, then, which perhaps best

fulfils the rather idealised Tocquevillian vision of the USA in
the work of Robert Bellah and other new communitarians in
America. Indeed, Bellah's *Habits of the Heart* (1985) was cited
with approval in the Commission for Citizenship report. The
decentralisation of the institutional structure designed to
shape individuals into citizens – defended throughout by the
Commission – is echoed by the way nearly everything except
the legal and monitoring functions of the race relations legislation is pushed down and devolved to the level of local authorities to implement. It is these authorities who exercise
most of the jurisdiction over the arms of the legislation in education, housing and social policy. It is simply taken that it is
not the direct role of the state – beyond those test cases that
came up through the CRE anti-discrimination law – to get involved in state-directed intervention, or in making top-down
centralised judgements about the implementation of the
policy guidelines. Jurisdiction thus goes down to the local
sphere and the legislation has been interpreted and implemented in different and inconsistent ways.[43]

Within this frame, the devolution of the sphere of race relations and multiculturalism has been the perfect vehicle for re-
ligion-based Asian politics, particularly in strongly Asian cities
such as Leicester or Bradford, where the first Muslim Asian
mayor was elected in 1985. The relative decline in the physical
power of local government has been accompanied by a rise in
the symbolic power of local constituency-based ethnic groups
that use their concentration to attract the attention of the
major political parties. Both the Labour and Conservative
Parties shifted their attitudes during the 1980s to be more accommodating and woo ethnic votes, by the direct involvement
of ethnic figures in local politics, and by pursuing new policy
lines that spoke to the perceived interests of the communities.
A significant number of marginal inner city constituencies
turn on the votes of the Asian or Muslim electorate.[44]

Education has been the key site of these politics. As the
sphere which is inherently a site of the cross-over between
public and private, a line which in Britain is so little defended
or defined – and conceived in reverse order of importance to
that in France – it has allowed for developments and possibilities that would be unthinkable in secular France. The law explicitly makes provision for independent voluntary-aided

schools under religious instruction, providing such schools are integrated into the national education system. More to the point, there is nothing legally to stop state schools, on the discretion of their headteachers, recognising the wishes of organised parents from minority cultures over non-participation in certain classes, food provision or special uniform provisions. Girls have generally been the target of these debates. There has been a marked tendency towards understanding and accommodating these concerns through the 1980s. In the main, this has been an accommodation on pragmatic grounds, although it is sometimes dressed in the language of multiculturalism. Conservative authorities, themselves not particularly enthusiastic about the usually left-wing-inspired rhetoric of multiculturalism, nevertheless have found it prudent not to turn these issues into inflexible fights over symbolic line-drawing. Even the much-feared centralisation and traditionalism of more recent educational reforms has been substantially tempered by the multicultural adaptation forced by applying its goals in practice.

The recommendations and philosophy of the Swann report of 1985 can, then, be read as highly indicative of the consensus position, despite the fact the recommendations were not necessarily pursued as central government policy.[45] As a classic, multi-authored institutional compromise – that was also left to the mercy of the press and had a difficult and controversial beginning to life – the report was remarkably vulnerable as a target for criticism from both the traditionalist right and the anti-racist left.[46] These display a symmetry in the kinds of concern they raise: either that multiculturalism is a dangerous cover for seditious left-wing ethnic politics and the trendy thinking of the education establishment, and hence a damaging influence on the promotion of traditional British values in schools; or that it is a liberal sop designed to deflect real concern about racism and prejudice with the artificial promotion of cultural goals, while doing nothing about the deep-seated socio-economic causes and institutional racisms that structure British public life.

What Swann really reveals, however, is the rather bland, but wide, core consensus of ideas that can be agreed to by both the left and right on the terms and theoretical assumptions of achieving social integration in what it describes as the given

accepted 'reality [of a] multi-racial and culturally diverse'
Britain (EFA p. 3). It is concerned with marrying this and a
more engaged approach to the roots of educational under-
achievement and social insecurity that prolong an unstable
and potentially dangerous place for ethnic minorities in the
country. Again, this approach takes the form of a search for
'social harmony' and unity around common 'democratic'
ideals, arguing that the long-term obstacle to these ideals are
majority prejudices (EFA, p. 4). The report is written in the
typically paternalistic but uplifting style of elite reflection on
these questions. It is, on the one hand, trying to pull the
popular conception of the nation along with a rather rosy multicultural picture. On the other, it argues that the ideal is far
from being achieved, and sets up an alarmist and somewhat
exaggerated counterpole of the dangers of 'fragmentation
along ethnic lines which would seriously threaten the stability
and cohesion of society as a whole' (EFA, p. 7). Majority intolerance and minority separatism are thus rather implausibly
taken to be equal threats. The pluralism the report defends is
an idealised cultural pluralism, that finds its perfect place in
the vaguely structured sphere of local institutions:

> We consider that a multi-racial society such as ours would in
> fact function most effectively and harmoniously on the basis
> of pluralism which enables, expects and encourages members
> of all ethnic groups, both minority and majority, to partici-
> pate fully in shaping the society as a whole within a frame-
> work of commonly accepted values, practices and procedures,
> whilst also allowing and where necessary, assisting the ethnic
> minority communities in maintaining their distinct ethnic
> identities within this common framework. (EFA, p. 5)

Pluralism, here, is again defended on the basis of its being the
best means to a certain goal. And the report even goes on to
argue that the reasonable openness and tolerance of British institutions was one of the primary reasons for the attractiveness
of Britain to New Commonwealth immigrants in the first place.
   The most significant theoretical stance taken in this general
statement of principle is its defence of the importance of
ethnic 'identity' within the common democratic framework envisaged within the idea of pluralism. The assimilation of ethnic

groups to the majority white British culture is rejected on these grounds. It is asserted that 'the ethnic minority communities cannot in practice preserve all elements of their cultures and lifestyles unchanged and in their entirety [because] it would be impossible for them then to take on the shared values of the wider pluralist society'. But then it goes on to claim:

> in order to retain their identities when faced with the pervasive influences of the lifestyle of the majority community, ethnic minority groups must nevertheless be free within the democratic framework to maintain those elements which they themselves consider to be the most essential to their sense of ethnic identity – whether these take the form of adherence to a particular religious faith or the maintenance of their own language for use within the home and their ethnic community – without fear of prejudice or persecution by other groups. (EFA pp. 5–6)

There is no exploration of what identity is, or why it is valuable to persons, other than to say it is a matter of democratic free choice: in virtue of their 'freedom'. The harder question of specifying what is to be found 'unacceptable' in cultural practices is left to the 'inevitable' sociological process that the majority cultural context will impose on the minorities.

This shallow theorising of identity thus explicitly avoids trying to theorise hard cases as the French discussions have done. It is a normatively driven 'sociological' argument, very characteristic of much multicultural liberal argument of recent years, particularly of a postmodern or feminist kind.[47] Where the report does assert something stronger is in its defence of the new 'empirical' reality of multi-racial Britain, and how pluralism 'must' therefore be the solution now. Crucially it recognises as basic to this that the existence of established ethnic minorities means there are different modes of attachment to 'being British', of 'diversity within unity':

> we are perhaps looking for the 'assimilation' of *all* groups within a redefined concept of what it means to live in British society today ... We are not seeking to fit ethnic minorities into a mould which was originally cast for a society relatively homogenous in language, religion and culture.

Lest this radical break with a traditional conception of Britain be considered too sharp, the caveat of underlying continuity is added:

> Nor [are we seeking] to break with this mould completely and replace it with one which is in all sense 'foreign' to our established way of life. We are instead looking to recast the mould into a form which retains the fundamental principles of the original but within a broader pluralist conspectus. (EFA, p. 8)

The undertheorised vagueness of this mould and its internal social mechanics are very characteristic of the British consensus about multiculturalism; but they do lay bare the reason for its effectiveness as a consensual focal point. This can be appreciated if one considers how the focus of the report shifted during its writing from the very specific problem of the under-achievement of Black Caribbean children, and the effects of racism, to the wider vision of multicultural education. The theme of anti-racism in the interim Rampton Report of 1981 was considered to be far too politically controversial and militant; the government rejected its findings, and several of the panel members, including the chairman, resigned. This, of course, was a self-defeating, self-marginalising strategy on the part of the anti-racist lobby, forfeiting any voice in the final report: another example of what might be called the 'exit syndrome' in British left-wing politics.[48] The remaining progressives were forced to the centre, and the recommendations the finished Swann report finally made thus epitomise the spirit of practical and affirmative compromise that was forced to develop in order to overcome these initial difficulties. Hardly anything is retained from the anti-racist agenda, designed to identify institutional racism and prejudice in the educational system. Moreover, out with the bath water goes any concern for the 'welfare' dimension of such integration policies, of identifying socio-economic conditions as the source of racial disadvantage and disorder. In its place, an affirmative, and conciliatory philosophy of 'education for all' is proposed, that raises only cultural issues, not socio-economic ones. This, then, bases the combat of discrimination on educating all children – black and white – about the 'new reality' of Britain as a multi-racial and multicultural society, and its diversity of faiths, cultures and ethnic origins. Nearly all the specific proposals focus on interests pursued by the Asian community: minority language provision, concerns about girls' education and the recognition of cultural practices. The emergence of the Swann report's new synthesis marks the take-over by the global concept of multiculturalism, of the centralist compromise position on race relations first established in the early 1970s, and hence its distinction from the more militantly left-wing anti-racist agenda that was also the fruit of the 'liberal hour' of the original legislation. Of the two, multiculturalism is much closer to the centrist, equilibrium position in British politics. As such, it is a far better expression of the pragmatic evolutionary approach to balancing the social change and accompanying dangers of a multi-racial society. It is also, therefore, an inherently conservative philosophy; a clue to why, in a decade of right-wing government, the multicultural race relations consensus was able to hold ground, and easily fight off the challenge of the more traditional right.

Where the report went further than this, it found its recommendations falling on deaf ears. Actually instituting multicultural 'education for all' in all-white schools, for example, has never become a reality. In practice, these kind of recommendations can be pursued, but only in local authorities which actually face the problems they reflect. The pluralist structure of education has certainly allowed ethnic groups to influence the practice of schools at a local level, but only on grounds of localised pragmatism, rather than as a genuinely translated expression of the report's new vision of British society. The politics of education in Britain, therefore, do reflect the numerical and political concentration of ethnic minorities and the nature of city life. They do so certainly more accurately than the kind of centralised, symbolic decision-making that is the ruling logic in France, and which has accordingly blown up certain issues concerning the Muslim population out of all proportion to its numerical and demographic source. The issue in Britain is only politicised, if at all, at local levels; although there have been certain recent new developments, that I will look at later.

The focus on education as the main institutional expression of multiculturalism has also helped lead questions about the

practice of multiculturalism away from the specific issues of
hard cases it often throws up (about women and children
within Islam, for example) in favour of a more general pragmatic development of loose policies of tolerance designed to
achieve the best outcomes. Ethnic minority practices generally
are not challenged on this ground. There has been no systematic need *a priori* to pass judgement on the acceptability of a
practice in advance of it becoming a sociologically significant
problem. When cases do come to court, there is a presumption in favour of the ethnic minority practice, on the grounds
of the 'reasonableness' of cultural pluralism and tolerance,
unless such practices are adjudged 'repugnant' in some way.[49]
This allows for more sociological arguments – such as those
put forward by the Swann report – and an interpretation of
'equality before the law', as entailing the 'complex equality' of
groups (an echo of Michael Walzer) allowed freely to pursue
distinct practices.[50] Once again, the constitutive power or ap-
propriateness of deontological human rights-based considerations are consistently played down.

However, the presumption of liberal toleration is overrid-
den by cases that raise the question of personal harm, defined
in material and physical terms. One example was the unam-
biguous outlawing in 1985 of Islamic female circumcision
practices. The material and physical terms of this justification,
and the lack of a rights-based frame, explain the relative
toughness of British laws on female circumcision compared to
France, where the authorities vacillate because *excision* is a
practice in the private sphere. This is in contrast to the relative
leniency of laws about bigamy and ethnic marriage practices
in Britain, which in France are ruled out as contravening the
positive rights of citizenship. Moreover, in Britain there has
been little attempt, unlike in France, to reconcile the logic of
these arguments with that of international human rights or international private law. Britain sees these kinds of question as
falling under its territorial rather than moral authority, and
thus under the criteria of defending public order and national
sovereignty, rather than international human rights standards.
And nowhere is there any suggestion that the universal ethical
nature of these questions might somehow put into question
Britain's moral prerogative to make judgments on such nationally particular grounds. Such a step, which would follow if

the judgments were to be brought in line with international legal norms, is resolutely avoided by the national courts.

The pluralist political structure, then, is taken to be a better guarantee of the higher interests of ethnic minorities than the essentially 'foreign' criteria of human rights, disembodied as they are in Britain from any constitutional framework. Such assumptions can only be made, however, if the tolerant pluralist structure is assumed over time to have a benign effect on the cultural practices and behavioural motives of ethnic minorities, and the individuals that constitute them. This is an assumption which therefore rejects the less-optimistic, 'realist' argument that these individuals will always pursue their self-interest, thereby reinforcing their cultural practices and perpetuating further ethnic conflict in society. It is here that the core underlying belief in the beneficial effects on the ethnic minorities of pluralist toleration over time is reached: why in particular such leeway is granted to them at local and community level to pursue their own collective aims. It is assumed that, over time, members of ethnic groups will perceive the benefits to them offered by the tolerant institutional framework, and affirm it themselves; moreover, this is more likely to happen if they are involved in some form of community-based action, than if not. Pursuit of their own interests in the educational and local political spheres – indeed, the civilised pursuit of wealth through commerce and the market – will, by the classic motion of the invisible hand, bring benefits for society at large. Good citizens and a harmonious society will be the outcome.

Such an idea is underlined by the privileged position given to the official place and role of church organisations in Britain. Again, this is in direct contrast to the French case, where the place of the church is a site of such political conflict between the state and ethnic groups. Rather, the mainstream British churches have used the expansion of the numbers of recognised churches within Britain to promote a picture of Britain as a multi-faith society, a strategy which also maximises the role of a declining Church of England as a leader in these initiatives.[51] Initiatives such as the *Faith in the City* studies have emphasised the mediating role of churches in the inner city as a vehicle for the integration of ethnic minorities and the encouragement of good citizenship virtues through the enlightened self-interest of religious aims.[52] This has been the spirit of the main Muslim and Hindu organisations in Britain, aligned behind the idea of promoting cultural tolerance and awareness of diverse religions at the same time as extending religious claims in areas such as education. These organisations are often unproblematically courted and funded by the state. An example is the Inner Cities Religious Council, a forum funded by the Department of the Environment. It liaises closely with the UK Action Committee on Islamic Affairs on questions of education, health, housing and social services.[53]

The mainstream religious organisations of the ethnic minorities are perhaps the best embodiment of the local and voluntary participatory ideals sketched out in the report on *Encouraging Citizenship*. This vision of the 'good citizen' could not be further from the secular political definition of citizenship found in France. The two public theories thus offer opposed conceptions of the source of public order and the origin of a sentiment of public duty, with reverse ideas about the importance of the state and public sphere in relation to the private and the local. It is surely remarkable that the two countries should have produced such different ideas about the moral education of their citizenry.

FAITH, TRUST AND CIVILITY: THE MULTICULTURAL POLITICS OF AN *ANCIEN RÉGIME*

By casting the policies of France and Britain towards the dilemmas of cultural pluralism as two distinct public philosophies – alternative national versions of philosophical liberalism – an axis of comparison can be established that allows for very general insights about the nature of politics in the two countries. As a scheme of interpretation it is, of course, a synthetic heuristic device. But the benefits of such a scheme should already be clear: it allows a comprehensive comparative viewpoint that most of the literature internal to each country fails to provide. Where they differ markedly is in the level of philosophical reflection that has been engaged in to justify policy statements and proposals. While the reports of the *Commission de la Nationalité* and *Haut Conseil à l'Intégration* amount to fully worked-out theories – with a built-in foundational 'metaphysics' – the British reports read much more like the slippery and glossy statements of political manifestos written by committee. British pragmatism, however, is a naturally self-effacing philosophy. Observers should not be fooled by the apparent ad-hocracy. British multicultural race relations has a heavily evolved and politically subtle rationale; its 'metaphysics' – its sacred core – are simply not ever made explicit. In this final section, I aim to make the jump and spell it out.

What is remarkable is how few political or academic observers of multicultural race relations show a real understanding of the essence of these institutions in their ideological interpretations of the kind of society Britain is and should be. The new right are frequently heard arguing that race relations are an artificial 'liberal' piece of social engineering and hence a corruption of the true English national political tradition: ignoring how classically conservative and 'organic' these institutions are in many ways.[54] The new left, meanwhile, lament the fact that such British institutions are not more explicitly justice-based and formalised in rights and constitution: overlooking how much of the success and stability of the framework has been down to its shifting, evolutionary utilitarianism.[55] The radical left, meanwhile, write the whole liberal project off as institutionalised racism and oppression. None of these viewpoints gets close to understanding how the institutional structure of multicultural race relations hangs together and works, in either a positive or negative sense. What I have tried to spell out in my reading, is a vision of Britain based on an idiosyncratic but self-consistent combination of ideas – driven by an underlying instrumental rationale – that is both a faithful re-interpretation of the 'long tradition', and an avant-garde vision of a new kind of society. It is a paradoxical triumph, for sure.

On the one hand, there is a set of legislation dominated by the conservative impulse to preserve a reasonable social order, and a faith in the wisdom of existing political structures that rely on a *laissez faire* libertarianism and anti-formalism to achieve a benign form of social progress. Yet, on the other, this is coupled with a rather radical willingness to countenance the idea of Britain as a multicultural society, with no place for exclusionary discourse on culturally nationalist grounds, and which pursues its goals through progressive legislation that is well in advance of public opinion. It is the one – and probably only – sphere of the political scene in which the liberal centre held its own and advanced in the 1980s, and which now, with the narrowing of the ideological waters in the early 1990s, is unquestioningly the dominant position. Yet it is also a paradoxical part of this picture that, viewed from an international perspective, there is anything but a convergence of the British public philosophy with progressive legislation elsewhere. The normative logic of the British philosophy resolutely refuses the introduction of any higher normative authority, such as the universal perspective of international law and human rights; it is even less internationalist than the already exceedingly nationalist French position. Britain's open and tolerant ethos of multiculturalism is tightly closed within a strict, territorially-bound national sphere.

As in France, the distant figures of classic political philosophers and theorists loom high in the underlying British philosophy of integration. Many of their well-known motifs can be read between the lines of the official arguments and justifications, where they have been re-used and connected together as the implicit compromise 'equilibrium philosophy' on which left and right are able to converge as a common framework. The motifs have been most apparent in the way these classics have been re-read through various contemporary – and distinctly 'British' (albeit some of them by adoption) – political thinkers, such as Ralf Dahrendorf (a prominent member of the *Commission on Citizenship*), Joseph Raz, John Gray and others. As with so much else in British political institutions, the true antecedents of the logic embedded in British multicultural race relations are Hobbes and Locke. As a political philosophy, Hobbesian thought first and foremost advances an analytical theory of the cement of society and the moral social order. It is a theory of individual behaviour and social interaction that leads to the conclusion that the source of moral order is embodied in the need for the arbitration of a sovereign law-giver. Historically, this is a set of theoretical ideas embedded in the early modern natural rights tradition, which has had a long-standing influence on British political thought.[56] The development of British political thought can indeed be interpreted as the progressive mediation and softening of the harsh original vision of the state of nature and the origin of law, by first Locke and then others, to accommodate the possibilities of an enlightened social condition developing out of the basic individualist presuppositions that ground its understanding of man and society.[57]

It is these 'responses to Hobbes' that are reflected in the legislative framework of multicultural race relations. The first is the key role of sovereignty in the framing of the British political question. The 'invisible' sea boundaries of the British nation provide a very distinctively bounded territorial basis, whose justificatory significance is not often made explicit. The obsession with border control and the peculiar ethical prerogative Britain asserts to set its own solutions in its own terms – and the fact that internationally the only obligation or responsibility that Britain has ever fully recognised is its obligation to the Commonwealth – should be seen in this light. Such nationalism is not the exclusive property of the right; socialists are apt also to dream of a sovereign socialist economy, and defend Britain's island-bound multiculturalism.[58] Hobbesian theory claims there will be moral and social anarchy if the sovereign authority of the law-giver is not recognised; in Britain, this clearly means the symbolic role of the Queen as head of state as much as parliament as the constitutionally unfettered maker and breaker of laws.

The upshot of this is the idea that social order questions involving ethnic minorities have a bottom line requirement about the need for 'loyalty' to Britain. At base, this is not a cultural imperative, but a territorial nationalist one. It has two dimensions: on the one side, it subordinates the necessity often felt by ethnic minorities for a cultural diaspora, to the home base superiority of British law; on the other, it unambiguously gives the right of the minority to consider itself 'here to stay', if it affirms its loyalty to British law and the sovereign authority. The richer interpretation of the Hobbesian formula is that the law-giver also gives moral 'recognition' to the subject who submits to the law; the recognition of his or her liberty, and the call of duty to the public order. It was exactly on this theme that David Selbourne's *The Principle of Duty* (1994) made such a surprise splash in the new spirit of the 1990s. This, then, is the underlying rationale of the fundamental category of 'legal subject' that runs through the nationality law, with primacy over the categories of 'citizen' or 'national'; and which is wholly bound up with the maintenance of the idea of

British sovereignty. As the use of these terms suggests, these are very much the classic concerns of an *ancien régime*.

The natural corollary of a Hobbesian theory of the state is a concern with the concentration of moral power that such a theory presupposes. France has no problem with this question, and tends to think unproblematically that a democratic state, in which the will of the citizens is sovereign, will naturally make for enlightened state jurisdiction over social and cultural behaviour which offends basic constitutional principles in the public sphere. Britain's political structure, built on its famously negative logic towards these questions, reverses the question. It is a condition of the open society that the morality of state power is continually questioned and limited where appropriate. In part this is because the state is not identified as the will of the people as in French democratic theory. British constitutional history from the Magna Carta, through the belief in the freedom of the market to modern corporate and property rights, has been consistently concerned with defining the limits of central political authority; all the more so, since there is no real, clear distinction, as in France, between the public and private spheres of society.

The two-step logic of externally-bounded sovereignty and subjecthood coupled with the limited nature of political authority internally, mirrors perfectly the lexicographic relation of nationality law and multicultural race relations. The assumption that society should pose a continual challenge to the dominant moral status of the state, and that as a consequence political structures should be devolved and pluralist as a result, is a central theme of the English pluralists.[59] Their response to Hobbes is to deny that sovereignty should be anything more than a central power to preserve order and peace, and hence emphasise the moral authority of corporations, guilds and the organisations of civil society in assuring the legitimacy of the political regime. In another way, the traditional idea of political representation in Britain, expressed most famously by Burke, performs the same function: that political representation, in parliament or local politics, is not a direct representation of sectional interests, but the creation of an elitist 'community of trust' between the representative and his or her public. This qualifies and frees the representative to interpret the long-term ideals of the community, free of strings.

This particularly British version of pluralism reflects both the justification for the 'moral' obligation to legislate taken in the national interest by elitist legislators, and the benign multicultural tenet that 'enlightened' ethnic leaders will represent their communities for the public good rather than narrow sectarian interests.

These thoughts are clearly echoed in the dominant reliance on local and community-level organisations as the natural sphere in which members of the ethnic minorities are enabled to become good citizens. In this sense, ethnic minorities have clearly become the guilds and corporations of contemporary urban Britain: their well organised church and social institutions are indeed given a privileged political and social role in their social integration, skilfully managed through the community relations of the main political parties and the state, and kept for the main part in very benign forms. This is also why cultural outlets for political grievances are the main safety valve for social tensions, outlets that have certainly been best used by parts of the Asian communities. And it should be recalled that tensions provoked by basic poverty or deprivation are, in the main, handled far less well.

These political and institutional structures are clearly underpinned by a distinct notion of freedom as their core guiding value. In any defence of the rights of ethnic minorities or of the protection of the value of cultural identity, the standard of *freedom* is always stated as the bottom line.[60] It is here that the more fundamental 'metaphysical' ideas found in the British approach are broached. It is a conception of freedom that has little to do with much of the recent egalitarian or rights-based reflections on the subject in a Rawlsian vein, but has had perhaps its best recent expression in the work of Joseph Raz, himself writing self-consciously in the tradition of J. S. Mill and H. L. A. Hart.[61] Characteristically, it is a theory which begins with the question of the nature and limits of political authority, a question often played out – as in the classic debates in the 1960s between the liberal Hart and the conservative Law Lord Devlin concerning homosexuality – over the question of public morality. One is reminded of the centrality of Hart versus Devlin over the role of the state to be played in questions of public morality: the need to defend, define and

limit a paternalist and perfectionist conception of state jurisdiction, and reconcile it with the recognition of cultural and
moral pluralism, without forsaking the virtues of the British
common law tradition. In short, the fact that judges should
not be simply empowered to put into judgment the worst
reactionary common opinions of the man on the Clapham
omnibus.[62]

Addressed by Raz, in a way which reflects very closely the kind
of legislation that has evolved in the multicultural race relations
legislation, the question of freedom comes down to the primacy
of individuals to pursue their own choices within an accepted
framework of moral pluralism and the incommensurability of
certain viewpoints; choices that nearly always depend on a rich
social and cultural setting and cannot be reduced to individualist
presumptions. The only limits that are set on this are the direct
harm of some practice to the 'social' conception of autonomy
that is here conceived. In many cases, state intervention on the
grounds of human rights, or the dominant liberal individualist
presumptions of the majority population, destroy the possibility
of social autonomy found in rich cultural practices and, in Raz's
terms, create more harm than good.[63] The longer-term goal of
liberal autonomy for all, may in fact be best served by a more
lenient and sympathetic attitude towards ethnic minority practices than a deontological theory would allow. A consequentialist
perfectionism is thus taken to be the guiding logic of state intervention into any multicultural dilemmas, a logic that admits of
both sociological factors and a principled normative theory of
the nature of autonomy and individual morality.[64] The utilitarian
logic that lies behind this thought is the idea, from J. S. Mill, that
individuals, ethnic minorities and society as a whole are better
off for having the chance to make 'experiments of living' with
diverse ways of life and cultures; in short, that a paternalist tolerance is the best way of maximising outcomes – often measured
in the richer utilitarian terms of 'well-being' – for everybody.[65]

It is obvious enough that negative freedom and *laissez faire*
are still very much part of the applied philosophy guiding
British politics; but why is there such a strong presumption
that the working out of this process will inevitably lead to
benign and harmonious results? Part of the answer certainly
lies in the continued currency of the classical early utilitarians,
Adam Smith and David Hume, on the origin of moral senti-

ments: in the clear feeling that the key to the ethnic minorities' benevolent integration is fostered by their own enlightened self-interest. But, as all the discussion about the *morality* of freedom suggests, there has to be rather more to the picture if it is to argue for benign outcomes over society as a whole, especially if the problem of toleration is raised. In part this is because toleration is far more concerned with the attitudes and predispositions of the majority population to the minority; and thus that the inculcation of good dispositions in the minority alone will not be sufficient to ensure their acceptance in the society at large.[66]

France has tried to deal with this problem by situating the core value of autonomy in the republican theory of moral political citizenship; majority and minority alike (categories, of course, which the French refuse to recognise) will find an identity in the public egalitarian identity of the good *citoyen*. In Britain, where the categories of majority and minority are maintained as the central classification of progressive legislation, the value of autonomy, rather, must be located in some form of mutual recognition between the parties: the toleration of the other *despite* their cultural differences. The idea takes us back to the root text of the British compromise over religion that enabled a Protestant regime to avoid the catastrophic ravages of religious war in continental Europe: Locke's *A Letter Concerning Toleration*.[67] Locke offers a number of arguments that are of great relevance today, but perhaps the most important here are the religious and sociological assumptions he makes. He argues that the public order will be served best if the ruling power does not try to stamp out dissenting or conflictual religious practices; and that, consequently, individuals have to be trusted (the double sense of the term *fides*) with their own faiths, which are only answerable to God in the final judgement. In short, Locke argues for lenience towards cultural forms in the evolution towards more benign forms and the presumption of good conscience as the root of liberty. Moreover, the condition for such toleration is that the sovereign rule of British law is unquestioned by the dissident faith. Toleration does not presume that the state has to like the practices it permits; rather it has to live with them in order to assure the moral public order. The origin of trust, civility and a multi-faith society lies ultimately with this thought: with the idea that members of minority faiths, who often believe in bizarre and repugnant practices, have to be recognized themselves as having *souls* that can be saved. Or, in words more familiar to our modern idiom, an autonomy of their own.

This interpretative key is, I would contend, the best way of making sense of the peculiar normative and explanatory claims of the British philosophy of integration. It is exemplified by the pragmatic concerns of toleration and the recognition of autonomy, as the best means to a moral social order, freedom, and the benefits of social flourishment and progress. British legislation has all along been concerned with this kind of line, even if it is rarely articulated, and only ever snaps into action when provoked by violence on the streets, or the 'seditious' disloyalty of groups to the sovereign power. It has only very rarely intervened in strong, positively directed ways, to restore, aid or reform undesirable practices. For the most part, wider social forces have been allowed to take their effect. The legislative philosophy is also one which believes in the integratory powers of letting groups join together and bargain through local forms. On the other hand, there has on the whole been a declining concern with tackling poverty or welfare questions as a means to this end. Britain fails systematically to match up to evaluatory criteria based on human rights, universal deontological reasoning, or the prescriptions of republican political participation. It is pervasively divided along colour and culture lines, just as it always has been on class lines. Its smugness about the defeat of racism publicly might just mean the sentiments have become privatised and unspoken.

Yet the very real benefits of this multicultural *ancien régime* are there for all to see; where there are ethnic minorities on the streets and in large concentrations, a truly multicultural society has flourished. In many ways this is a society marginal to the dominant elite and conservative ruling classes, who live remote from it, and would rarely offer any enthusiastic words on the subject. But for many ordinary citizens, being British is something that has been profoundly changed by post-colonial immigration. And perhaps even a Tory heart can feel some obligation to this vision. After all, it was a Conservative Home Office minister, John Patten, who declared after the Rushdie affair: 'At the heart of our thinking is a Britain where Christians, Muslims, Jews, Hindus, Sikhs and others can all work and live together, each proudly retaining their own faith and identity, but each sharing in common the bond of being by birth or by choice, British'.[68] In essence, these are the same kind of multicultural platitudes that anyone on the radical vegetarian and hippy left would be happy to endorse. This is surely an example of one of the apparent paradoxes of British politics and society, that have made it so impenetrable to homegrown and foreign commentators alike.

My concern here, and in the previous chapter, has been to build up the two distinct public philosophies as positive theories in their own terms: to show how they came to be put together and established themselves over time, and indicate how they work and justify themselves. My reading illustrates many of the abstract theoretical propositions put forward in Chapter 2. The remainder of my study will look at these philosophies with a more critical and evaluatory eye, along lines that I have begun to suggest. My reading here is based on the final section of Chapter 2: studying the evolution of a policy framework once established, and the ensuing questions of path dependency and institutional performance. Clearly, the two public philosophies are both powerful versions of philosophical liberalism, well-armoured with justifications that are canonical to the liberal tradition. Yet there are certain questions raised by the particular problem of the recent immigration and integration of ethnic minorities that also expose the limitations of these conceptions in adapting to the new problems of recent years, and to the political and social changes going on in an international perspective. In both cases, this problem is at root the inability to transcend their own peculiar, nationally defined institutional structures and embrace or combine the normative logic and developments of liberal institutions conceived at an international level. As I will show, the institutional solutions of both France and Britain – for all their merits – have a series of very deep and seemingly intractable problems, that follow directly from the kind of public philosophies they have enforced with their policy frameworks.

Notes

1.   The root text of these approaches is the enormously influential collection by the Centre for Contemporary Cultural Studies, *The Empire Strikes Back* (London: Hutchinson, 1982).

2. Michael Oakeshott, *On Human Conduct* (Oxford University Press, 1975); see also Roger Scruton, *The Meaning of Conservatism* (Harmondsworth: Penguin, 1980).

3. Thomas H. Marshall, 'Citizenship and Social Class', in T. H. Marshall and T. Bottomore, *Citizenship and Social Class* (London: Pluto Press, 1992 [1950]). A major new collection discussing his influence is Martin Bulmer and Anthony Rees (eds) *Citizenship Today: The Contemporary Relevance of T. H. Marshall* (London: UCL Press, 1996). See also the very penetrating critique of Marshall by Michael Mann, 'Ruling class strategies and citizenship', in Michael Mann, *States, Wars and Capitalism: Studies in Political Sociology* (Oxford: Blackwell, 1988).

4. E.J.B. Rose *et al.*, *Colour and Citizenship: A Report on British Race Relations* (London: Oxford University Press, 1969); Gunnar Myrdal, *An American Dilemma: The Negro Problem and Modern Democracy* (New York: Doubleday, 1944).

5. Report of the Commission on Citizenship, *Encouraging Citizenship* (London: HMSO, 1990).

6. See Will Kymlicka and Wayne Norman, 'Return of the Citizen: A survey of recent work on citizenship theory', *Ethics*, vol. 104 (Jan. 1994); Jürgen Habermas, 'Citizenship and national identity: Some reflections on the future of Europe', *Praxis International*, vol. 12, no. 1 (1992); Geoff Andrews (ed.), *Citizenship* (London: Lawrence & Wishart, 1991).

7. This is problem in the orthodox accounts of the story: for example, Zig Layton-Henry, *The Politics of Immigration* (Oxford: Blackwell, 1992); or Dilip Hiro, *Black British White British: A History of Race Relations in Britain* (London: Grafton, 1991). A more accurate picture is made by 'foreign' comparative American studies of the subject, especially Gary Freeman, *Immigrant Labour and Racial Conflict in Industrial Societies: The French and British experience 1945–1975* (Princeton University Press, 1979); Ira Katznelson, *Black Men White Cities* (Oxford University Press, 1973) pp. 123–51; and Anthony Messina, *Race and Party Competition* (Oxford University Press, 1989). See also, in French, John Crowley, 'Consensus et conflits dans la politique de l'immigration et des relations raciales du Royaume-Uni', in Jacqueline Costa-Lascoux and Patrick Weil (eds) *Logique d'états et immigrations* (Paris: Editions Kimé, 1992), and *Immigration, 'relations raciales' et mobilisations minoritaires en Royaume Uni: la démocratie face à la complexité sociale* (Paris: IEP thèse de doctorat, 1995).

8. My reading owes much to the writings of two of the most perspicacious commentators about multicultural Britain: Bhikhu Parekh and John Rex. Of the former, see 'The social logic of pluralism', in Bhikhu Parekh *et al.*, *Britain: A Plural Society* (London: CRE, 1990), and many other essays; of the latter, see especially, *Ethnic Identity and Ethnic Mobilisation* (Warwick: CRER Monographs in Ethnic Relations, no. 5, 1991) and *Ethnic Minorities in the Modern Nation State* (London: Macmillan, 1991).

9. See also the historical accounts in Colin Holmes, *John Bull's Island: Immigration and British Society 1871–1971* (London: Macmillan, 1988);

and Ann Dummett and Andrew Nicol, *Subjects, Citizens, Aliens and Others: Nationality and Immigration Law* (London: Weidenfeld, 1990).

10. Linda Colley, *Britons: Forging the Nation 1707–1837* (New Haven, Conn.: Yale University Press, 1992).

11. Shamit Saggar, 'Re-examining the 1964–70 Labour government's race relations strategy', *Contemporary Record*, vol. 7, no. 2 (1993).

12. Speech of 20 April 1968, reprinted in *Race: A Quarterly Forum*, vol. 10, no. 1 (July 1968).

13. See Philip A. Sooben, *The Origins of the Race Relations Act* (Warwick: CRER Research papers in Ethnic Relations, no. 12, 1990); E. J. B. Rose *et al.*, *Colour and Citizenship*, for a perspective from inside the policy process.

14. John Rex, 'Race, law and politics', in his *The Ghetto and the Underclass: Essays on Race and Social Policy* (Aldershot: Avebury, 1988).

15. See Shamit Saggar (ed.), *Race and British Electoral Politics* (London: Prentice-Hall, 1996).

16. Quoted from the general instructions issued to immigration service staff, in Commission for Racial Equality, *Immigration Control Procedures: Report of a Formal Investigation* (London: HMSO, 1985) p. 13.

17. Ibid, pp. 128–33.

18. See Richard Skellington, *Race in Britain Today* (London: Sage, 1992) ch. 1, 'Demographic trends'; D. Owen, *Ethnic Minorities in Great Britain: Settlement Patterns* (Warwick: CRER, 1992).

19. See Dummett and Nicol, *Subjects, Citizens, Aliens and Others*, pp. 241–53.

20. Tom Nairn, *The Break-up of Britain: Crisis and Neo-Nationalism* (London: Verso, 1981); Patrick Wright, *On Living in an Old Country: The National Past in Contemporary Britain* (London: Verso, 1985); Martin Barker, *Neo-Racism* (London: Junction, 1985).

21. Harry Goulbourne, *Ethnicity and Nationalism in Post-Imperial Britain* (Cambridge University Press, 1991).

22. See John Gardner, 'Liberals and unlawful discrimination', *Oxford Journal of Legal Studies*, vol. 9, no. 1 (1989).

23. John Rex, *The Concept of a Multicultural Society* (London: CRER Occasional Papers in Ethnic Relations, 1985) and 'The political sociology of a multicultural society', *European Journal of Intercultural Studies*, vol. 1, no. 1 (1991).

24. See, for example, the 1967 White Paper on racial discrimination; Rose *et al.*, *Colour and Citizenship*.

25. Quoted in Christopher McCrudden, David J. Smith and Colin Brown, 'Groups versus individuals: the ambiguity behind the Race Relations Act', *Policy Studies*, vol. 12, no. 1 (1991).

26. Report by the Rt Hon. The Lord Scarman, *The Brixton Disorders: 10–12 April 1981* House of Commons, Cmnd. 8427; referred to here as BD.

27. See John Rex, 'Law and order in multi-racial areas: the issues after Scarman', in his *The Ghetto and the Underclass*.

28. Home Office, 'A Guide to the Race Relations Act 1976' (London: HMSO); and Ian MacDonald, *Race Relations: The New Law* (London: Butterworth, 1977).

29. Harry Goulbourne, 'Varieties of pluralism: the notion of a pluralist post-imperial Britain, *New Community*, vol. 17, no. 2 (1991).

30. See the discussion about the pros and cons of racial classification in Skellington, *Race in Britain Today*.

31. The cases are discussed in detail in Colin Bourne and John Whitmore, *Race and Sex Discrimination*, 2nd edn (London: Sweet & Maxwell, 1993).

32. See Laurence Lustgarden, *Legal Control of Racial Discrimination* (London: Macmillan, 1980); McCrudden *et al.*, 'Groups versus individuals'.

33. See the CRE guidelines: 'Monitoring an equal opportunities policy' (1986); 'Equal opportunities in employment: a guide for employers' (1987); 'Why keep ethnic records?' (1991).

34. Gary S. Becker, *The Economics of Discrimination* (University of Chicago Press, 1971); see also Thomas Sowell – the hero of Ray Honeyford – *The Economics and Politics of Race: An International Perspective* (New York: Morrow, 1983), for another very Chicago school-inspired perspective on the relation of society, politics and economy on progressive or regressive integratory outcomes.

35. John Rawls, *A Theory of Justice* (Oxford University Press, 1971); Ronald Dworkin, *Taking Rights Seriously* (London: Duckworth, 1977).

36. See Nathan Glazer and Ken Young (eds), *Ethnic Pluralism and Public Policy: Achieving Equality in the US and Great Britain* (London: Gower, 1986).

37. Mancur Olson, *The Logic of Collective Action: Public Goods and the Theory of Groups* (Cambridge, Mass. Harvard University Press, 1980).

38. Nathan Glazer, *Ethnic Dilemmas 1964–1982* (Cambridge, Mass.: Harvard University Press, 1983); Arthur D. Schlesinger, *The Disuniting of America: Reflections on a Multicultural Society* (New York: Norton, 1992); or Jim Sleeper, *The Closest of Strangers: Liberalism and the Politics of Race in New York* (New York: Norton, 1990). For rather different – and more convincing – multicultural readings of the USA, see Ronald Takaki, *A Different Mirror: A History of Multicultural America* (Boston, Mass. : Little Brown & Co., 1993); and Michael Omi and Howard Winant, *Racial Formation in the US from the 1960s to the 1980s*, 2nd edn (London: Routledge, 1994). Meanwhile, Richard Alba, *Ethnic Identity: The Transformation of White America* (New Haven, Conn.: Yale University Press, 1990); Douglas Massey and Nancy Denton, *American Apartheid: Segregation and the Making of the Underclass* (Cambridge, Mass.: Harvard University Press, 1993), suggest some of the underlying sociological reasons for this majority white anxiety.

39. Michael Banton, *Promoting Racial Harmony* (Cambridge University Press, 1985). Banton makes a fruitful use of Olson in his analysis.

40. Report of the Commission on Citizenship, *Encouraging Citizenship* (1990), referred to here as EC.

41. See Douglas Hurd, 'Citizenship in the Tory democracy', *New Statesman* 27 Apr. 1988) and 'Freedom will flourish where citizens accept responsibility', *Independent* (13 Sep. 1989). The Labour Party has been no less active in trying to capture the idea of citizenship for itself. On the ideas behind the politics, see especially the recent interventions of

Ralf Dahrendorf, a key intellectual contributor to the Commission: an interview with John Keane, 'Decade of the citizen', *Guardian* (1 August 1990); and 'The changing quality of citizenship', in Bart van Steenbergen (ed.), *The Condition of Citizenship* (London: Sage, 1994). For a critical view of these developments, see Colin Crouch, 'Citizenship and community in British political debate', in C. Crouch and A. Heath (eds), *Social Research and Social Reform* (Oxford: Clarendon, 1992); and Anne Phillips, *Democracy and Difference* (Cambridge: Polity, 1993), ch. 4.

42. Many of the contributors pick up on these distinctions in the idea of community and citizenship at local levels in Albert Mabileau *et al.*, *Local Politics and Participation in Britain and France* (Cambridge University Press, 1989).

43. Ken Young and Naomi Connelly, *Policy and Practice in the Multi-Racial City* (London: Policy Studies Institute, 1991).

44. Muhammad Anwar, *Race and Politics: Ethnic Minorities and the British Political System* (London: Tavistock, 1986); and the special report in *The Guardian* (22 July 1989), p. 4.

45. Swann Committee Report, *Education for All*, House of Commons, Cmnd. 9453; referred to here as EFA.

46. See discussions in G. K. Verma (ed.), *Education for All: A Landmark in Pluralism* (London: Falmer, 1989); Sohan Modgil *et al.*, *Multiculturalism: The Interminable Debate* (London: Falmer, 1986); and Bhikhu Parekh, 'The Hermeneutics of the Swann Report', in Verma (ed.), *Education for All*.

47. For example, Iris Marion Young, *Justice and the Politics of Difference* (Princeton University Press, 1991).

48. See Albert O. Hirschman, *Exit, Voice and Loyalty: Responses to Decline in Firms, Organizations and States* (Cambridge, Mass.: Harvard University Press, 1970).

49. Sebastian Poulter, 'Ethnic minority customs, English law and human rights', *International and Comparative Law Quarterly* (Jul. 1987) and *Asian Traditions and English Law: A Handbook* (London: Runnymede/Trentham, 1990).

50. There is indeed much in common between the rationale of the British institutional framework and the ideas of 'complex equality' and 'institutional separation' defended by Michael Walzer, *Spheres of Justice* (New York: Basic Books, 1983). See also the discussions in David Miller and Michael Walzer (eds), *Pluralism, Justice and Equality* (Oxford University Press, 1995).

51. See Brian Pearce *et al.*, *Law, Blasphemy and the Multi-Faith Society* (London: CRE/Inter – Faith Network of the UK).

52. Reports of the Archbishop of Canterbury's Commission on Urban Priority Areas: *Faith in the City: A Call for Action by Church and Nation* (London: Church House, 1985); *Living Faith in the City: A Progress Report* (London: Church House, 1990). Tariq Modood, 'Establishment, multiculturalism and British citizenship', *Political Quarterly*, vol. 65, no. 1 (1994) discusses some of the pitfalls and limitations of the religious dimension to integration in Britain.

53. Danièle Joly, *Britannia's Crescent: Making a Place for Muslims in British Society* (Aldershot: Avebury, 1995); Philip Lewis, *Islamic Britain. Religion, Politics and Identity Among British Muslims: Bradford in the 1990s* (London: Tavistock, 1994).

54. For example, Ray Honeyford, *Integration or Disintegration? Towards a Non-Racist Society* (London: Claridge Press, 1988); and articles in the *Salisbury Review* by E.J. Mishan, 'What future for a multi-racial Britain?' (Jun./Sep. 1988) and Anthony Flew, 'The race relations industry' (1984). For the essentials of this view of Britain, see Roger Scruton, 'What is right?', *The Times Literary Supplement* (10 Apr. 1992).

55. For example, John Keane, *Democracy and Civil Society* (London: Verso, 1988); Chantal Mouffe (ed.) *Dimensions of Radical Democracy: Pluralism, Citizenship, Community* (London: Verso, 1992); Stuart Hall and David Held, 'Citizens and citizenship' in Stuart Hall and David Held (eds) *New Times: The Changing Face of Politics in the 1990s* (London: Lawrence & Wishart, 1989). Here, the essentials of the view are spelt out by Steven Lukes, 'What is left?', *The Times Literary Supplement* (27 March 1992).

56. See Richard Tuck, *Natural Rights Theories* (1979) and *Philosophy and Government 1572–1651* (1993) – both published by Cambridge University Press.

57. Ralf Dahrendorf, *The Modern Social Conflict: An Essay on the Politics of Liberty* (London: Weidenfeld & Nicolson, 1988).

58. For example, David Miller, *Market, State and Community* (Oxford: Clarendon, 1989).

59. David Nicholls, *The Pluralist State* (London: Macmillan, 1994); and Paul Hirst (ed.), *The Pluralist Theory of the State* (London: Routledge, 1989), which features the figures of Maitland, Cole, Figgis and Laski.

60. See Dahrendorf, *The Modern Social Conflict*.

61. Joseph Raz, *The Morality of Freedom* (Oxford: Clarendon, 1986).

62. Lord (Patrick) Devlin, *The Enforcement of Morals* (Oxford University Press, 1965); H. L. A. Hart, *Law, Liberty and Morality* (Oxford University Press, 1968).

63. Raz, *The Morality of Freedom*, chs 14 and 15. See also the philosophical reflections around the theme of autonomy in the Swann report: G Haydon (ed.), *Education for a Pluralist Society: Philosophical Perspectives on the Swann Report* (London Institute of Education).

64. A number of writers have pursued the idea that Raz's work is particularly appropriate for understanding British liberal philosohy towards race relations: for example, Gardner, 'Liberals and unlawful discrimination'; John Gray, *Beyond the New Right : Markets, Government and the Common Environment* (London: Routledge, 1993); and Raz himself in 'Free expression and personal identification', *Oxford Journal of Legal Studies*, vol. 11, no. 3 (1991) and 'Multiculturalism: a liberal perspective', *Dissent*, vol. 41, no. 1 (1994). But see also the (rather harsh) critique of Raz (and Mill) in Bhikhu Parekh, 'Superior people', *The Times Literary Supplement*, 25 Nov. 1994).

65. James Griffin, *Well-Being: Its Meaning, Measurement and Moral Importance* (Oxford: Clarendon, 1986).

66. Raz, *The Morality of Freedom*, pp. 401–7.

67. See the essays on Locke by John Dunn, in *Rethinking Modern Political Theory* (Cambridge University Press, 1985) and *Interpreting Political Responsibility* (Oxford: Polity, 1990); James Tully, *An Approach to Political Philosophy: Locke in Contexts* (Cambridge University Press, 1993); and Susan Mendus (ed.) *Justifying Toleration: Conceptual and Historical Perspectives* (Cambridge University Press, 1988), especially the essays by Richard Tuck and Joseph Raz.

68. John Patten, 'Letter to Muslim leaders in Britain', quoted in M. M. Ahsan and A.R. Kidwai (eds), *Sacrilege versus Civility: Muslim Perspectives on 'The Satanic Verses Affair'* (Leicester: The Islamic Foundation, 1991).

5 France into the 1990s: Following the Integration Line *jusqu'au bout*

In the years since the first nationality debates of the 1980s, the republican philosophy of *intégration* in France has gone from strength to strength. With the right sweeping to power in the 1993 elections – and the sheer exhaustion of the left after a decade of socialist disappointments – one might have expected the focus of policies to shift. In fact, if anything, the right's victory enabled the philosophical triumph of the 1980s to concretise and establish itself politically as legislation and policy; a process cemented by the passing of the new *Code de la Nationalité* and accompanying immigration restrictions, that completed the logic of the consensus soldered under the leadership of the left at the end of the previous decade.

The definitive triumph of this particular public philosophy across the board politically was no small achievement. In achieving the three conditions for such a triumph of ideas mentioned in Chapter 2 – soldering a large consensus, dominating rival theories, and establishing itself over time – the French republican philosophy of *intégration* has now achieved a cognitive dominance in the public debate of the issue, that largely pre-sets an exclusive political vocabulary and way of conceiving the problems at stake. As we shall see, the triumph has been so forceful as to render much internal French discussion blind to its own parameters. Many of the problems that have arisen in French policies towards ethnic dilemmas in recent years can thus be traced directly as *pathologies* of the dominant public theory, which, with the confident self-interpreting functionalism of its historical and philosophical line, has been zealously applied to new, emerging political and social circumstances.

In Chapter 3, I sketched the scenario of how the dominant set of ideas that emerged in France during the 1980s came to hold centre-stage. France's public philosophy of integration combines high universalist ideals with a 'mythical' retelling of a long historical tradition that grounds these ideals, and their working-out in practice, in the institutional particularity of the French nation. French national political identity is thus constantly foregrounded as the primary *enjeu* in French responses to ethnic dilemmas. This is seen both in the continuing operation of this institutional frame on the integration of new 'problematic' immigrants; and in the highly normative ideal model of the individual as '*citoyen*', imposed on new members of French society, that stylises the form of their relations with their own culture and participation in the political sphere. Such a normative theory exerts a price on those it is applied to: a price perhaps not always worth paying.

The republican philosophy of *intégration* is the peculiarly French political answer to the problem of social integration. A public philosophy of integration must take as its primary concern ordering the behaviour of the nation as a whole, and hence the unity of the majority population. In the French case, particularly, there is a heightened concern about the regionalist decentralisation of the nation, the pressure of European Union, and the emergence of political pluralism. France is peculiar, however, for taking as the axial focus of social re-integration a group which may always play a highly symbolic role in problematising questions of national order and identity, but need not necessarily be the *central* question: *les immigrés*. As I will show, the playing out of the neo-republican theory of *intégration* of the 1980s – with *les immigrés* caught half-way between *étrangers* and *citoyens* – has had numerous institutional effects, of both a political and social kind. Into the 1990s, these effects have reinforced the peculiarity of the French nationalist solution in respect to the rest of Europe, and only succeeded in deflecting concerns about regional devolution. Evaluating these consequences will be the task in this chapter; a case where the political logic, as befits such a rationalist nation, has been pursued with admirable self-consistency and application *jusqu'au bout*.

NATION AND NATIONALITY LAW: A VERY FRENCH OBSESSION

The coalescence of the new republican consensus in French politics at the end of the 1980s was above all a triumph of ideas and agenda-setting. It was to take until summer 1993 for the triumph to bear its full political and legislative fruit. Although the basic framework of ideas and concepts of the '*nouvelle synthèse républicaine*' had gained a pre-eminence in public discussions by the end of the 1980s, the final elements of the political consensus took a year or two more to fall into place. Indeed, the elaboration of these basic ideas in the *rapports* of the *Haut Conseil à l'Intégration* during the period 1990–3, traced the conversion of the wider technocratic elite to the arguments and justifications that had been promoted by the new generation of republican intellectuals since the mid-1980s. All that was left was for the whole package to receive confirmation by the electorate, and find its political consummation in law and new legislation.

It is worth stepping back and re-tracing the political events that were to lead to this final triumph. The report of the *Commission de la Nationalité* was received with great public attention and widespread support across the political spectrum when it was published in 1988. Its concrete proposals for reform – primarily making young Algerians between the ages of sixteen and twenty make a declaration of wanting French citizenship, and doing away with the *double droit du sol* for children of Algerians born before 1962 – were put on ice, however, as shifting political circumstances removed the immediate political uncertainty that had prompted its formation. New elections in 1988 had brought an end to the period of left – right *cohabitation* and, with a Socialist prime minister once again installed under Mitterrand, the central political motive behind the proposals – the attempt of the mainstream right to embrace a centrist position and forestall the rise of Le Pen – was gone again.

Not all socialists, meanwhile, were as yet fully on board the new republican bandwagon. For some on the left, the new individualist *contrat social*, first sketched by the *Commission* in 1987, was something that sat very poorly with their interpretation of the post-revolutionary republican tradition it tried to invoke. The individualism of the Commission's report, in particular its emphasis on the changing relation of the individual and the state, certainly mirrored the growing movement of politics and society in France as elsewhere, away from interventionism and centralisation. But this individualism was not clearly compatible with the dominant collectivism of traditional left-wing republicans, which still inspired much of the rhetoric on the left. For sure, this collectivism had – with the economic liberalisation of the 1980s and the coming together of the European Union – begun to look an absurdly arcane set of ideas. Yet it was still strongly represented in the *bicentenaire* celebrations of 1989, if only now as a nationalist defence of French particularity and resistance to outside international forces: most visibly in the public voice of the redoubtable left-wing republican stalwart, Régis Debray.[1] With this, as always, came a refusal to countenance any change to the so-called bottom line of the republican tradition: the *ius soli*. Any reform of the *Code de la Nationalité*, it was argued, would be a profound break with this national tradition; and for a time this reaction stalled any further progress in reform.

Again, what was needed was a certain squaring of the republican circle: a reconciliation of the new individualist proposals with a 'traditional' defence of French national particularity. The coming to power of the new prime minister Michel Rocard – the long-time representative of the technocratic, business friendly '*nouvelle gauche*' (new left) – was a first step in this direction. Prominent among the public intellectuals sustaining his new brand of centrist social democracy were 'nationalist' political economists such as Alain Minc and Michel Albert, defending the integrity and power of the French economy against the economic illusion of the *libérale* European Union, on the one hand, and the 'anglo-saxon' free market and North American dominance, on the other.[2] Here were grounds for a new nationalist line that bizarrely reconciled liberal capitalism with the bounded French collectivist spirit.

The events which made the squaring of the circle fully possible, however, were connected primarily to the continuing rise of the question of Islam in France, particularly the great rupture caused by *l'affaire du foulard* which burst open in November 1989. I shall go on later to make a full account of the strange trajectory of this affair, in which an enormous public scandal arose because of the banning from a French

public school of three Muslim girls who refused to take off
their religious headscarves in class. Here, I wish to note the instrumental role the crisis over Islam in France played in soldering the political consensus. There is no better indication of
this than the kind of effect the affair had on those on the left
reluctant to embrace the individualism of the original
Commission's proposals. The affair immediately inspired a
wave of fervent Republican militancy – in support of the ban –
particularly among the most mediatised intellectuals of the
left, a group of idiosyncratic radicals who showered the media
with off-the-cuff nightmare visions of Islam in France: visions
obsessed with the escalating fear of *islamicisme*, the corruption
of women's freedom by the veil, and the growing influence of
foreign Islamic powers in the socially deprived backwaters of
French cities.[3] Most extraordinary of all was the open letter
entitled 'Profs: ne capitulons pas!' sent to the *Nouvel
Observateur* of 2–8 November 1988 by a group of five leading
intellectual figures, including the usual suspects, Régis Debray
and Alain Finkielkraut, in which they asked – apparently in all
seriousness – whether the *affaire* was going to be 'the Munich
of republicanism'.

This reaction was in fact typical of the republican left's line
on Islam in France throughout this period. It helped generate
a public reception to this crisis which effectively pushed those
still sceptical on the left to embrace the individualist, new republican *contrat social* being offered in the official *rapports*.
They thus fell in line with the emerging consensus within the
French public and a broad spectrum of French politicians,
that a higher individualist price had to be exerted from
French Muslims for their citizenship and membership in the
French polity. Political participation, social integration and
social acceptance, would thus all be formally attached to a reci-
procal individual relation between the citizen and the French
nation-state. An ideal standard of citizenship would be set, allegiance demanded and a moral code imposed. This would,
among other things, ward off the high danger of political pluralism that the competing community-based allegiance of
Islam seemed to pose. Practically speaking, this entailed
reform to the one site where such allegiances can actually be
demanded formally by law: accession to French nationality and
the core symbol of full French membership, *le code et la carte*.

Michel Rocard himself put an end to any lingering multi-cultural tendencies on the mainstream left in his launching of the *Haut Conseil à l'Intégration* in 1990. Declaring the ill-fated idea of '*droit à la différence*' dead, he proclaimed that henceforth the focus of progressive thinking should be on the '*droit à l'in-différence*' (the right to be indifferent), the reconciliation of cultural diversity with universal rights and equality. Around this time, the new social movements of the left – such as *SOS Racisme* – that had been so instrumental in raising multicultural and anti-racist issues in the 1980s, began framing their own rhetoric in wholly republican terms.[4] The *rapports* of the *Haut Conseil* were thus to come out to almost no dissent, across a wide cross-section of political opinion that had shifted to identify itself with the new republican philosophy. And the terms of the theory of integration elaborated between 1990–3 by the *Haut Conseil* did indeed inevitably push any possible practical measures back towards the question of nationality law, left aside in 1989. This is because the idea of citizenship it envisaged – particularly the high standard of autonomy imagined at the root of individuals' ability to participate and integrate in the French nation – is impossible without full *formal* and *recognised* national status. This was, by definition, the problematic issue for so many North Africans and others – whether formal 'citizens' or not – caught between the stigmatising label of *étranger* and the elusive ideal-type category of *citoyen*. It was this theoretical paradigm of republican *intégration* that, with the left now also on board, had been embraced by the leading public intellectuals, the ENA-educated Parisian elites, and all the most prominent politicians of the late 1980s and early 1990s. It was thus *this* consensus, and the set of 'progressive' republican ideas it built itself around, that paved the way – as much if not more than Le Pen's manipulation of the disaffected sections of French society – for the return of a sharply right-wing government, armed with the number one priority of reform of immigration controls via a new nationality law. Like it or not – and no matter how much they protested at the eventual legislation – it was a victory assented to in full substance by the left in advance of their electoral defeat.

The sweeping return to power of the right in 1993 marked a new seizure of the centre ground in French politics: compatible on the one hand with the new republican consensus stretching left, and on the other with the nationalist agenda, that had been pursued exclusively by Le Pen in the 1980s to the detriment of the RPR and UDF, stretching right. The reform of the *Code de la Nationalité* was the perfect symbolic issue to solder this new centring of French politics. It was seen as the electoral pivot of their triumph: the fact that they were finally going to do something about reforms that been stalled in 1987, and again in 1989. It was the right's – and particularly *ministre de l'intérieur* Charles Pasqua's – first priority. With the rapid promotion of the new *Code de la Nationalité* and the 'Pasqua laws' on immigration control during the Summer of 1993, the triumph of the philosophy of *intégration* was complete. In effect, events had come full circle, back to the work of the *Commission de la Nationalité* and *Haut Conseil à l'Intégration*, now taken as the canonical texts by all the new code's proponents.

The technical preoccupation with defining *who belongs* as French national and citizen – the redrawing of borders and boundaries – is a policy line that patently fails to address many of the social symptoms of the immigration/integration question: the socio-economic decline and isolation of the *banlieues*, unemployment, growing youth delinquency, the attraction of militant Islamicism. Yet, in the climate established by both Le Pen and the neo-republican nationalist resurgence of the 1980s, it was a policy line that had become a hugely potent, vote-winning affair, since everybody across the political spectrum could at least admit that something had to be done about the flow of new *clandestins* and immigrants; even if the really important social issues have little directly to do with border control. The two issues of *immigration* and *intégration* had become indistinguishably mixed up in everyone's minds. When the central policy question becomes how to transform the members of ethnic minorities into citizens – '*de l'immigré au citoyen*' as the slogan goes – the process of integration is unavoidably thought of as hinging on the moment the new immigrant enters the nation and applies for formal status. Unfortunately, the more significant and wider questions raised by the problem of integration – resoldering social order, trust and civility across cultural differences – only begins in earnest once the newcomers have fully secure status and formal rights; that is, when they are, to all extents and purposes, already citizens. However, the *surenchère* of the formal category of *citoyen*, into a fully fledged moral and political definition of the ideal liberal individual – with characteristics well over and above those of a simple juridical subject – has created a difficult and distant ideal that fails many of the new 'liberated' *citoyens* it is supposed to support.

A great deal of very pious left-wing dissent was heard with the presentation of the new code. It was said – again – that the new law would touch the fundamental *ius soli*, destroying a core element of national identity.[5] With little else to do but make noises at the political sidelines – and an extraordinary degree of *mauvaise foi* – the now out-of-power left washed its hands of the fact it was largely responsible for setting up the conditions of the new republican consensus, and the return to a strongly nationalistic criteria of membership on which the new code puts the seal. In fact, the proposals put forward by Pasqua in the early summer of 1993 (which had been voted by the Senate in 1990 but not gone any further) were practically the carbon copy of the original proposals published in *Etre français aujourd'hui et demain* in 1988. Marceau Long and other members of the Commission, such as Salem Kacet, were brought out to justify its working out in practice. Long, notably, refused to be drawn on whether the practical translation of the proposals remained faithful to the original text.[6] Technically, then, it was not the abrogation of the *ius soli*, as the critics somewhat ingenuously complained. Rather, the changes brought in the voluntary requirement to ask for French nationality, removing the right for parents to ask for it for their children, and the *double droit du sol* for children of Algerians themselves born before independence, in favour of proof of five years' residence and *enracinement*. Other changes were purely restrictive in nature: lengthening the waiting period and conditions before family regroupment could be asked for to two years; lengthening to two years the waiting period for citizenship after a foreigner marries a French citizen; and passing a new immigration law to bring French legislation into line with the Schengen agreement. Toughest of all in the changes to the code was the addition of certain conditions requiring a clean criminal record before citizenship could be given, and the refusal of French nationality to any one condemned to six months of prison for various crimes, among which was drug-trafficking.

The proposals were defended as promoting social cohesion and integration, and regulating French nationality rules in line with the new individualism and individual responsibility in a less collectivist state. Nowhere was there any suggestion that these were laws inspired by Le Penist rhetoric or social prejudices. Above all, they were defended as being for the French and applied to the French; reprising the exact arguments of the Commission.[7] It was also said the laws 'merely' brought France into line with other countries, having been so much more 'open' than other nations in the past. This is a typical, self-styled French myth, which simply cannot be true, otherwise Germany would not be so far ahead in numbers of resident foreigners, refugees and immigrants. This is proof, perhaps, that migration flows have less to do with the supposed openness of naturalisation and citizenship laws (something for which the French always criticise Germany), and more to do with the kind of economic and social 'deal' that a host nation offers. In 1993, there were 5.87 million foreigners resident in Germany compared to 3.6 million in France, plus much higher numbers of resident refugees and asylum-seekers.[8]

The legislation was passed without difficulty in July 1993, and with one or two important but minor challenges made by the constitutional court at a later point, went right through to the statute books. Part of the Immigration Act concerning Schengen was thrown out because of its incompatibility with human rights norms, but this did not derail the main thrust of the reforms.[9]

What had been impossible in 1987 and 1989/90, had therefore become easy by 1993, with only a few minor constitutional objections able to hold up the sweep of legislation. A new political consensus and legislative change was thus built on the foundation of ideas and concepts established in the late 1980s. In other words, this political success was *path dependent* on the original public theory of *intégration* established as the main consensus point in French politics at the end of the 1980s. It was thus a consensus that hinged on its re-formulation of the integrity and cohesion of the French nation, and the conditions for the successful integration of cultural diversity. With the new legislation freshly in place, it was now possible to look back and reinterpret the adjusted line of new 'classical' republicanism, as wholly consistent with French history and the continued effect of the French *creuset*, re-understood now in an individualist, contractarian way. To emphasise this point, the sharp way in which a different right-wing line was resoundingly rejected by all parties at this time might also be noted: Giscard d'Estaing's latest attempt to launch another presidential comeback in 1991, by seizing the right-wing populist vote with a nativist argument that *ius sanguinis* was the true foundation of the French nation.[10]

Taking the new *Code de la Nationalité* as the authentic continuation of the theory of *intégration* elaborated in French politics throughout the 1980s, it is possible to go on and pinpoint the self-consistent effects that putting into practice such a set of ideas has had, and hence to consider the institutional performance of this set of dominant ideas. For all the talk of the code being for the benefit of social cohesion and cultural integration – the desired effect of establishing better definitions of French boundaries and national membership – the justifications and wording of the legislation clearly have a symbolic, deontological grounding, rather than one justified by the desired consequences. Again, they embody the characteristic *a priori* style of French politics. *Nationalité réussie*, as in the original report, is said to depend on the new immigrant fulfilling certain moral and legal criteria as preconditions for *intégration*. There are certainly clear, principled benefits to this kind of stance: particularly considering its anti-relativism and the prohibition of certain undesirable practices that might be allowed on consequentialist terms. Here, however, I am primarily concerned with the *effets pervers* that might follow from this institutional starting point, and thus the various examples of negative pathologies that such a rigid path of conformity can be seen to cause.

There are several ways in which the obsessive focus on boundary and membership definition has deflected political efforts away from where they should be focused. The central irony of France's public philosophy of *intégration* is that, despite explicitly addressing the core theoretical question of integration – the re-securing of moral order from conditions of value pluralism – the institutional solution found in fact deflects the target of legislation and policy away from what should be its key concern: the behaviour and unity of the majority population. Unlike the 'self-effacing' hidden logic of the British institutions, the problem in the French case is that its focus – an obsession with regulating the status of *étrangers*, and

hence fixing the coterminous boundaries of French *nationalité*
and *citoyenneté* – in fact mistakes the symptom of the nation's
integration problems for its cause. This is a pathology which,
over time, has deflected elite political concerns away from the
social and political realities they should be addressing, towards
the symbolically powerful and electorally rich issue of *les immigrés* in France.

Truth and relative proportion can be the first victims of politics when it is pursued in highly symbolic ways. This is the
great danger in the French debate, in which the overcharged
rhetoric of *immigration* and *intégration, nationalité* and *citoyenneté*, has become a kind of institutionalised *langue de bois*.[11] The
most abiding triumph of Le Pen in the 1980s was thus to
impose on the contemporary French political consciousness
and vocabulary a kind of fixed opposition between the term
étrangers and those with full membership in the French nation,
the coterminous *nationaux* and *citoyens*. '*L'étranger*', is a term
which works at numerous philosophical and political levels: it
is at once the term for 'the Other' (opposed to 'the self', 'I',
and 'us'), the 'outsider', the 'strange' (*fremde*, in German),
and – more concretely in politics and jurisprudence – the 'foreigner' and 'immigrant'.[12] As in Albert Camus' famous novel,
'*l'étranger*' *par excellence* is '*l'arabe*', '*l'algérien*', '*le musulman*', or
worse, '*le raton*' or '*le bougnoule*'. From this, it has always been a
short step to wilder binary oppositions between civilisation
and barbarism, secularism and the '*intégriste*', democracy and
terrorism. Indeed, the high-flying rhetoric of certain writers
concerning Islam in France has in latter years become mixed
up with a wholly paradoxical stance in *defence* of Muslims involved in the war in Bosnia, read as another manichean struggle between civilisation and barbarity.[13] If, for whatever reason
– most likely to do with colour, culture, religion, or socio-
economic predicament – the new member of society fails to
match up to the high ideal of *citoyen français* spelt out in the
rapports and surrounding discussions, there is always the likeli-
hood that this problematic member will slip from being an accepted *citoyen* to the category of *étranger*, forever marginalised.

Language matters: these are the linguistic stakes attached to
the dominant problematic of integrating difficult immigrants
into French society.[14] They are stakes, moreover, which, with
the emergence of the full-blown republican theory of *intégra-*

tion, have been raised to the highest philosophical and historical levels. It is no surprise, perhaps, that the fulfilment and maintenance of such high ideals is open to sullied translation in practice. A graphic example, already mentioned, is the problem of collecting accurate and representative population statistics when a political embargo, for well-principled philosophical reasons, is put on their collection according to racial or ethnic criteria. Facts and figures, the very stuff of truth-based political reasoning, are only available for those officially classified as *étrangers* (non-nationals) in juridical terms; a category which thus fails to represent the vast majority of North Africans in France who are full citizens, often of the second and third generation. In popular parlance – and even social scientific work extolling the triumphs of French *intégration* – these persons are also referred to as *étrangers*: witness the figures recently quoted for inter-cultural marriages between 'French' and 'North Africans'.[15] During the last Socialist government under Mitterrand, civil servants were, during a particularly key debate, ordered to shred all available official statistics on persons according to ethnic origins (which *are* kept unofficially), in order to defuse the arguments of the extreme right about the number of *étrangers* present in France. Such apparent absurdities – which are caused by the parameters of a political vocabulary set by the philosophical commitment to certain rhetorical forms – do nothing to ease the social acceptance of ethnic minorities present in France. Indeed, they only encourage and perpetuate the use (and abuse) of the term *étrangers* for persons who have been French for over twenty-five years by others still hostile to their presence. Above all else, it sadly tarnishes the idea of *nationalité réussie* for all the smiling young North African *beurs* brandishing their French *cartes d'identité* on the front of official French documents about integration.

Between the (probably) exaggerated numbers of *clandestins* present in France, and the equally shady and unfixed numbers of full French citizens of North African and other origin, there is a huge margin for manipulation, misrepresentation and exaggeration for political ends. The right were undoubtedly trading on such fears when they pursued the code and immigration control as their number one symbolic priority in coming to office. Given different factual circumstances, and a different focus of concern about the bases of French cultural and social integration, such a focus might not have been possible. The same goes generally for the concern and uncertainty about the now much larger flows of migrants and refugees that are trying to move across Europe to the richer countries (note again France's exaggerated self-reputation on this score), and the immediate electoral payoff garnered by electoral candidates in the 1995 presidential elections by criticising the Schengen agreement.[16] It is a perfect indefinable variable for the kind of rhetoric in which Le Pen and others have traded, and which has now been absorbed into the mainstream consensus.

The fixed terms of the legislation, of course, also have certain institutional effects when they are put into practice. Notable has been the bureaucratisation of the whole procedure of attaining French nationality. This can be observed both in the necessary publicity that now has to be made to inform young immigrant teenagers about applying for their entitlements at the right age, and the significantly closer involvement of the police and local town halls: in particular all the new bureaucratic offices and procedures that have had to be set up to deal with the new process. The police now have to provide certain additional information about new applicants, and have greater opportunity for blocking the application because of criminal records or perceived attempts to corrupt or illegally jump through the legislation. New police powers have been set up to monitor borders (in co-operation with other national police forces – the main 'achievement' of the Schengen accord). For the first time in French history a police force has been created exclusively for dealing with policing immigration: the DICCILEC. Police are now able to get involved in decisions on asylum, and are now entitled to root out and take the decisions themselves on what are 'manifestly ungrounded' applications for asylum, before the dossier gets to the official agency for asylum requests, OFPRA. Further, town hall officials are now entitled to question the legitimacy of marriages between French citizens and foreigners, and delay their ratification if there is a suspicion of their not being genuine.[17]

The message that comes from these new restrictions is clear: whatever positive presumption there used to be about voluntary immigrants being entitled to full *citoyenneté* has been re-placed by grudging suspicion and a deliberately difficult and technically inaccessible procedure. This is an effect of the in-stitutionalisation of the legislative provisions, rather than the text itself. Other consequences follow from the new principled conditions. For example, there is the inequality of refusing French nationality to a young offender of foreign origin (who is just as entitled to be French), when his next door neighbour born immediately French because of his parents, could never risk losing his nationality in the same way. Similarly there is now one set of rules for French marriages; and one for others, deemed to be potentially bogus because they involve a foreign person who might be gaining illicit access to French citizen-ship. The symbolic hierarchy that this poses on rights which should not necessarily be attached to citizenship as such, but should be a human right of some kind, is of course not lost on those who are subject to it.[18]

In other ways, the new nationality legislation is not any more inviting for those immigrants and members of ethnic minor-ities who happen to have access to it. The steep 'ideal' condi-tions that are imposed – the voluntary individualistic proof of assent, the proof of a real *enracinement* in the country, the heavy moral and political baggage put on the simple right to reside, vote and be a French citizen – also lay out a kind of logic and hierarchy that can have negative effects for those who fall short. As has been said, to become a citizen technic-ally does not 'mean' that you have become an unconditional full *citoyen* as such. Such a term can only apply to those who in some sense fulfil the model that is set out for them in the ideal-type scenario of full integration. To take the texts liter-ally, the 'proof' of this would be articulate participation as a rational individual in democratic political deliberation, and the full embracement of all that is distinctly French about the country's political culture. There are numerous success stories of just such model citizens, and one is always struck by how classically and elegantly French the discourse of representa-tives of cultural and ethnic minorities in France is. The ideal role model is the fully autonomous individual French political actor, broken from his or her tribal and ethnic origins: a Harlem Désir (the media friendly leader of *SOS Racisme* who is of mixed *antillais/alsacien* origin) or Kofi Yamgnane (the black African first *Secrétaire d'Etat à l'Intégration*).

But why should the mark of successful integration be measured in this way; in terms of the ideal-type full participatory citizen and member of the polity? The very presence of such standards and success stories also reflects badly on those who do not fit the model. There is a tendency for the French system to impose what might be called 'total citizenship' on the ideal-typical identities of individual French persons, as the condition of full social acceptance. It is as if all that is of moral significance is that which can be translated and debated in the French public sphere; that is, as a political debate relevant to the bounds of the French nation.[19] But, again, why should the moral quality of a person be measured in terms of his or her political participation, or how articulately he or she debates or votes? Surely it should be measured in terms of more general social behaviour and levels of civility? The slanted demands of French citizenship are well expressed in the right's favourite slogan of the mid-1980s: that to be French *'cela se mérite'*. Needless to say, this overlaying of basic rights with particular duties and obligations goes against the sense of what rights are meant to mean, in philosophy as in law: that they are unconditional guarantees, given to people in virtue of their being persons with dignity as individuals, not in virtue of their membership in this or that social group.[20] It is, of course, an open discussion as to who should have the right to vote, and what should be the exact allegiance or membership requirement for voting. But, although it is true they normally have to be operational in some concrete national political institutional setting, a good many of the basic rights covered by the universal declarations – declared by many republicans to be a French invention[21] – are in fact granted regardless of membership in the nation, to people as humans not as citizens. This basic cornerstone of international law is in fact what jars most in the way the new highbrow citizenship laws and definitions have been set up in France: in particular, the continual attempt to recuperate universal human rights within the bounds of positive French republican law. Such a move clearly excludes certain people from the idea of rights: those persons not regarded as formal members.[22]

Indeed, there is an internal inconsistency here with the practice of social rights in France that does indeed operate in conformity with international European norms and legislation. These jar within the new republican context, since social rights in the past have been granted in virtue of residence, with relatively good social welfare standards for foreigners, denizens, residents and so forth. This has been an important area of contestation of the Pasqua laws on normative grounds.[23] Through European court rulings, many nationally defined rights have been extended to non-nationals (and non-citizens) in virtue of their residence status in France alone. The legislation at the European level is not redistributive in nature, but rather the translation of regulatory universal Euro-norms into the national context, that incur obligations for the nation-states. Indeed, since Maastricht, officially residents should also be able to enjoy the right to vote in France as well, although this has been blocked in practice. The category of citizen is here adjudged to have no effect on social rights. The developing conflict of principles, between the new nationality and citizenship laws, and the extension of residential rights – itself driven by the fact of new migration and social mobility – is an important challenge to the coherence and applicability of the French public philosophy of integration. This general conflict between the parliamentary legislative sphere and the rights-based reasoning of the courts in France has indeed been a growing 'sore spot' of political tension in recent years. Their opposed legal logics sit ill at ease with one another, and would surely need to be resolved one way or the other. Symptomatically, though, there was nothing in the new *Code de la Nationalité* to make any better sense of this tension.

These various problems with the new legislation and the justificatory foundations on which it relies, give the legislation the air of an Act that is considerably more vulnerable than suggested by its easy passage through parliament and – with one or two minor challenges – the constitutional courts. The various problems that the new code and laws have faced indeed indicate that the smooth unfurling of the historical and philosophical line set out in the public philosophy of *intégration* has begun to be disturbed and distorted by difficult elements of the social and political reality it applies itself to. Put another way, the underlying republican philosophy of citizenship and nationality is not necessarily very responsive to the changing demands of rationality and truth raised by issues not dealt with in the theory. These new elements would affect and perhaps force reform to current republican practices, if these practices could be detached from their path dependent historical and philosophical grounding. However, politically speaking, the language and terms of the republican philosophy of *intégration* are so well rooted that the code and laws are likely to remain fixed, with increasingly degenerate and pathological consequences.

It might be worth summarising the consequences and effects considered so far. Firstly, the dominant concerns do not match up to the truth and facts of the situation: the social problems that most need addressing, the real numbers involved, and the symbolic artifice on which many of the arguments are built up (treating Algerian immigrants as equivalent to pre-First World War Italians or Polish, for example). Secondly, the consequences of the new institutions have not been included in the justificatory theory: that is, the negative perception those targeted would have and the reactions this can cause, the vindication it appears to give to the extreme right line, or the actual effects of creating new disciplinary and bureaucratic procedures to enforce all the philosophically charming ideas about voluntarism and individual 'contractual' consent. Thirdly, it fails to take into consideration the *effets pervers* of not achieving the ideal: the kinds of use and abuse that can be made or felt as a result of excessively idealised images of citizens and politics. And fourthly, it has not taken into consideration the new external circumstances, the presence of new legal norms, and the wider context of boundaries and membership in Europe, in connection with social welfare and residential status questions. Several years down the road, and the effects of these pathologies can be clearly observed. The over-zealous use of historical justification in particular, has rendered France inflexible to modifying its aims, or encompassing different institutional paths. There are high costs involved in explicitly awakening the spectre of historical national identity as being the central *enjeu* of a certain issue such as new immigration.[24] The increasingly nationalist and wilfully particular course of French politics in the last few years seems to bear this out.

What can be done to challenge the overwhelming dominance of this now standard internal perspective and interpretation of French politics and society, is to challenge it *counter-factually* with the two other possible resolutions that might have been produced to resolve the questions that arose about the *Code de la Nationalite* during the 1980s. These, certainly, were definitively beaten as rival ideas and philosophies, although in terms of their *prima facie* potential benefits for the question of integrating cultural diversity in France, they appear to have great if not greater rational appeal. What their defeat reveals, again, are the deeper underlying factors that caused the republican philosophy of *intégration* to be adopted.

The first alternative is what became fashionably known as '*nouvelle citoyenneté*' (new citizenship) in debates from the mid-1980s onwards. This idea proposed a separation of the coterminous notions of nationality and citizenship, by laying the accent on citizenship alone, and thus removing the heavy cultural and historical attachments it had, and making it entirely dependent on residence alone: '*J'y suis; donc, je vote*', went the Cartesian slogan.[25] Among its promoters were representatives of other 'national' groups within the French polity, such as the Portuguese representation at the *Commission de la Nationalité* hearings. Another inspiration was in fact German. Jürgen Habermas and others had begun promoting this kind of conception of citizenship as a resolution to the German impasse felt over the constitutional founding stone of nationality law: the fact that ethnic 'Germanness' was the principal criteria for access to German nationality and hence full citizenship. As many critics have pointed out, this has led to strikingly low levels of naturalisation for second and third-generation immigrant children.[26] If citizenship – and all the legal, social and political rights that came with it – could be detached from the national *ethnos* and fixed instead in the *demos* at European level, there could be a way out of Germany's constitutional problems on this point, and the troubles in dealing with its huge numbers of immigrants, asylum-holders and foreign residents.[27] Some such reasoning, shorn of its Euro-idealism, has been the guiding logic behind Germany's generally positive line towards the effectiveness of European institutions for getting Germany out of its own constitutional problems; indeed the guiding line behind Kohl's use of Europe to embed Germany further in a 'post-national' European context. Habermas, of course, simultaneously signalled the welfarist dilemmas of this sort of solution: the fact the remoteness of Europe as a public political sphere, and the way it only exists as a mediatised and bureaucratic entity, tends to remove the power and meaning of political and civil rights because they cannot be meaningfully exercised within this context.[28]

For France, however, one can see how this kind of line might be a highly attractive response to many of the problems the nationality and integration questions pose. It avoids setting high symbolic stakes on citizenship, defuses nationalism, and sets better and more realistic conditions for the social and political participation of ethnic groups. It fits better with the overarching level of Euro-norms. It would work to overcome the increasing problem that finds ethnic minorities – who have been forced to act as individuals within the new system – reacting by no longer seeing it in their own interests to act as good citizens, but rather acting as free riders wherever possible.[29] *Nouvelle citoyenneté*, instead, would work to remove barriers to identification with France, but lower the elitist cultural standards. However, a shift to this kind of conception within France would have needed a far more positive evidence of a process moving towards European integration, which by 1993 was in fact starting to slow down. It is a conception which has no grounding in French history, and would indeed resite the boundaries of the political outside the republican state; and this, at a time when all the other tendencies are 'bringing the state back in' on matters of immigration and integration. To relinquish the disciplinary control over new immigrants, residents, and foreigners – that the French state has always claimed as its own, right through their education to the fulfilment of the requirements for full citizenship – is a step which no current state in Europe is prepared to do. Control over migration and the status of immigrants – although it raises all kinds of post-national possibilities – is in fact the very last thing that is likely to go cosmopolitan and boundless in any future possible Euro-state. Freedom of movement is something given to money and business interests, first and foremost, after all. By 1993, the idea of *nouvelle citoyenneté* had disappeared from the French public political agenda, ruled out as an option by the path dependency on the nationalist republican justification of new policies, which automatically rejects the idea's implicit assertion that France is no longer an exceptional or particular case in Europe.

A second counter-factual possibility might have been to take the opposite tack. This would entail separating nationality from citizenship, and putting the emphasis on foreigners and immigrants attaining nationality more simply, without all the symbolic and moral conditions put on the idea of citizenship. Some argue that this in fact is the true juridical tradition in France, with roots in the *Code Napoléon* that pre-date the highbrow republican conflation of citizenship and nationality in the late nineteenth century.[30] Nationality, rather, should pertain to residence, human rights and social rights; that should not be accorded to immigrants as abstract citizens but in virtue of their being French legal subjects. This in effect would make French nationality law look far more like Britain's, with citizenship a somewhat empty category granted to anyone who has right of entry and residence. All the political and moral overtones of citizenship would thus be removed: newcomers would become French without the need to prove themselves as good or model citizens in the political and public sphere.

The benefits of such a conception would undoubtedly be for its pragmatism and effectiveness in promoting internal integration; removing a great deal of the heavy symbolic potency of the current definitions of nationality and citizenship. It has potential at the European level, given that it fixes the national status of residents, allowing them easier access to the kinds of rights that the Euro-standards guarantee. Clearly though, such a pragmatic defusing of the high standard of nationality, and the process outlined for its achievement, was ruled out of the question in the current French political climate. All the efforts of the late 1980s had been on the sacredness of the idea of nationality, with the status it confers built on an investment in the moral and political definition of being a French citizen, and the redefinition this enables of the integrity of the 'universal' French nation. The counter-factual option is again ruled unlikely because of path dependency. It is perhaps possible that such a conception of French nationality might be reawoken, should European Union not progress, and the current conception prove inadequate to reflect the new cultural diversity found in France, with the general decline of the public, political sphere as the site of integration. It seems likely that to achieve this, it would have to mobilise a revisionist historical vision of the nation equally as powerful as the one that became dominant in the late 1980s with the French model of *intégration*. There were some such attempts to redefine the nation in these terms in the early days of the Mitterrand period, reconceiving *l'Hexagone* in terms of regional and cultural diversity in the new atmosphere of decentralisation that was briefly encouraged. However, this was to fall foul of the controversy over the *droit à la différence*.

The defeat of these two attractive options poses the question as to what sustains the path dependency of the dominant republican idea. Surely the benefits of a better framework for addressing social problems and the reality of pluralist diversity in France would be enough to break out of the institutional path? The strength of the historical pull in itself would not be enough to stop a revision of the new French 'tradition' concerning immigrants but, as I have emphasised throughout, there is far more at stake in the problem of pluralism than centralised control over the integration of immigrants. The one question that neither of these two alternative options addresses is the consequences a revision of pluralism in France and the decentralisation of symbolic unifying powers would have on the threat of regional autonomy or fragmentation. This indeed is the real agenda about all the concern for the unity of the nation. Underneath all the rhetoric about *immigrés*, the myth of the *creuset français* is, in the end, much more concerned with the problem of turning *basque, bréton, picard* or *méridional* peasants into Frenchmen, than immigrants who chose to come. An indication of this is the enormous political and legal fuss over the on-going 'sore spot' of the Corsican question. Quite apart from the sporadic independentist terrorism on the island, it is revealing that even more moderate requests by Corsican representatives' to be referred to as the '*peuple corse*', have always been flatly turned down and rebuked in the strongest terms at the constitutional level.

As it is, the dominant republican philosophy and the new *Code de la Nationalité* hold centre-stage, unchallenged now by any other potential conceptions, despite all the evident difficulties that the dominant political self-conception displays. Over time, we can expect the ever-deeper embedding of this conception. Paradoxically, the resolution of the nationality law question – which ended France's national peculiarity concerning immigration control – has in fact guaranteed the internal strengthening of a very particular national conception of political and social integration in the country. The new code's accent on a political and moral conception of citizenship and national membership is very foreign, as we have seen, to the pragmatic European norms about residents, foreigners and migrants, which are also directed at international co-operation. France, meanwhile, remains resistant to any form of multiculturalism permeating its political institutions. For this reason – alongside Britain, for contrasting but equally nationalist reasons – France has fought the introduction of Euro-wide legislation on the status of migrants, residents and foreigners, preferring to keep resident foreigners under its own legal jurisdiction. And yet while its formal citizenship laws differentiate them as second-class (non-) citizens, on the one hand, their social rights are guaranteed by European legislation and well-established French practices, on the other. This outcome is neither consistent, nor a justifiable way of promoting better integration in a European and international context.

Other strange fruit of the dominant philosophy have confused the picture further in the last few years. The mainstream right-wing victory and tough new legislation of 1993 was designed to bury for good the threat of Le Pen and resolve the hot issue of immigration. In the period after 1983, it did indeed seem that the immigration had finally been cooled down and pushed off the political agenda. That was until the results of the first round of the 1995 presidential election, in which a resurgent Le Pen took over 15 per cent of the vote (a small 5 per cent behind the eventual winner, Jacques Chirac), and was able to seize all the headlines, playing a pivotal role in the run off. These figures tell their own story: 75 per cent of his voters citing *les immigrés* as the primary reason for their vote for him. In the months since, the *Front national* has made several more important political advances, with Le Pen dominating the headlines in the summer of 1996 after a series of racial attacks in Marseilles.

This failure to quell the issue is not so difficult to explain. With all the strident nationalist republican rhetoric and symbolism in the air, it is difficult to tell apart any more, Le Penist philosophy, the new Gaullism of Chirac, and the neo-republican philosophy of the intellectual elite.[31] This irony was well illustrated in Pierre Bourdieu and Jacques Derrida's highly publicised attempt to confront all the 1995 presidential candidates with their apparent endorsement of the exclusionary logic of the Le Penist rhetoric. The irony is compounded further by the 'conversion' of several of the leading neo-republican intellectual figures associated with a self-elected elite political club '*Phares et balises*' ('beacons and buoys') – most notably Emmanuel Todd, and former *Esprit* editor, Paul Thibaud – to the Gaullist camp: now defending or advising Chirac as the 'true' republican leader. It is truly the smart public intellectual who changes his spots with those in power. Yet the new *Code de la Nationalité* has been plagued with problems. After a new public scandal surrounding the violent break-up of a hunger strike by a group of black African *sans papiers* (illegals) in a Parisian church, new laws on border control are again on the cards. In the meantime, the level of the on-the-spot spot police controls on black and coloured individuals on the Parisian *metro* and elsewhere has reached extraordinary levels. This keeps the issue well and truly in the public eye; and continues to provide fuel to Le Pen's cause.

In reaction to these problems, it can come as no surprise to see France taking a sharply introspective and nationalist course in its politics. Politicians and civil servants have routinely criticised European welfare standards as corrupting and lower than those in France (an extraordinary adoption of the classic Scandinavian welfare argument). As well as asserting the state's control over immigration and nationality claims, they now argue the national sphere is the best way of protecting people's social rights. A strong new anti-European movement, the 'New Europe' led by de Villiers, an aristocratic centre-right candidate, borrowing the nationalist and anti-immigrant line of Le Pen, has made its presence felt in French electoral politics in the last few years. It now gets its votes among the urban *bourgeoisie*, not the provincial *couches populaires* (working-class zones). In the late 1990s, the big votes seem to be in Euro-scepticism, something rather unthinkable in France in the 1980s.[32] The strongly pro-European wisdom of a generation of French technocrats who were the original architects of the European Union seems to have faded. Maastricht struggled to pass in 1993; a year or two later, it would have stood little chance. In all these matters, French politics is maybe only converging with Britain's – and that of other members of the EU – in its nationalist logic. What is certain is that the triumph of the republican philosophy of *intégration*, cemented into place with the new *Code de la Nationalité* in 1993, has played no small part in legitimating, encouraging and establishing this nationalist *repli sur soi-même* across the political spectrum in France. All this is occuring at a time when most other progressive political thought in Europe has been trying to go in the opposite direction.

MORAL ORIENTALISM: THE PROBLEMATIC PLACE OF ISLAM

The republican philosophy of *intégration* offers a conceptualisation of French social and political reality that is highly particular and stringent in its logic. Given its strongly idealised, *a priori* formulation, it is no surprise that there are elements of the reality it seeks to encompass and shape which fit badly and come off poorly in its application. Throughout recent years, the most obvious symptom of this has been the place of Islam in France, and the problem of Muslim culture within the overall picture of the smooth assimilatory integration of cultural diversity within the French nation. The difficulties that have occurred have arisen despite the high concern given to the place of Islam in official reports, and the concerted institutional efforts made to accommodate it within the secular structure of France; despite the early phase of interculturalism and pragmatic compromise that worked well in the early days of *insertion*; and, despite indeed the best efforts of all those concerned to promote the new model of French *intégration* as open to cultural pluralism, and not a repetition of French colonial behaviour in North Africa. The inability to define and resolve the problem definitively – with institutional solutions going one way and the next, taking on evergreater symbolic significance – is symptomatic of the issue's unresolvable place in the dominant political framework on offer.

The story of this issue has not been a wholly negative one in its evolution through the 1980s into the 1990s, but by the mid-1990s, with the new government conducting arbitrary roundups of suspected Islamic militants in France, a growing concern bordering on paranoia about the Algerian situation, and the continued growth of extreme militant Islamic movements in the most deprived *banlieues*, the signs and general tendency were not good. The dominant line taken in the republican synthesis, forcing Islam and the wishes of those with declared Islamic allegiances into an inappropriate 'classic' political republican mould, has proven to be inflexible and counter-productive. This mould, notably, rejects the three most prominent demands made by Islamic youth representatives and activists during the period: a recognition of multiculturalism, and equality of cultural diversity; *nouvelle citoyenneté* in a European perspective; and a *recentrement islamique* (a recentring) on the Arabic world.[33] A mode of *cohabitation* for France's second religion, and a reconciliation of its problem spots with the dominant wishes of the French majority and the moral requirements of membership, has therefore not been found. Instead, mainstream French political intervention, represented by the reports and the legislation that has been passed – together with the increasing public and media hostility towards Islam in France – has simply blown the problem up into one of exaggerated and dangerously unstable proportions.

This particular pathology of the French republican philosophy has continued to be an open sore. It is an inflexible blindspot that has, in the end, always put the deontological sacredness of the republican ideals ahead of a rational and pragmatic compromise. And, throughout the period, the issues raised by the *affaire du foulard* of 1989 have remained the most potent focus of these problems. Although the *affaire* initially seemed to have been resolved, the tensions it released keep coming back to centre-stage: returning like a bad dream, on each occasion the inflexible official line grating against the sore, adding more fuel to the militants' fire, further aggravating the general tendencies, and embedding majority public opinion deeper in anti-Islamic concerns.

The repetition of the *affaire* a second or third time, of course, has an air of farce rather than tragedy. First time round, there was certainly a sense of there being a great deal genuinely at stake about the self-definition of France when the issue burst on the scene in November 1989, after a headmaster in Creil (later an RPR politician) in the northern *banlieue* of Paris refused access to school to three Muslim girls in veils.[34] As I have noted, the huge public debate which ensued split the Socialist party, played a very substantial role in soldering a larger republican consensus (given the right were in no mood to compromise with the Muslim lobby), and fuelled endless fantasies in the weekly news press.[35] Indeed, in more aggressively secular accounts of the affair, it was referred to as *l'affaire du hijab, hijab* meaning the full religious headwear worn by Muslim women in some of the more militantly Islamic states, not the small *foulards* – headscarves – the girls in fact wanted to wear. This misrepresentation was typical of the case. As it was, its most important aspect was perhaps its fixing in the political debate an opposition between a principled, rights-based individualism and the *communautarisme* said to characterise both the Muslims' position and any compromising political stance which dealt with them as a distinct cultural group with political interests and claims. The way in which this opposition was set up and used for political capital is very reminiscent of the 'cross-purposed' discussion in contemporary political philosophy of liberalism versus communitarianism, which reduces very complex issues about the way liberal societies balance individuals and groups to a deceptive binary paradox.[36] In France, the philosopher who made the most of interpreting the current French concerns in this light was Pierre-André Taguieff, the most notable intellectual figure to emerge out of the coverage of the two affairs.

In a way, the individualist republican conclusion was one whose path had been well prepared by the 'Rushdie affair', which burst only nine months earlier, in February 1989, with almost as much force in France as in Britain. Crucially – a fact rarely observed by secular liberal intellectuals on both sides of the channels – the affair had rather different political and institutional foci in the two countries, entirely consistent with the distinct national philosophies I have documented in Chapters 3 and 4. As I shall explore later, more than anything this affair revealed the underlying problems with the British ideas of sovereignty, public order, and public morality without clear distinctions between public and private spheres. In France, rather, it was all about the right of free speech and literature; the dangers of *communautarisme* for the liberties and freedoms of the individual, with a nervous eye at the waxing crescent of the Islamic world; the sacrilege of *auto-da-fé*, and the impossibility of fervent French Muslims ever being good *citoyens* as they were photographed baying for Rushdie's blood.[37]

This has been the long-term, abiding image of Muslims that emerged from these two affairs, something which reinforces only too well all the other international images of modern Islam with which the West feeds its new geo-political worries.[38] However, this was not the initial outcome of the *affaire du foulard*, institutionally or politically in France. An alternative political solution to the eventual triumph of the republican position in fact won the day in the early stages, wholly pulled by the pragmatic demands of the situation. This has proven to be an unstable solution. It was insufficiently well rooted, or co-herent with other parts of the general public philosophy, to ward off the republican concerns about the new pluralism and the diminishing centralised powers of the state and govern-ment, and the reaffirmation of the state's monopoly on moral judgement and the political identification of citizens. This struggle between two competing logics is a fascinating demon-stration both of the strength of the newly dominant mode of dealing with the questions, and the seeming impossibility of solving a particular problem rationally when the best response runs against the dominant reasoning of the central public phi-losophy. Indeed, in this case, it is the central republican phi-losophy that is the cause of the problems the local adaptation is trying to solve. More generally, also, it is a case study of the dangerous relation of *a priori* moral and political principles to difficult cases and institutional outcomes.[39]

The republican ideal theory wishes to create autonomous citizens. In the French case, this is an image of citizens where there is a close intersection of 'good' citizenship with the affirmation of nationality, through a certain kind of political participation in which the culture of the 'autonomous' individ-ual is subordinated to the direct relationship of the individual to the social contract and common polity. By 'autonomous' a high degree of self-controlled individual rationality is pre-supposed, together with a certain freedom from sub-national collectivist and cultural forms: the freedom despite one's particular upbringing to exercise voice and exit, and choose one's own culture (a favourite argument of liberals against communitarians). Education for autonomy becomes the key target of the state: this primarily means *l'école*, of course. Ideally, the republican state wants to make as much social and cultural behaviour as it can subject to its moral education. It thus tries to confront cultural practices in the public sphere, because practically and legally it can have little direct jurisdiction over what goes on in the private sphere. It is troubled by a version of George Berkeley's ontological worries: is the violation really a violation if the public cannot see it? Clearly also, for reasons of poverty and deprivation, it does not want immigrant children to be locked away under terrible conditions at home: it wants to get them out to school, get them educated. Successful education implies the end-product of the *citoyen* as the fully autonomous individual political actor, who demonstrates his or her competence by full public participation and unfettered voice. A neat example of this is a favourite anecdote of the black African former *Secrétaire d'Etat à l'Intégration*, Kofi Yamgnane – and its unintentionally hilarious pro-republican *verlan* (backwards slang) punchline – from his well-publicised autobiography. A group of rough *banlieue* youth are sent off to Africa by Yamgnane to do voluntary work, and rudely mock his arch republican send-off speech. Three months later, they return, having finally understood what it means to be a true *citoyen*. A spokesman for the youth comes back to Yamgnane to apologise, saying: '*Le blicrépu, enfin quoi, la République, c'est vraiment bonnard*' (roughly translated, 'The repub, yeah well, the Republic, it's really cool you know').[40]

The problem comes with certain kinds of behaviour which go against this ideal-type of realised autonomy in the public sphere, where certain types of unreformed cultural behaviour appear to negate the hoped-for autonomy to which all citizens are entitled. The example of young girls wearing the veil in class is presupposed as exactly this kind of behaviour: an unthinking reproduction of cultural norms that deny the full liberty of women as individuals; doing what the father (church) told them to do; the opposite of a freely-voiced political voice; finally, an affirmation of religious affiliation in a sphere (*l'école laïque*) which is supposed to be kept clear of religion. One should note that France's secular tradition alone does not determine the shape of the issue: the key element is the symbolic threat to autonomy that wearing a veil in school allegedly poses, which wearing a crucifix or 'Jesus Loves You' T-shirt does not.

The state presupposes it knows the real interests of the girl; its education programme is designed to fulfil it. And it marks this particularly symbolic act of behaviour as being particularly damaging for the girls: it is the thin edge of the wedge of compromise that would have to be made with Islamic customs of child-raising if the religion were listened to. The state assumes it has a monopoly on what is best morally; the alien culture fails to match up by definition. This is what may be described as 'moral orientalism': assuming, because of certain visible forms of behaviour that are different from those taken to represent the normal path to full autonomy in the public sphere, that the foreign culture is less moral, less likely to enable autonomy for the girls. This assumption is of course highly problematic, both anthropologically, and also given the power relations involved in a western society as far as immigrant culture is involved. It may indeed take very high levels of autonomy and personal responsibility in the girl to be able to choose to wear a veil in school – effectively a political act – just as in other circumstances where it is the unthinking social norm, it would not at all be an autonomous act. In a western context, where there is no escape from western media, culture and living customs, and where young North Africans are more likely to be turned on by *le rap et le tag* (rap and graffiti) – or even *la drogue* or *la dépouille* (drugs or mugging) in worst-case scenarios – wearing a veil and displaying a high level of personal piety would seem a rather comfortingly moral and autonomous choice; perhaps even a mark of bold individualism.

The initial reaction of the French authorities completely ignored this possible interpretation of social behaviour, and decided rather that the wearing of a veil was not only damaging for the autonomy of the girls concerned, something for which the state must step in to prevent their culture or families doing this to them; it was also damaging to the sacred public space that the school is supposed to represent. This was also the dominant republican line hammered home by most public intellectuals – many of them media *philosophes* – in the press. Paradoxically, then, the outcome of this decision was in fact to expel the girls and send them back to their homes, back into the untouchable realm of the private sphere: surely from the point of view of the state's ideal world, the worst outcome of all. The state wants to promote autonomy, but by ruling out certain questionable behaviour, it takes away with one hand the very possibility of what it wants to give with the other. No space is left for the Muslim, branded as morally deficient, for the 'learning' of autonomy. Because the ideal-type and principles are too distant, the real case fails.

For a sociologist observing such behaviour there is no way to tell if the girl is acting autonomously or not. 'Autonomy' indeed would not be a sociologically meaningful criterion for evaluating her behaviour; a sociologist would be more concerned with levels of *anomie* in the persons concerned, the effect a certain policy line might have on the tolerance levels of the majority population, or gauging the militancy of the Islamic community. These indeed were arguments put forward in the 'dissenting' line argued for publicly by Pierre Bourdieu and Alain Touraine, among others. For the moral philosopher, of course, autonomy is everything: the whole edifice of consent, rights and democratic legitimacy depends on its assumption about the moral autonomy of persons being an ideal and reality. What to do about the little girls with the veils, then? Some way surely had to be found to promote autonomy more widely: even if the Muslim practice is repugnant, it cannot be extinguished by simply banning it and sending the girls home.[41]

The evasiveness of the *Haut Conseil*'s reflection about Islam in France is here very important. Extraordinarily, it offered hardly any explicit discussion of the legal and institutional *foulard* case beyond the redefinition of the idea of *laïcité* discussed in Chapter 3, despite the fact this live case is the tacit backdrop of all its formulations. All its explicit discussion about the law concerning Muslim practices is restricted instead to those extreme cases which themselves uphold the moral orientalist view of Islam, and not one which holds that some kind of mutually beneficial compromise position might be reached. Applying human rights as positive law, and using them to enforce French jurisdiction over problematic Muslim residents on French soil (again contradicting the inclusiveness of the nationalist citizenship logic), it comes to some not very difficult judgements about the extreme case of *excision* (as more widely symbolic of immoral Muslim practices) that in fact ignore the usual public/private distinction, and go further than law has ordinarily been prepared to do in regulating these 'behind closed doors' practices.[42] This debate has continued to rage amongst Parisian intellectuals and feminists, perhaps in the hope it might hold the key to the entirely distinct problem posed by the *foulard* case: a much harder question, where 'harm' is much less easy to prove in any tangible sense. The intellectual attraction of the *excision* case, for feminists in particular, is that it offers a rhetorical lever for an archetypal radical move: equating actual physical harm with psychological or mental harm, a broader critical criterion, which can then be applied to a far wider range of invisible cases of oppression and power.[43] However, it is the indeterminate question of 'harm' in the case of the *foulard* – about what counts as restricting autonomous behaviour in the public sphere – that is far more revealing of the limits of the French republican theory, and ought to have been the focus of ethical discussions.

The first actual institutional resolution that emerged as a political response to the impasse about autonomy did not reflect at all these formulations of the *Haut Conseil*, but did make some sense of the expanded notion of *laïcité* the *Conseil* defended. For a while, it instituted a logic very foreign to the centralised state monopoly on judgement that the republican philosophy of *intégration* seeks to defend. The Socialist minister Lionel Jospin, faced with a great split in his own party ranks, called for an extraordinary *avis* (judgment) from the constitutional forum *Conseil d'Etat*, on the constitutional interpretation of the problem. The decision – which in effect set up an extraordinary precedent of devolved interpretative jurisprudence for all future cases – deemed that the wearing of a veil in itself was not in contradiction to French laws of *laïcité*, but that headmasters could, under certain circumstances, prohibit the wearing of the veil for reasons of classroom disturbance, or ostentatious proselytism. This in effect was not a clear decision at all: it was, rather, a devolving of responsibility to decide to the local levels, leaving open a great deal of interpretative leeway in local decisions. In practice, it opened the way to a certain amount of more widespread veil-wearing, a few cases where local authorities pursued a hard-line only to have it thrown out at the *Conseil d'Etat* level again, but in general a defusing of tensions over this particular issue.[44]

A different kind of justification and logic had been put into operation. Assuming that the education of 'autonomous' citizens remained the guiding aim of the French political system, the new approach was in fact pursuing a different route to this end. Rather than presuming that wearing a veil by definition snuffs out the potential autonomy of the Muslim girl, it presumes – against the precepts of moral orientalism – that the wearing of a veil could in fact be compatible with autonomy under the right conditions. It presumes, in other words, that the background social influences of schooling and living in a modern French city will continue to work on the girl and change her relation to the symbolic culture she is affirming. The act of wearing the veil becomes a public one; recognised by the school, but challenged. A justification must be produced: that she is doing it in good faith, and is responsible for the decision; that this much at least is out of the hands of the father and of the state. An unquestioning reproduction of cultural behaviour is challenged and must represent itself as an 'autonomous' response – *giving reasons* – which then become a valid political and public expression of personal identity, in the face of peer pressure. A learning process is begun; and a road to autonomy kept open, since it is assumed that the girl cannot choose to continue wearing the veil in good faith, without feeling some sort of responsibility for the decision. It would be impossible to lie about one's own free choice, and then lie to oneself about having chosen to lie.[45]

The terms of the public debate had however been set by the initial controversy. The growing level of intolerance in the press and public towards the wearing of veils has over a period of years re-affirmed the issue as a perennial symbolic battle-ground, not only between Islam and France, but between different sections of the Muslim community. Figures in the *Le Monde* survey of 13 October 1994 confirm that majority French opinion about Islam has hardened in the period 1989–94, and that Arabic opinion in France has become more divided. The more militant Islamicists have used the issue to further their aims: there has been plenty of coverage of these organisations in the press in the last few years, and a burgeoning literature about Islam in France.[46] The presumption that the wearing of a veil is by definition immoral, morally backward and retrogressive has strengthened. The all-important context of this symbolic act is forgotten, lost in sweeping generalisations about its ethical symbolism. Moral orientalism has gone from strength to strength, fuelled by further international tensions and flashpoints.

Those groups which were initially prepared to defend the veil, have themselves reneged on this rather small concession towards interculturalism in the intervening years. *SOS Racisme* was at first a strong supporter of the Muslim case, pointing out the obvious racism and stereotyping perpetuated in the republican arguments. Its own position, however, was blown apart by the Gulf War, when it found a large majority of the *beurs* sympathetic to Iraq, and extremely hostile to French participation in the Western operation in the name of the new world order.[47] Saudi Arabia's involvement discredited it amongst the Islamic grass roots; the country withdrawing funding for many of the more radical Islamic groups which, in France as elsewhere, expressed support for Saddam's attempted *jihad*.[48] It is no small irony, meanwhile, that *SOS Racisme* – whose public support had by then dwindled enormously – meekly followed the rival integrationist group *France Plus* into stating a strongly reaffirmed republican line, suggesting proposals even tougher than ones eventually made.

The other significant organisation of compromise to come out of the original affair, the CORIF – designed to help begin reflection on the institutionalisation and regularisation of the statute of Islam in France – itself came to grief due to the toughening republican line in French politics. It was initially set up in a manner designed to outflank the dominance of the *mosquée de Paris* (financed by Algeria), and bring together all the different representatives of Islam in France. However, in the intervening years, the internal divisions amongst Muslims in France got steadily worse, and in 1995 Pasqua openly re-endorsed the Algerian-backed mosque and returned to supporting only this *charif* as the legitimate leader of Muslims in France. The CORIF, meanwhile, was effectively wound up. The outcome, of course, only isolates marginal groups and leaders, who have now been left out of any political dialogue, further aggravating their militancy. Proposals concerning a new institutional status for Islam in France – so central in the official *rapports* – seem to have been shelved. An important opportunity appears to have been lost.

The culmination of these developments was the new government's return to the hardline, after the brief period of pragmatic compromise. This coincided only too well with the heightened tensions about Algeria, new controls on immigrants, and high-profile police operations against militant groups. A new circular was sent around schools by the minister, François Bayrou, in September 1994, apparently banning once again the ostentatious wearing in schools of religious symbols which 'encourage proselytism': notably only Muslim veils seem to fall under these criteria. A new *affaire* broke out, with new occasions for the militants to win converts, and for the majority population to harden its opinions. The compatibility of a Muslim and French self-identity was once again put into doubt. With local legal decisions in Lille and Lyon in the spring of 1995 again contradicting the political decision at the centre, there seemed now to be an almost permanent stand-off between the constitutional and legislative arms of the state, with neither able to provide a definitive resolution. Effectively, in other words, it has become a permanent symbolic pathology, well out of control and unlikely to find the resources from within its own reproducing logic to find any kind of solution. Relations between the state and the majority population on one side, and Islam on the other, are worse than ever: a graphic example of an irrational outcome all round.

HIDDEN BY UNIVERSALISM: THE NEW FRENCH UNDERCLASS

'Monsieur le futur Président:
le racisme, l'exclusion, les banlieues –
parlons-en réellement!'

Libre Antenne 101.9FM

Advertising hoarding, Paris, April 1995: 'Dear Mr Future President: Racism, exclusion, the deprived suburbs – let's talk about it for real!'

The power that ideas took in the debate over *intégration* in the 1980s and 1990s in France has had further structuring consequences on the framing and management of the social questions that have arisen concerning France's ethnic dilemmas. These ideas have not only been central in cementing the national political consensus that emerged during this period; they have also imposed themselves on the way questions are treated politically at local and applied levels.

The lack of serious thought given to the local and applied levels of policies in the official reports – symptomatically underlined by the skewed focus of the *Code de la Nationalité* on state-centred naturalisation and border control – is highly characteristic of the new public philosophy dominant in France. Inevitably this void in the official representation of the social and political realities at stake has had an effect on the shape of French social policy. Since the discrediting of the previous policy model of *insertion*, there has been an increasingly sharp *décalage* between the highbrow republican rhetoric of the centre – the general symbolic issues involved in the definition of *citoyenneté* or *laïcité* – and the void of appropriate and consistent discourse and methods at the local level.[49] The new ideals, as I have shown, were themselves built on a rejection of the logic and method of *insertion*, which was predicated on a rather narrow index of socio-economic factors, and a particular kind of intervention in certain key public spheres (notably priority education, housing, welfare assistance, and associations – including Muslim ones) as a means towards an improved social integration of immigrants and their families. The new synthesis of *intégration*, with its seductive grand philosophico-historical debates about French identity and its universalist mission, has often rejected many of these means, because of their alleged particularism and tendency to promote ghettoised *communautarisme*; not to mention the creation of special interests, and the alleged clientalism and corruption it produces. Yet local authorities, in charge of managing the strong French track record in targeted, redistributive welfare policies and urban intervention, know no other way of pursuing such policies in reality.

To a certain degree, the highbrow citizenship (framework) can be adapted to local circumstances. There have been interesting examples of practical adaptation in strongly immigrant cities like Marseilles and Lille, with the setting-up of 'citizen-ship bureaus' to promote access to language provision and civil education, and the tailoring of immigrant associations' strategies to the new framework on offer. Yet the swamping of public discourse with a high-minded republican universalism has in other ways cut the language of classic state intervention – and hence its underlying normative justification – out from underneath it. The arguments for targeted, socially specific, redistributive welfare policies – pursued for example through the special ZUP (*Zones à Urbaniser en Priorité*) and ZEP (*Zones d'Education Prioritaires*) programmes for deprived inner city and *banlieue* areas – have been fatally weakened. In many ways, the nationalist republican rhetoric, obsessed with cultural issues and denying any 'ethnic' or community-based arguments, has seized back symbolic power for the central state, which the logic and necessities of more applied social policy was tending increasingly to dissipate. Yet, paradoxically, it is doing this at a time when its actual powers of welfarist intervention are clearly in decline, and other political tendencies are going in the opposite direction.

Other costs have thus been felt structurally within France and at the local level. It is ironic that the French continue to combine a faith in the comparative superiority of their universalism and political principles – the translation of the rights of man into the functioning framework of the democratic *République* – with a proud belief in the superiority and effectiveness of their local management of welfare provision: the marvellous public housing, the lack of ghettos, the high and superior 'Scandinavian' style welfare provision. The French have always reaped flattering self-comparisons with 'anglo-saxon' British and American *libéralisme sauvage* (unfettered, 'wild' free-marketeering) on exactly these scores. No one, least of all the sociologists of race and ethnicity in the USA and Britain, would deny the enormous poverty and inequality problems these countries have.[50] But the self-deception of the French in these matters is quite remarkable. The 1980s, the decade in which republicanism triumphed in the sphere of national identity and social cohesion, was also the decade in which a thorough '*libéralisation*' (in the French use of the word) swept the country, condemning France to exactly the same high levels of unemployment, social marginalisation, homelessness and disparities in wealth that have become the norm elsewhere. The welfare state, in France as elsewhere, is in terminal decline. And one of the striking consequences has been the appearance of ghettos and racialised poverty of almost exactly the kind French politicians and intellectuals claim 'couldn't happen here': a world not at all reflected in all the positive republican policy statements about *intégration* and individualist social success for immigrants.[51]

It would seem reasonable to think poverty, concentrated deprivation, long-term unemployment, and the cultural or racial specificities of these social ills, might be thought of as impediments to a policy of *intégration*. As it is, the lack of discussion of these factors as causally relevant to the achievement of integration is quite remarkable in the official *rapports*, which have focused instead on the very philosophical issues of membership, cultural pluralism, or what it means to be French. Antiracism, where it is discussed, is not thought of in terms of concrete, anti-discriminatory measures, let alone any kind of 'positive' discrimination. It is, rather, framed in law and legislation in terms of bland, universalist ideas: racism as a violation of human rights.[52] The language of French legislation and the dominant rhetoric of the politicians has little power or range to describe what is actually going on in the *banlieues*: rising levels of crime, delinquency, drugs, gangs, and so on. Parts of Paris have became practically no-go areas for police and local officials. Several race riots took place in Paris and other urban centres in the early 1990s. The recent film *La Haine* (1995) offered a chilling portrait of racially scarred urban violence and alienation.[53] The main benefactors from these problems – apart from the organised criminals – have been the radical Muslim groups who provide the one stop-gap against these tendencies, promoting recruitment by acts of direct welfare, disciplining the youth, and providing a focus for the social feelings of resentment and frustration.[54] It is remarkable then that among the social preconditions for integration – and all those *a priori* values attached to political participation and the education of good citizens – little thought appears to have been given to overcoming such poverty as a primary condition.

Only recently has some serious sociological work been done on the bases of integration, and the actual disintegration of the social fabric of the lower sections of French society: in particular its connection to racism and the rise of extreme right politics and higher levels of public intolerance.[55] The startling evidence of this work is that the fears of national disintegration because of cultural differences and the 'threat' of Islam, have indeed largely masked the fact that cultural pluralism itself would be much less a problem were poverty and social conditions addressed as the central focus. In other words, that poverty and Islamic fundamentalism are one and the same problem; and that without the variable of extreme poverty, and concentrated social conditions in decline, Islam in France itself would not be such a problem. The rhetoric of republicanism has done much to obscure this issue, and its symbolic universalist posturing and inflexibility about Islam has boosted exactly those elements of radical Islam most benefiting from the declining socio-economic conditions.[56]

Theorising the most important bases of integration as something other than relative levels of poverty and deprivation, has thus helped the official policy line escape considering what is becoming *the* fundamental question concerning the relation of state to polity in advanced post-industrial societies with increasing disparities in social inequality and a declining welfare state. That is, the question of the responsibility of the state in balancing the maintenance of social order with the continued march of *libéralisme*. A trade-off can be made, as in the USA, that allows enormous levels of disorder and depravity to coexist with enormous affluence and wealth; with two separate bounded and marked worlds, that only collide in the centre of the major cities. The American literature on urban poverty and the underclass comes as a salutary shock to the European reader, and one wonders how long it will be before Europe – France included – resembles the nightmarish scenarios sketched of Los Angeles or Chicago.[57] As certain French sociologists have pointed out, it would be wrong to exaggerate and claim that an American-style underclass of the same kind already exists in France.[58] Yet even here, the presumption that the state is always *unquestionably* responsible for the poorer layers of society is by no means guaranteed. A functional class suffering from chronic poverty can and has been permitted to come into existence, simply because the state can no longer afford – and can no longer secure democratic assent – for the high levels of welfare that might be able to hold together the political community as a whole.[59] The French debate has almost wholly concentrated on the cultural dimensions of the lower sections of this political community (a community still genuinely believed by all to exist). Yet, socio-economically speaking, the *de facto* functional role of the permanently poor excluded by *libéralisation* from this community is beginning to root itself in France as elsewhere. It is not without accident that the most visible symptom of this new French 'underclass' is referred to as the *sans domicile fixe*: a group who have lost the territorial identity that, with the idea of *ius soli* so powerful in the republican conception, is a basic tenet of French national citizenship. The reports do not even begin to think about these issues. And this despite the fact that treating the question of *intégration* in socio-economic terms would in fact have the side-effect of downplaying the theoretical importance of race or culture in the question of securing an integrated social order.[60]

The centralisation of the reports – in an effort to secure a state-dominated control over the discipline of immigrants and marginal cultural groups – has in fact taken place in a period in which France has steadily become decentralised in other ways. Financially speaking, this is a process now well under way, allowing huge disparities between different *départements* and authorities within France. The rhetoric continues to be centralised and highly republican, but this practice has been forced by the need to placate the more powerful regional and provincial demands within France. National culture, however, has been jealously guarded at the centre, since the discrediting of the *droit à la différence* movement in the early 1980s. The new financial structures further exacerbate the growing poverty of the *banlieues* and peripheral areas. The centre focuses its rhetoric largely on symbolic cultural issues – as well as border control, something that the state can still do relatively well – because the days when the centre could control the spending of local town halls are well over. These have all been devolved to the local level, where there is a concentration of wealth and finance in the rich central city authorities, and a lack of resources in the peripheral *banlieues* which need the expenditure.[61] Similar to the developments occurring between different tax districts in American cities – although in reverse to the USA which has empty inner cities, and rich, financially isolated suburbs – the geographical and urban financial structure of France is having a serious effect on the deterioration of social conditions for the most deprived elements of French society. Paris, of course, is the classic example: the administrative city of Paris is an increasingly rich bourgeois haven, surrounded by the growing magnitude of social problems accumulating in the *banlieues* of the overall Parisian conurbation. The ironic disparity between the heavily centralised republican rhetoric and the reality of who holds the purse strings, is not least among the bizarre irrationalities of the new public theory to hold court in France. Not forgetting, of course, that Chirac's Paris has now become Chirac's France.

The slowly growing parallels with the USA are not without other similarly ironic manifestations. Look again at the triumph of liberalisation in France; look at the new urban geography of French cities, with their concentrated areas of deprivation, and long lines of American-style fast food drive ins, motels, and *grandes surfaces* that pepper the outskirts. It should come as no surprise: France is in many ways the most Americanised and USA-resembling country in Western Europe. The psychological resemblance goes deeper. One need only think how much the political and legal rationality of institutions in France owe to translated ideas of the original constitution of its 'sister republic'; not to mention its cherished love of individualist liberty, and the symbiotic fascination of its intellectuals from Tocqueville to Derrida and Baudrillard.[62] The relation is of course a love–hate one, a fatal attraction that continues to pull, even as the rhetoric of French nationalism and business autonomy fights the invasion of American English from her culture and public life.

The schizophrenic passion with which this fight is conducted – and the belief that is invested in French particularity in the face of Europeanisation and globalisation – indicates perhaps the strength and tenacity of the nexus of ideas that, during the 1980s and 1990s, has pulled France to strike such defiant poses in its public policies. At a time when there are indeed numerous other post-national, transnational and international currents decisively shaping policies on immigration and integration elsewhere, the domestic charm and power of nationalist French political ideas continues to be a pull that is keeping other institutional paths and possibilities well in check. Yet it is a passion not without hope. The French population is still capable of voting overwhelmingly – as it did in 1993 and 1995 – for right-wing liberalism and the end of socialism, and yet a few short months later, descend into the streets to strike and throw stones; this time in defence of a welfare state and idea of political community that the nation can no longer afford. This is surely something the French do like nowhere else in the western world.

THE STUBBORN VIRTUES OF A REPUBLICAN PHILOSOPHY

In this chapter, I have focused primarily on the negative consequences of the political ideas that have emerged as the dominant consensus in France in the last few years. Clearly this is not the whole story. France is a particularly welcome subject matter for this kind of analysis. It is a rare example of where a clearly formulated and articulated public philosophy can be shown to have succeeded politically, established a dominant framework for policy, and had distinct and observable consequences over time. Public philosophies which are much less consistent, or only latent – as in the British system – are much less clearly readable for critical evaluation. In France, however, the philosophy has been made explicit and followed through in a self-consistent and determined way. What fault lines have emerged can be clearly delineated and held up to the light. Indeed, such criticisms can often be fed back directly into the public debate that surrounds the public philosophy, since the positive standards and ideals to which the philosophy commits itself are themselves obvious to behold.

It is thus worth giving some space to the positive heuristics of the French philosophy of integration as it has come to be practised in recent years. Setting ideal standards does have benefits. No one could claim that they did not know what they were getting when embracing the membership of the French nation and its political rules: they are explicit and spelt out. In public life, in access to jobs and hierarchies, the French are consistent and apply their universalist principles more zealously than in other countries, with perhaps better-looking progressive legislation. Racist and ethnically slanted prejudices draw sharp rebuke in any public situations. The growing power of the Le Penist minority has to be set against the clear anger expressed by the majority public against these views, and their readiness to mobilise. There is indeed something to be said for having the issue of racism out in the open as it was in France, in the full glare of public debate. It is significant that groups such as East Asian immigrants have often thrived, economically and culturally, in the republican environment. France can indeed boast of high levels of inter-racial marriage and high numbers of successful naturalisations, compared to other European countries. It can boast of high levels of educational achievement, and high levels of integration in public and official life (not in the media and culture as in Britain).[63] France holds high ambitions and ideals for all its citizens, and openly celebrates the success stories of immigrants who made it into the elites through sheer merit. The country is genuinely proud of its multi-racial football and athletics teams.

Having explicit ideal-ends and a perfectionist, state-defined concept of the good polity, is a very foreign thing to much of the Anglo-American liberal tradition. It sets high political standards and expectations. It has long guaranteed the quality of political life and debate in France as better than elsewhere. Politics here is intellectual and demanding; there is a high involvement of academic specialists and intellectual reflection. It is this, of course, that opened the way for the highbrow philosophical reflection on integration in the 1980s. But the problems concerning integration and immigration have been open to the public at large, continually debated, turned over, and contested in the true spirit of democracy. The new republican synthesis has not been an easily won or deceptive consensus, but one largely made through the force of its arguments and its powerful rehabilitation of certain classic French political ideas. It is in many ways an attractive and convincing vision, and its pathologies should not detract from the basic power and validity of the French model as a genuine and defensible version of philosophical liberalism. Its main deficiencies are sharply drawn: a tendency to over-encourage symbolic and philosophical rhetoric rather than factual or empirically-rooted debate; a tendency to over-idealism, and inflexibility over linguistic terms, which renders difficult the application

of philosophical ideals; a tendency to mistake rights and principles for the true substance of politics; an excessive focus on
political life and the power of the state, in an age when politics
and traditional political power is in decline; a lack of focus on
the social dimensions of integration, particularly the critical
effect of poverty in frustrating it; a denigration and problema-
tisation of culture and religion as valid political components
of individual motivation, and hence a tendency to create political conflicts in these areas.

In other ways, no less connected to the heuristics of the
public philosophy, France's commitment to universalism has,
as I have mentioned, scored notable successes in its handling
of ethnic dilemmas. France is indeed probably the most ethnically diverse and racially mixed country in Western Europe.
France's positive role in international terms has been as a
consistent upholder of an objective standard of human rights,
and it has always been well represented in any international
commitment to humanitarian aid. Another particular indication of the payoff of the French inflexibility over arguments
based on race and culture has been a highly principled
official and scientific resistance to the return of genetics research – particularly this form of research as a better
scientific explanation or justification for social policy and
social control than sociological reasons – something which is
currently drawing enormous public funding in the USA and
elsewhere.[64]

The politically engaged, anti-relativistic mission of French
political thought has also been an important antidote intellectually to the recent tendency of Anglo-American thought –
ironically itself under the influence of a previous generation
of French cynics and sceptics – to dissolve everything into the
most facile relativism: postmodernism and all that. A great
deal of further self-damage has been done by intellectuals in
Britain and the USA using these modes of thinking for the
serious use of intellectual work in politics. This is something
which is not ever even questioned in French political life, used
as it is to the continual involvement of reasoned knowledge
and argument in political debate. Moreover, with *les lumières*
as a standard reference point, nearly all French political and
social research is strongly normative in nature. Serious
deficiencies in its empirical and sociological credentials can

be found as a result of this. However this willingness to direct reflection towards normative goals and political argument undoubtedly increases the relevance and effect of such intellectual work.

It is often said that France has given the world 'the most beautiful political idea the world has ever seen: *la République*'.[65] With great self-confidence, many – like the philosopher Emmanuel Lévinas in this quotation – still pronounce the now culturally pluralist and liberal France of the 1990s to be the nearest achievement in reality to the best visions of political philosophers. More importantly for this study, it is a political system whose logic is visible and clearly worked out, and whose deviations and pathologies are therefore clearly evident. Only France could provide the fixed point of study in this comparison, against which elements of the public philosophies in Britain or elsewhere – far more opaque and peculiarly worked-out theories – have to be matched. The difficulties of taking France's admirably ideal philosophy of integration *jusqu'au bout*, reveal that the virtuous practice of policy model construction does not always coincide with the virtues of responsive political adaptation and reform. Making better sense of politics must involve trying to discern where such rationalised formulations, arguments and ideals do indeed have positive effects, and where on the other hand they are the root of serious political problems and pathologies.

Notes

1. Régis Debray, *Que vive la République* (Paris, 1989).
2. See, respectively, Alain Minc, *La grande illusion* (Paris: Grasset, 1989) and Michel Albert, *Capitalisme contre capitalisme* (Paris: Seuil, 1993).
3. Concerns prefigured scientifically in the main conclusions of Gilles Kepel, *Les banlieues de l'Islam* (Paris: Seuil, 1987) pp. 379–84. For a near hysterical rundown of the threats to *la République* from Islam in France – typical of the French media in recent years – see the dossier 'Immigrations: Les cinq tabous' in *L'Express* (8 Nov. 1991). The five taboos are cast on special language and culture classes; national service in foreign countries; female circumcision; polygamy; and tolerating fundamentalism.
4. David Blatt, 'Towards a multicultural political model in France? The limits of immigrant collective action 1968–1994', *Nationalism and*

Ethnic Politics, vol. 1, no. 2 (1995); Miriam Feldblum, *Reconstructing Citizenship: The Politics of Nationality Reform and Immigration in Contemporary France* (State University of New York Press, 1999).

5. For example, Jack Lang, 'L'insulte faite à la France', in *Le Nouvel Observateur* (6–12 May 1993).

6. See the debate in *Le Nouvel Observateur*, ibid; Salem Kacet, *Droit à la France* (Paris: Belfond, 1993).

7. *Le Monde* (16 Jun 1993); see also Philippe Seguin, 'La République et l'exception française', *Philosophie politique*, no. 4, pp. 45–62 (1993).

8. Reuben Ford, 'Current and future migration flows', in Sarah Spencer (ed.), *Strangers and Citizens. A Positive Approach to Migrants and Refugees* (London: IPPR/River Oram Press, 1994).

9. *Le Monde* (16 Aug 1993).

10. *Le Monde* (21 Sep 1991).

11. France historically has been susceptible to this kind of reification of philosophical ideals. See the anthropologist Paul Rabinow's *French Modern: Norms and Forms of the Social Environment* (Cambridge, Mass.: Harvard University Press, 1989), which as he describes as a 'fieldwork in philosophy' inspired by Foucault and Bourdieu.

12. Numerous French writers have reflected on the linguistic roots of these binary oppositions that permeate French political life. See Emile Benveniste, *Le vocabulaire des institutions indo-européenes* (Paris, 1969, 2 vols) vol. I, pp. 355–62, on *xenos* and the foreigner; Emmanuel Lévinas (ed. Séan Hand) *The Lévinas Reader* (Oxford: Blackwell, 1989); recent work by Abdelmalek Sayad, *L'immigration ou les paradoxes de l'altérité* (Paris: De Boeck, 1991); and Tzvetan Todorov, *Nous et les autres: la réflexion française sur la diversité humaine* (Paris: Seuil, 1989). Virginie Guiraudon offers a reconstruction of the binary opposition of *étrangers* and *citoyens* in terms of the revolutionary tradition, in 'Atavisms and new challenges: (re) naming the enemy in contemporary French discourse', *History of European Ideas*, vol. 19, no. 1–3 (1994).

13. For graphic examples, see *Nouvel Observateur* regulars Jean Daniel and Bernard H. Lévy moralising on Islamic veils one week, for example, 'Les femmes et l'Islam' (22–8 Sep 1994), and on Bosnia the next. Or the succession of bestselling intellectual polemics on the subject: Alain Finkielkraut, *La défaite de la pensée* (Paris: Gallimard, 1987); Alain Minc, *Le nouveau moyen age* (Paris: Gallimard, 1993); Guy Sorman, *En attendant les barbares* (Paris: Fayard, 1992). Many of these paradoxes are discussed by Sami Naïr, *Le regard des vainqueurs: les enjeux français de l'immigration* (Paris: Grasset, 1992).

14. See Simone Bonnafous, *L'immigration prise aux mots: les immigrés dans la presse au tournant des années 80* (Paris: Kimé, 1991).

15. Ironically enough repeated in Emmanuel Todd's triumphant discussion of inter-marriage figures between 'français' and 'étrangers', which he takes to be one of the scientific 'proofs' of successful integration and the superiority of the French model over Britain, the USA and Germany: Todd, *Le destin des immigrés: assimilation et Ségrégation dans les démocraties occidentales* (Paris: Seuil, 1994).

16.   See Bernd Baumgartl and Adrian Favell (eds), *New Xenophobia in Europe* (The Hague: Kluwers, 1995), especially the concluding overview, for a comparative survey of the political capital made from these developments. See also the post-election analysis by Pascal Perrineau, *Le Monde* (25 Apr 1995).

17.   Georges Ubbiali, 'Towards the institutionalisation of prejudice', in Baumgartl and Favell (eds), op. cit.

18.   The survey of 'immigrant' youngsters in *Le Nouvel Observateur* (6–12 May 1993), 'Leur idée de la France', confirms this.

19.   The criticism of 'total citizenship' comes from Ralf Dahrendorf, 'The changing quality of citizenship', in Bart van Steenbergen (ed.), *The Condition of Citizenship* (London: Sage, 1994). See also the Belgian critique of the French *surenchère* of the public sphere in Albert Bastenier and Felice Dassetto, *Immigration et espace public: la controverse de l'intégration* (Paris: L'Harmattan: 1993); and Paul Yonnet, *Voyage au centre de la malaise française: de l'anti-racisme à la destruction du roman national* (Paris: Gallimard, 1993).

20.   Jeremy Waldron, *Liberal Rights* (Cambridge University Press, 1993); Luiji Ferrajoli, 'Dai diritti del cittadino ai diritti della persona', in Danilo Zolo (ed.), *La cittadinanza: appartenenza, identità, diritti* (Rome: Editore Laterza, 1994).

21.   François Furet in Furet *et al.*, *La République du centre* (Paris: Calmann-Lévy, 1989); Luc Ferry and Alain Renaut, *Des droits de l'homme á l'idée républicaine* (Paris: Presses Universitaires de France, 1985).

22.   Although the problem is particularly marked in France, this is a general problem for nation-states in the face of new migrations: see Tomas Hammar, *Democracy and the Nation State: Aliens, Denizens and Citizens in a World of International Migration* (Aldershot: Avebury, 1990); Yasemin Soysal, *Limits of Citizenship: Migrants and Postnational Membership in Europe* (University of Chicago Press, 1994).

23.   'Discriminations peu constitutionelles', in *Plein Droit*, no. 26 (Oct–Dec 1994), which sets out GISTI's attack on the Pasqua laws, which they argue are a challenge to French social rights norms on social security provision.

24.   See, in particular, Françoise Lorcerie's brilliant account: 'Les sciences sociales au service de l'identité nationale. Le débat sur l'intégration en France au début des années', in Dénis Constant-Martin (ed.), *Cartes d'identité: Comment on dit 'nous' en politiques* (Paris: Presses de la fondation nationale des sciences politiques, 1994) which discusses in particular the crucial roles played by Dominique Schnapper, Pierre-André Taguieff, Gérard Noiriel and Claude Nicolet. See also Danièle Lochak, 'Usages et mésusages d'une notion polémique: la référence à l'identité nationale dans le débat sur la réforme du code de la nationalité 1985–1993', in Jacques Chevallier *et al.*, *L'identité politique* (Paris: Presses universitaires de France, 1994).

25.   Proponents of the ideas of 'nouvelle citoyenneté' included: Jean Leca, 'Questions sur la citoyenneté', *Projet*, no. 173–4, (1983). Catherine Wihtol de Wenden (ed.), *La citoyenneté et les changements de structures sociales et nationales de la population française* (Paris: Fondation Diderot,

1988); Said Bouamama, *Vers une nouvelle citoyenneté: crise de la pensée laïque*, and Said Bouamama, Albano Cordeiro and Michel Roux, *La citoyenneté dans tous ses états* (Paris: CIEMI/L'Harmattan, 1992). Other non-French writers to discuss these possibilities are Rainer Bauböck, *Transnational Citizenship: Membership and Rights in International Migration* (Aldershot: Edward Elgar, 1994); and Ulrich Preuß's large-scale project on 'Concepts, foundations and limits of European citizenship' at the University of Bremen.

26.   Rogers Brubaker's account, *Citizenship and Nationhood in France and Germany* (Cambridge, Mass.: Harvard University Press, 1992), appears however to follow the rather jaundiced French perspective on German politics, that is not very sensitive to the positive developments and quite substantial shifts that have taken place in Germany concerning immigration and naturalisation in the late 1980s and early 1990s. See Kay Heilbronner's retort, 'Citizenship and Nationhood in Germany', in Brubaker (ed.), *Immigration and the Politics of Citizenship in Western Europe* (New York: University Press of America, 1989). See also Laura Murray, 'Einwanderungsland Bundesrepublik Deutschland? Explaining the evolving positions of German political parties on citizenship policy', *German Politics and Society*, no. 33 (1994); Christian Joppke, 'Towards a new sociology of the state: on Rogers Brubaker's *Citizenship and Nationhood in France and Germany*', *European Archives of Sociology*, no. 36 (1995); and a more critical German perspective in René Del Fabbro, 'A victory of the street', in Baumgartl and Favell (eds), op. cit.

27.   Jürgen Habermas, 'Citizenship and national identity: some reflections on the future of Europe', *Praxis International*, vol. 12, no. 1 (1992).

28.   *ibid*. This problem is also a key issue in Jean Leca's writing on France, see 'Individulisme et citoyenneté', in Pierre Birnbaum and Jean Leca (eds), *Sur l'individualisme: théories et methodes* (Paris: Presses de la fondation nationale de la Science politique, 1986)

29.   Jean Leca, 'Une capacité défaillante d'intégration', *Esprit* (Jun, 1985).

30.   See Danièle Lochak, 'Etrangers et citoyens au regard du droit', in Catherine Wihtol de Wenden (ed.), op. cit.; and 'La citoyenneté: un concept juridique flou', in Dominique Colas (ed.), *Citoyenneté et nationalité: perspectives en France et en Québec* (Paris: Presses universitaires de France, 1991); Smain Laacher (ed.) *Questions de nationalité: histoires et enjeux d'un code* (Paris: L'Harmattan, 1987).

31.   See the latest interventions by Pierre-André Taguieff, *La République menacée* (Paris: Textuels, 1996); and Christian Jelen, *La France éclatée* (Paris, 1996).

32.   A tendency for which Emmanuel Todd is now premier spokesman: *L'invention de l'Europe* (Paris: Seuil, 1996, 2nd edn).

33.   See Robert-Jean Leclerq, 'Natures des revendications et des enjeux culturels portés par les minorités actives issues de l'immigration maghrébine en France pour la période 1978–1987', in Bernard Lorreyte (ed.), *Les politiques d'intégration des Jeunes issue de l'immigration* (Paris: L'Harmattan, 1989).

with the Jewish and Catholic schools that have always organised their own schools unimpeded by state restrictions.

There is a clear sense here of touching the soft underbelly of the British philosophy of integration. The French are undoubtedly right to worry about the kind of ideals that guide education, and seek to encourage them as a norm and basic standard for French society as a whole. It is far more difficult to impose meaningfully the ideal standard of tolerant public order – a racial and cultural equilibrium – as an inspirational standard for public institutions. It is not, in this sense, a philosophy that can be plausibly promoted as an outcome of public reason or democratic deliberation. It is to be regretted perhaps that the Swann Report did not make a clearer stand on its philosophical groundings, or the ideal of autonomy on which it appears to be founded.[55] The British philosophy must be judged solely by the outcomes it achieves, and not the ideals which it fails to clearly set itself. Not having such an ideal does have its cost. Unlike France – and unlike the USA, as was most famously studied by Gunnar Myrdal – Britain does not have an implicit British ideal or creed against which the dilemma of sub-optimal realisation can be matched. Myrdal was not naive in spelling out the palpable presence of this ideal as a constituent self-identity and source of social cohesion, that cut across all the terrible failings the USA has had on racial matters. Civil rights did eventually win the argument along these lines, as a symbolic victory mainly achieved through the Supreme Court.[56]

Because Britain's philosophy explicitly tries to play down issues as the best way to deal with them, it is all too likely to settle for the 'quite life' if the ethnic minorities themselves do not participate, agitate or assert their demands for a principled response.[57] It may be that the outcome of this is greater liberty, pluralism and tolerance all round – as J. S. Mill would have wished – but this is an entirely contingent outcome. As I have argued, the last twenty-five years of 'very British' race relations and multicultural legislation have achieved a very substantial extension of these benefits. But twenty-five years on, the medium-term solution is noticeably wearing thin and having uncomfortable results in many places. Yet the issues remain distant to the drawing of party political cleavages, and the substance of national political debate. The perception generally – for all the series of failings spelt out above – is that the legislation has, on balance, got things about right. The mirror continues to reflect back a flattering self-image. But for how much longer?

THE QUEEN IS DEAD

British race relations writers often write as if the real proof of their radical critique of institutionalised racism in Britain will come the day the youth of Brixton and elsewhere take to the streets to riot again. For sure, every summer, as the heat piles on in July and August, the streets of South London buzz with talk of a big revolt 'just like 1981'. It is the romantic *sina qua non* of London's ubiquitous counter-culture; just as much as the Notting Hill carnival is its joyful celebration, no matter how much the authorities and conservative media would like to close it down. Such an idea that the proof of the inadequacy of the current multicultural race relations compromise will result in urban revolt is, of course, a fanciful idea, which runs entirely against the actual general outcomes of the legislation taken as a whole since the 1970s. It is an equally common myth that the framework will finally be challenged by the ethnic subjects revolting against their subjectivity: finally showing the British authorities what true full citizenship really *means*.

The truth is that the last place a radical overhauling of the ethnic minority system in Britain is going to come from is the communities themselves. Britain is not South Central LA, not least because the numbers concerned are so small. Relatively speaking, the political system has allowed ethnic minorities a very high profile and level of access for pursuing their own aims. With the notable exception of the absence of a concerted focus on poverty and social conditions, the establishment has very carefully offered these minorities a range of symbolic concessions in order to secure and stabilise the country. As in France, it is obvious of course, that the legislation and the form it takes has been formulated with the white majority population primarily in mind, and the identity and the integrity of the nation as a whole: in Britain an instrumental depoliticisation and decentralisation of the issue; in France a *surenchère* of the problems to divert them away from other connected threats to national integrity. In the British case, there is an undoubted 'feel good factor' about the public affirmation of anti-racism and multiculturalism; together with the uneasy feeling that rather large sections of the conservative and working-class population would – as they have in France – very openly endorse racist or xenophobic political options if they were allowed to surface.

The ethnic minorities in each country – as the focus of policy provisions and public debate – are thus symbolic vessels for larger issues concerning the national unity and social order of the countries, at a time when both 'old' nations are coming under increasingly serious internal and external threats from Europe and their own peripheral regions.[58] Unlike in France, British politics has clearly distanced any thinking about race relations or multiculturalism from the potential threat of the break-up of Britain. It would also be absurd to claim cracks in the race relations legislation are themselves likely to cause great cracks in national unity as a whole. This would not be the case if the politics of the two issues were deliberately connected together. Rather, it seems from the evidence of the justifications given in the British philosophy of multicultural race relations – and the kinds of paradigmatic problems that this institutional structure has led to – that the institutional solution is a *Great* British solution *par excellence*. This is both because it is a characteristically instrumental and well-tried colonial compromise, and because it is locatable in all the best traditions of British politics and the state. It reveals only too well the shortcomings and failings of this *ancien regime*, precisely because it is its pride and joy: and this at a time when a wider break-up of the old-fashioned philosophy seems to be getting increasingly close.[59]

The subjects are therefore not likely to revolt against their subjectivities and overturn the sovereign. The possible threats to the race relations and multiculturalism framework come, as for British politics generally, from exogenous factors: external and peripheral challenges. Clearly, the story of Britain's increasingly desperate wriggling out of its European obligations has all too predictably been repeated in the sphere of race relations. Time and time again, it has been seen in all the obstructiveness about immigration controls, the rejection of European human rights standards, and the latest comedy with

SCORE and the 'export' of race relations to Europe. Again, like in France, the story reveals the fact that the sphere of immigration and integration will be the last that the nation-state is likely to devolve to a supra-national level, for all the international dimensions of the question. It is a very basic and primal question of political control over the declining national sphere; especially since all the positive legislation that has been constructed – and which has had some success over the medium term – has been done so strictly within a nationally-bound, immigration-controlled context. This represents an enormous institutional investment, both symbolically and in terms of the stability of its achievements; upsetting it would be highly unsettling. It should be expected that any government will be every bit as stubborn about the defence of British race relations, as they are of the pound sterling currency.

The very nationalist defence of border peculiarities and the idiosyncratic legal-political method of dealing with ethnic dilemmas has thus become but one more dimension of Britain's curious Europhobia, which plays such a pivotal role in current party politics.[60] In the broadest sense, the obstructiveness about the progressive possibilities in Europe for race relations, multiculturalism or citizenship, reflect the general feeling that the underlying question at stake in all this is British *sovereignty*. In miniature, of course, this is reproduced with the pacified situation of ethnic minorities in Britain. Their political identities – and the sphere of involvement as 'good citizens' that has been given to them – is wholly dependent on their bottom-line acceptance of subjecthood, and fidelity to British law. The intervention of European citizenship and rights provisions is a direct and tumultuous challenge to this established order. It is a normative logic that could have no place in the institutional set-up that has been established in Britain, without overturning the whole institutional trade-off and equilibrium. It is difficult to see how Britain can even begin to bring itself in line with Europe – as it must over migration flows, denizens' rights, anti-discrimination provisions, and the recognition of human rights norms – without fundamentally upsetting the institutions of multicultural race relations. In a literal sense, 'sovereignty' over ethnic and racial minorities – just as sovereignty over 'foreigners' more generally – has already in many ways passed beyond national borders. The limit of what a lot of other countries can do is 'dump' these foreigners outside their borders, hardly a great proof of the triumph of a nationally sovereign law's empire.

Not all the challenges to the existing compromise come from the external European sphere. Sovereignty within the Union (United Kingdom) of 'Great Britain and Northern Ireland' – Britain as I call it – is not really what it used to be. It is no coincidence that the twin unthinkables of Scottish (and maybe Northern Irish) independence, on the one hand, and the end of the British monarchy, on the other, should have suddenly emerged so sharply in recent years, with new and unexpected vigour. The presence of Europe, and geo-political turbulence elsewhere, have certainly been a part of this. But no small measure of this fragmentation is due to the enormous sea change that the 1980s Thatcher government brought to the British pluralist political institutions and the social equilibrium that has kept them balanced for centuries.[61] It is ironic that the race relations and multiculturalism compromise – itself a typical example of the old tried and tested way of dealing with threats to British social order and national unity – was one of the things that Thatcher's reforms did not touch. Clearly, here was an old conservative philosophy that was working only too well: a devolved issue, peripheralised, privatised and depoliticised from the beginning.

It was always the way to deal with class and regional conflict too, until the new Thatcherite regime came along and upset the conciliatory, incorporating, but marginalising strategies of Conservative predecessors. Instead, on the question of class conflict and regional relations (as opposed to race relations), Thatcher upturned all the established rules. She set in motion a Tory 'long march' of institutional revolution, centralising government and its powers like no other previous government of the century, destroying the powers of local authorities (that is, traditional English pluralism), concentrating wealth in the south-east, using Scotland as a legislative testing ground, running down all the northern industrial areas. In the words of new right turned New Labour guru, John Gray: 'It made the Attlee government of the 1940s look positively Burkean in comparison'.[62] It is a well-known story. But the shock of it for conservative philosophy must surely be the hardest thing to overcome. Here was a Conservative government destroying much of the basis for conservative philosophy and its tradition in Britain.[63]

It should come as no surprise then, that the upshot of all this, ten years on with Labour now in power, is the serious threat of devolution – itself riding on the wave of Euro-inspired citizenship talk – which also demands internal constitutional change, a more explicit statement of rights and political identities, and a challenge to the idea of British political citizenship being based on subjecthood. None of these changes is going to happen in a direct, Jacobin manner. But a whole series of challenges to the existing institutional set-up have now been let out of the bag. If, the thinking goes, the Conservative Party destroys its own central philosophy and basis for ruling the nation – the careful incrementalism and balance that enabled them to pursue medium to long-term consequentialist and pragmatic outcomes – what else is there left but to re-conceive the nation in rational, constitutional and rights-based (deontological) terms? Such a redefinition of the nation could not but pass through a fundamental devolution to the periphery nations. This would now be most probably strongly supported in Scotland and Wales, with Ireland moving towards reunification. What is more, the Commonwealth is crumbling: both Canada and Australia are likely to vote for republicanism in the near future. Could it be, as with the Communist leaders in the Soviet Union of old, that the 'Queen' is in fact dead, but that nobody has noticed yet?

As a largely untouched relic of the old philosophy, race relations and multiculturalism now, unsurprisingly, might be looked at with a certain amount of nostalgia. Clearly, as an expression of the localised, devolved form of pluralism, it too has lost much of the basis for its equilibrating powers. One might expect the sectional mobilisation of the poor and disenfranchised Muslims to be the likely pattern for the future, rather than the smooth local representation of minority interests by interlocutory ethnic politicians. Perhaps future governments will be tempted to tamper with the old structure, set up for a political system that has largely been destroyed, and impose a new anti-pluralist centralism. In the sphere of education, this was already attempted in the last few years. This sphere saw the crude imposition of a national curriculum, Christian obligations, and a squeeze on the hitherto well-

maintained presence of multiculturalism; although as yet pragmatic compromise at local levels continues to dilute the effects
of this.

Post-Thatcher, post-Maastricht, twenty-five years on from
their invention and insightful liberal/conservative construction, it is almost impossible to imagine the complex legislative
compromise of race relations and multiculturalism being
made this way today. Times have changed: the relation of sovereign and subject; the old conservative management techniques; the secure national boundaries; the curiously
idiosyncratic legal categories and institutional channels. All
these well-balanced, and originally well-founded compromises
– the distinctively British way – have had their time, and are
now seriously deficient in respect of certain external
influences, and internal changes of circumstance. It is no
small paradox that the ideas behind the *avant-garde*, liberal
legislation, pioneered by Euro-friendly and civil rights inspired
liberal politicians like Roy Jenkins, should look so different
now. Twenty-five years later, they now have to be seen in the
light of the much more constitutionally rounded, rights-based
norms of European law and legislation, and after Thatcherism
has removed many of the social institutions and pluralist equilibrium on which the legislation was finely balanced. In this
light, the legislative compromise begins to look – as with the
swinging sixties generally – like the anachronistic invention of
some long time past.

Notes

1. See Sarah Spencer, 'The implication of immigration policy for race
   relations', in Spencer (ed.), *Strangers and Citizens. A Positive Approach to
   Migrants and Refugees* (London: IPPR/River Oram Press, 1994).
2. Adrian Favell and Damian Tambini, 'Clear blue water between "Us"
   and "Europe"?', in Bernd Baumgartl and Adrian Favell (eds), *New
   Xenophobia in Europe* (The Hague: Kluwers, 1995).
3. Commission for Racial Equality, *Immigration Control Procedures: Report of
   a Formal Investigation* (London: HMSO, 1985).
4. Richard Skellington, *Race in Britain Today* (London: Sage, 1992) p. 153.
5. Reuben Ford. 'Current and future migration flows', in Spencer (ed.),
   Strangers and Citizens; Guardian, 14 Feb. 1995).
6. This is the rationale behind many of the articles in Sarah Spencer
   (ed.), *Strangers and Citizens*. See also *The Economist*'s endorsement of its
   conclusions: 'Immigration: unclaimed benefits' (30 April 1994).

7. Allan Findlay, 'An economic audit of contemporary immigration', in Spencer (ed.), *Strangers and Citizens*.
8. Britain is therefore an exception to Gary Freeman's ideal-type model of immigration politics, 'Modes of immigration politics in liberal democratic societies', *International Migration Review*, vol. 29, no. 4 (1995), something he himself is aware of: 'The consequences of immigration politics for immigrant status: A British and French comparison', in Anthony Messina *et al.*, *Ethnic and Racial Minorities in Advanced Industrial Democracies* (London: Greenwood Press, 1992).
9. Reuben Ford, 'Current and Future Migration Flows', p. 68.
10. Anthony Lester, 'European human rights and the British constitution', in Jeffrey Jowell and Dawn Oliver (eds), *The Changing Constitution* (Oxford, University Press, 1994 3rd rev. edn).
11. See cases discussed in Hugo Storey, 'International law and human rights obligations', in Spencer (ed.), *Strangers and Citizens*.
12. In particular Ann Dummett (ed.), *Towards a Just Immigration Policy* (London: Cobden Trust, 1986); Brian Barry and Robert Goodin (eds), *Free Movement: Ethical Issues in the Transnational Migration of People and Money* (New York: Harvester Wheatsheat, 1992); Sebastian Poulter, 'Ethnic minority customs, English law and human rights', *International and Comparative Law Quarterly* (Jul. 1987).
13. See Yasemin Soysal, 'Immigration and the emerging European polity', in S. S. Anderson and R. A. Eliassen (eds), *Making Policy in Europe: The Europitication of National Policy* (London: Sage, 1993); and the introduction to Martin Baldwin-Edwards and Martin Schain (eds), *The Politics of Immigration in Western Europe* (London: Sage, 1994).
14. See Danièle Joly, *Haven or Hell? Asylum Policies and Refugees in Europe* (London: Macmillan, 1996). A comprehensive comparative survey of East and West European countries on these questions in Bernd Baumgartl and Adrian Favell (eds), *New Xenophobia in Europe*, especially the comparative conclusion and the articles on traditional humanitarian countries such as Germany, Switzerland, Denmark and Sweden.
15. Reuben Ford, 'Current and Future Migration Flows', pp. 61–8; Hélène Lambert, 'Asylum seekers, refugees and the European Union: Case studies of France and the UK', in Robert Miles and Dietrich Thränhardt (eds), *Migration and European Integration* (London: Pinter, 1995).
16. Stephen Castles, 'Migrations and minorities in Europe: perspectives for the 1990s. Eleven hypotheses', in John Solomos and John Wrench (eds), *Racism and Migration in Western Europe* (Oxford: Berg, 1993); Stephen Castles and Mark Miller, *The Age of Migration: International Population Movement in the Modern World* (London: Macmillan, 1993).
17. See Ann Dummett, 'Immigration. UK objectives for future European Community policy' (unpublished mimeo, 1992). A new article by Michael Banton explores the reasons behind these national variations and their policy consequences: 'National variations in conceptions of racism', *Migration* (1997).
18. Catherine Neveu, 'Is 'black' an exportable category to mainland Europe? Race and citizenship in a European context' in Rex and Drury (eds), *Ethnic Mobilisation in a Multicultural Europe*.

19. See again Baumgartl and Favell (eds), *New Xenophobia*, especially the conclusion: 'National visions, international perspectives and comparative analysis'.

20. Muhammad Anwar, 'Race relations policies in Britain: agenda for the 1990s' (Warwick: CRER Policy Papers in Ethnic Relations, no. 21).

21. Michael Banton, 'The race relations problematic', *British Journal of Sociology*, vol. 41, no. 1 (1991) argues just this.

22. John Edwards, *When Race Counts: The Morality of Racial Preference in Britain and the US* (London: Routledge, 1995).

23. John Bourne and Colin Whitmore, *Race and Sex Discrimination*, 2nd edn (London: Sweet & Maxwell, 1993).

24. Commission for Racial Equality, *Second Review of the Race Relations Act 1976* (London: HMSO, 1990).

25. *Mandla v. Dowell Lee*, House of Lords, 2 AC 548 (1983).

26. See John Solomos, 'From equal opportunity to anti-racism: racial inequality and the limits of reform' (Warwick: CRER Policy Papers in Ethnic Relations, no. 17); and 'Race relations research and social policy: a review of some recent debates and controversies' (Warwick: CRER Policy Papers in Ethnic Relations, no. 18).

27. Still the position defended by the journal *Race and Class* – notably Ambalavaner Sivanandan, *Communities of Resistance: Writings on Black Struggles for Socialism* (London: Verso, 1990) – and the long-term root of many of the factions within the race relations and multiculturalism lobby.

28. See the local studies made by Shamit Saggar, on the political manoeuvring within the fixed overall institutional consensus soldered by the 'liberal hour': *Race and Public Policy: A Study of Local Politics and Government* (Aldershot: Avebury, 1991), and 'The changing agenda of race issues in local government: the case of a London borough', *Political Studies*, no. 39 (1991) pp. 100–21. See also Paul Gilroy, 'The end of anti-racism', *New Community*, vol. 17, no. 1 (1990).

29. Michael Omi and Howard Winant, 'The Los Angeles "race riot" and contemporary US politics', in R. Gooding Williams (ed.), *Reading Rodney King, Reading Urban Uprising* (New York: Routledge, 1993).

30. Paul Gilroy, *There Ain't no Black in the Union Jack* (London: Hutchinson, 1987); Tariq Modood, *Not Easy Being British: Colour, Culture and Citizenship* (London: Runnymede Trust/Trentham, 1992).

31. See research by Pamela Conover and Donald Searing on citizenship and racial exclusion in Britain, 'Citizens and members: accommodation for cultural minorities' (unpublished paper presented at ECPR, Apr. 1995), who argue that this will be another tool in the repertory of exclusion.

32. See the new research by Tariq Modood, Sarah Beishon and Satnam Virdee, *Changing Ethnic Identities* (London: Policy Studies Institute, 1994).

33. CRE, *Second Review of the Race Relations Act 1976*.

34. Such as the well-publicised 'Counterblast' pamphlet by Fay Weldon, *Sacred Cows* (London: Chatto & Windus, 1989); see also press and

other articles collected in Lisa Appignanesi and Sarah Maitland (eds), *The Rushdie File* (London: Fourth Estate, 1989).

35. For example, Gilles Kepel, 'Les versets britanniques' in *A l'ouest d'Allah* (Paris: Seuil, 1994).

36. See Steven Lukes, 'Five fables about liberty', in Stephen Shute and Susan Hurley (eds), *On Human Rights* (New York: Basic Books, 1993); Ernest Gellner, *Postmodernism, Reason and Religion* (London: Routledge, 1993).

37. I am greatly indebted in my reading of the case to a brilliant MA thesis by Lucy Jordan, *Cultural Interrelation in The Satanic Verses and the Rushdie Affair* (Norwich: University of East Anglia, 1991).

38. For a sample of Rushdie's journalistic writings see his *Imaginary Homelands* (London: Penguin, 1991), especially the anti-racist polemics.

39. Oliver Mongin, 'La France en mal de fiction', *Le Monde* (3 Jul. 1992).

40. This paraphrases a comment made by Dr A. A. Muzuri, of Cornell University, in March 1989, quoted in Appignanesi and Maitland (eds), *The Rushdie File*, p. 220. See also Bhikhu Parekh, 'Between holy text and moral void', *New Statesman* (24 Mar. 1989); and Bhikhu Parekh and Homi Bhabha, 'Identities on parade: a conversation', *Marxism Today* (Jun. 1989).

41. Yunas Samad, 'Book burning and race relations: political mobilisation of Bradford Muslims', *New Community*, vol. 18, no. 4 (1992).

42. For important Muslim perspectives on the affair, see M. M. Ahsan and A. Kidwai (eds), *Sacrilege versus Civility: Muslim perspectives on 'The Satanic Verses Affair'* (Leicester: The Islamic Foundation, 1991); Shabbir Akhtar, *Be Careful with Muhammad!* (London: Bellew, 1989) and his intelligent reflection on Islam in the modern world: *A Faith for All Seasons: Islam and Western Modernity* (London: Bellew, 1990).

43. R v. Chief Metropolitan Stipendiary Magistrate, ex parte Choudhury, *All England Law Reports* (1991) 1 All ER. See the legal and religious discussions in Brian Pearce *et al.*, *Law, Blasphemy and the Multi-Faith Society* (London: CRE/Inter-Faith Network of the UK, 1990); and Bhikhu Parekh *et al.*, *Free Speech: The Report of a Seminar* (London: CRE, 1990).

44. Lord (Patrick) Devlin, *The Enforcement of Morals* (Oxford University Press, 1965); H. L. A. Hart, *Law, Liberty and Morality* (Oxford University Press, 1968 [1963]).

45. See the in-depth discussion of Sen's puzzle in Jon Elster and Aanund Hylland (eds), *Foundations of Social Choice Theory* (Cambridge University Press, 1986).

46. Bhikhu Parekh, 'The Rushdie affair: research agenda for political philosophy', *Political Studies*, no. 38 (1990).

47. T. Asad, 'Multiculturalism and British identity in the wake of the Rushdie affair', *Politics and Society*, no. 18 (1990).

48. See Bernard Crick (ed.), *National Identities: The Constitution of the United Kingdom* (Oxford: Blackwell, 1991).

49. See Yasmin Alibhai's very angry post-Rushdie comment, 'Why I'm outraged', *New Statesman* (17 Mar. 1989).

50. Geoff Dench, *Minorities in the Open Society: Prisoners of Ambivalence* (London: Routledge, 1986).

51. John Rex, *Ethnic Identity and Ethnic Mobilisation* (Warwick: CRER Monographs in Ethnic Relations, no. 5).

52. Harry Goulbourne, 'New issues in black British politics', *Social Science Information*, vol. 31, no. 2 (1992). See also A. Alund and C. U. Schierup, *Paradoxes of Multiculturalism* (Aldershot: Avebury, 1991).

53. Ray Honeyford, *Integration or Disintegration? Towards a Non-Racist Society* (London: Claridge Press, 1988).

54. Commission for Racial Equality, *Schools of Faith: Religious Schools in a Multicultural Society* (London: CRE, 1990).

55. See a plea of this kind in G. Haydon (ed.), *Education for a Pluralist Society: Philosophical Perspectives on the Swann Report* (London Institute of Education, 1987).

56. Gunnar Myrdal, *An American Dilemma: The Negro Problem and Modern Democracy* (New York: Doubleday, 1944); see also the discussions of the legal cases and its philosophy in Bernard Boxill, *Blacks and Social Justice* (Totowa, NJ: Rowman & Littlefield, 1992 [1984]).

57. The importance of mobilisation to democracy: see John Rex, *Ethnic Identity and Ethnic Mobilisation*; John Rex and Beatrice Drury (eds), *Ethnic Mobilisation in a Multicultural Europe* (Aldershot: Avebury, 1994); John Crowley, 'Paradoxes in the politicisation of race: a comparison of the UK and France', *New Community*, vol. 19, no. 4 (1993).

58. Robin Cohen, *Frontiers of Identity: The British and the Others* (London: Longman, 1994).

59. I deliberately echo Tom Nairn's brilliant and provocative discussion of the monarchy reflecting British myths and self-images: *The Enchanted Glass* (London: Picador, 1990).

60. Favell and Tambini, 'Clear blue water'.

61. David Nicholls, *The Pluralist State*, 2nd edn (London: Macmillan, 1994), especially the new introduction.

62. John Gray, 'Whatever happened to Englishness?' See the similar analysis made of the Thatcher decade by another English philosopher: Martin Hollis, 'Friends, Romans, Consumers', *Ethics*, vol. 102 (Oct. 1991).

63. Why the new right has had to go, in John Gray's terms, beyond the new right: see *Beyond the New Right: Markets, Government and the Common Environment* (London: Routledge, 1993).

7 Challenge to the Nation-State: The European Question

In this work, I have sought to cast light on a key area of public policy in Western Europe – the integration of immigrants and new ethnic groups – by comparing and contrasting the distinct political responses of two of the continent's most peculiar old nations: France and Britain. In the reversed mirror images of their ideas about citizenship and nationality, they have proven to be a particularly apt coupling. In the first half of the study, I identified the two dominant public philosophies underlying the policy frameworks in the two countries, showing how and when they came together in each case to solder a broad cross-party consensus on the best way of dealing with the policy dilemmas involved: particularly on the core language and conceptual terms for addressing these issues. I then went on to show how the triumph of the philosophy in each case has over time constrained and delimited responsive adaptation to new issues and circumstances, most notably international developments taking place outside their borders. The predominant picture that emerges from the second, critical, half of this study is rather negative. The interpretation I make of recent politics in both France and Britain suggests that the dominant central policy framework in each is set on a problematic and degenerate path in many respects. In each case, it seems that each country is moving further from the liberal democratic goals and ideals that inform the underlying public philosophy, rather than closer to them.

In their own way, France and Britain both conform to the stereotype of post-colonial ex-world powers, whose introverted internal politics on a question of keen international importance play out a long-term pathology of national decline. In both cases there is evidence of a self-deluding, rearguard, nationalist *repli sur soi-même* in reaction to this. It

240

has mobilised philosophical ideas and the peculiarities of their distinct national 'political cultures', in order to block off symbolically the European and international dimensions of their ethnic dilemmas. Each policy framework can be seen to rely on a good deal of mystificatory discourse, to sustain a political consensus that is less and less responsive to the social facts and demands of the situation. As I have shown, while the public philosophies are largely successful when judged in their own terms, a comparative perspective reveals a whole line of problems consistent with their particular way of approaching the problems. Most revealingly, perhaps, there is a glaring lack of concern in each case with the welfare and poverty dimension of ethnic dilemmas: the one area that the state has lost or relinquished most control over during the 1980s. This indicates that the strong build-up of culturally focused discourse in both cases – and the theorising of the problem of integration predominantly in terms of *cultural* dilemmas – is a diversionary mask or self-deception of some kind. There is the clear suggestion that both countries are going to face increasing problems fitting recalcitrant new developments within the same paradigmatic frameworks, and that the problems that they have already seen are likely to keep on recurring in ever more damaging ways. Moreover, it appears that the margin for adaptation and change is small, and that there is little sign of competing ideas coming along internally to mount a positive challenge.

It is the power of path dependency that blocks internal adaptation and responsiveness to these problems. The political stakes invested in the initial consensus on dealing with immigration and integration in the two countries have remained high and volatile. If changes are likely to come they will do so because of factors outside the nation-state, and outside the mainstream political system. That is, there are important international and sub-national influences on the politics of immigration and integration, that represent a challenge to the view centered on the nation-state. It is these factors which may prove the catalyst for breaking the myths of nationally-bounded citizenship that have so dominated the political outlook on these questions in France and Britain during the last twenty years.

BREAKING THE MYTHS: INTERNATIONAL AND LOCAL PRACTICES

Many people look to the European Union to break the inertia and path dependency of the national mind-set, and open an institutional sphere that enables new co-operation and social learning across national experiences. For sure, Europe has opened up another front for politics, as a potential political system and competing institutional framework of its own.[1] But it is far from clear that the European political system is yet in a position to challenge the predominance of the nation-state in policy-making on immigration and integration. It is valid, though, to ask *counter-factually* what might change in the current situation and policies if the European sphere were to impose itself successfully on this arena. In this light, it is possible to evaluate the actual, incomplete and uneven, results of European co-operation on immigration and integration, and pinpoint what is holding it back.

A lot has happened in the last few years to change the situation European nation-states once faced. The EU has imposed a new normative and institutional dimension on national law and politics. 1989 changed the face of the continent for good, causing vast new levels of international migration, an exponential rise in refugee and asylum-seekers, and new and unexpected minority problems. Large numbers of non-national permanent residents can now be found in all of the member states of the EU. At the same time, the relationship between Islam and the West has sharply deteriorated, with an appreciable knock-on effect on the Muslim populations in Western Europe. The problems associated with these new issues call for rather different institutional responses from those contained in the original nation-state-based ideas of integration for post-colonial immigrants or guest-workers. All of these factors, and others, have made it difficult, if not impossible, for some of the terms and elements of the original national policy frameworks to be applied as effectively as they were at the outset. They call less for social and political assimilation into the host country culture, and more for a devolution of responsibilities for rights and protection to agencies other than the traditional nation-state: whether local, federal or supra-national. They call for concerted international co-operation, and the bolstering of institutionally-enforced international legal rights and regulation. Issues such as freedom of movement, welfare benefits, work rights and legal protection for 'non-members' become more important than access to the full symbolic status of membership in the 'British' or 'French' nation. And, in an era of political deregulation and rolling back the state, it should come as no surprise that these developments do indeed follow on from the fact that the state has lost many powers over the rights, benefits and freedoms it used to control and redistribute.

Some commentators – most notably Yasemin Soysal – now argue that these factors are indeed more important in determining the shape and outcome of the politics of immigration in Western Europe than the old nation-state-based concerns. A 'post-national' institutional framework of citizenship policies is seen to be shifting the emphasis of national politics away from neo-nationalist barrier-building, and working to break down national cultural particularities in practice.[2] Despite the divergence of rhetoric in national-level politics, it is argued that at the ground level of practice there is in fact a convergence in the methods and means of managing immigrants and new ethnic minorities.

This is happening because of a two-pronged effect: at both international and local levels. At the international level, there are legal means – embodied in human rights accords and so on – which have enabled ethnic minorities to challenge the authority of national level institutions. Cases have successfully challenged parts of the new immigration laws in France and the limitations of anti-discrimination law in Britain. The European courts have been able to intervene decisively in cases concerning social policy or the residential status of foreigners in both countries. The moral high-ground of the 'international human rights regime' even makes special claims on public opinion across Europe: representing a source of consensual legitimacy that runs counter to the national monopoly. Ethnic minority groups are quickly learning to adapt to the new institutional channels on offer. Moreover, their forms of organisation are often diasporic and transnational in nature, and well suited to this new arena.[3] These challenges work in tandem with the effects of local-level practices on the top–down national policy frameworks. There is evidence in both countries that this is the real site where the theory of integration is put into practice: a place where the high ideals of the public philosophies are challenged and forced to adapt to organisational and practical realities, regardless of party politics, ideological posturing, and central *dictats*.[4] In particular, it is where the overbearing framework of the public language and culture of the 'official' problems gets adapted to the needs of the immigrant population. Local courts and agencies have had to adapt to the practical reality of upholding the rights of denizens and resident foreigners, however little persons of these categories fit into the official frameworks of membership and belonging. In France, local immigrant organisations have been very smart in turning and compromising the central line on *intégration* or *citoyenneté* to their own ends. Similarly, in Britain, ethnic minority groups have used the institutional frame work very skillfully to further cultural and religious goals, or wrest control over local party politics. These examples offer an alternative idea of democracy expressed through group mobilisation and social movements, and the development of new centre–society relations through the intermediary level of political and corporate organisation.[5]

Such arguments for the convergence of national policies of immigration and integration in a single supranational framework of post-national citizenship are gratefully echoed by the leading policy groups pushing for this at the European level. This, they would argue, is being pulled by the rational policy co-ordination among the elite civil servants and policy-makers who have to respond directly to the problems of new migration, refugees and the status of non-nationals. And it is being pushed from below by the success of ethnic groups and other lobby groups tailoring their actions to the given institutional structures: first at national level and now increasingly to those emerging at international level, such as the European courts and European social policy funding.[6] In short, the emergence of new institutions is created by a mix of lobbying and activist partisanship, responding to objective needs and circumstances. And the language in which this process is argued for, is the set of ideas associated with 'new citizenship', predominantly focused on the idea of formal legal guarantees regardless of nationality status. In practical terms this has been translated into the Starting Line Project for European citizenship and the attempt to get rights for non-nationals into the revised Treaty on European Union discussed at the intergovernmental conference of 1996–7. Other proposals seek to extend the developing immigration co-operation within the EU's 'third pillar' of justice and home affairs on the back of the Schengen agreement signed in the mid-1980s.[7]

However, as yet all of these proposals remain unrealised reforms. It is clear that there is a deep political resistance at national level to fully institutionalising these new kinds of channels and arenas. As I have underlined, the negative and degenerate power of the philosophies that sustain national policy frameworks is most visible when the ideas they express are used *politically* as the primary justification for deliberately stalling or derailing the new European-wide initiatives. I have mentioned the resistance to a general bill of rights for migrants at the *Conseil de l'Europe* or new European citizenship guarantees in the first pillar of the European Union Act. The resistance to co-operation when there is insufficient national self-interest pushing the nation's involvement from behind is becoming a serious problem. This is especially so as the EU falters after its positive drive in the early 1990s. Where it happens – the Schengen agreement, for example – it seems only to have reinforced the nation-state's hand in monopolising the control of immigration questions.

So who is right? Is it those who argue that post-national forces are now pulling the politics of immigration and citizenship? Or, is it rather those who believe the nation-state still holds the upper hand in directing and determining the shape of these politics across Europe? Roughly speaking, these are the two alternative interpretations of the situation offered respectively by Soysal and Brubaker.[8] My answer to this question is not a direct one, but it does nevertheless put its finger on the big political problem in Western Europe revealed by this study.

The predominance of nationally-bounded perspectives in French and British politics suggest that Soysal's theory is empirically incomplete, for these two cases at least. However, against Brubaker, I have shown that the resistance of nationally particular policy frameworks is not due to the fact they are 'rooted' unchangeably in long-term historical legacies, despite the fact they are often defended this way. These arguments are rather a kind of neo-national reflex, a rearguard reaction to the declining powers of the nation-state in this area.[9] The reflex is not without some grounding. The appeal to particularist, political culture-based arguments is a by-product of the political stakes raised at the time the dominant framework came together. In each country, there was a need to resolder a large national consensus, that reconciled an acceptable 'new' vision of the contemporary society with the culture, traditions and myths of an 'old' nation. This consensus had to adapt to the presence of new minorities, a hostile right wing, and other regional and peripheral threats to national sovereignty and unity. These factors together pulled the initial policy *synthesis* to take very nationally-bounded forms. At the time the consensus came together, in both France and Britain, this was certainly an effective and rational response to the problems as they stood: the social facts of the situation, and the building blocks of historical inheritance. Moreover, the wider normative stakes involved – the fundamental social order question raised by the problem of integration – also pulled a solution to the policy dilemmas that can be said to be rational in a wider sense. The solution found was a distinct and valid version of philosophical liberalism, that sought a wide political consensus through the power of its theory and the justifications offered. In other words, it represented the triumph of the public philosophy through a process of democratic deliberation.

In their pristine ideal states, then, the two public policy frameworks in France and Britain might both be taken as paradigmatic examples of rational liberal democratic politics. They can be read as combining open party political bargaining and public opinion formation, the independent interventions of the courts and judiciary, and the problem-solving technocratic pragmatism of 'behind-closed-doors' technocrats, to produce progressive and innovative new institutions. Indeed, a balanced combination of these three dimensions can be taken as the source of the *legitimacy* of public policies in a liberal democracy. However, the dynamic soldering of a dominant consensus in each country had costs that have been increasingly exposed over time. First, securing a consensus involved imposing a peculiar and restrictive language and institutional structure on the public perception of the problems.

Secondly, there were hard political compromises needed to marginalise the threat of the extreme right, that involved internalising some of their themes and preoccupations. Thirdly, each national solution invoked in its own way the spectre of history and cultural particularity as a way of generating a wider public identification. Although all this was done to create a wide public consensus at a certain moment, sustaining the consensus and the framework it supports over time has also entailed sustaining the architecture on which it was built. As I have shown, what may start out as an appropriate and justifiable institutional solution, may over time become less responsive to new circumstances and external changes.

An ideal policy-maker would be responsive to these new developments, and seek new policies appropriate to new demands; perhaps even a completely new policy framework. Ideal policy-making would pay close attention to identifying the facts of the situation and realistically conceptualising the outcomes of different policy lines. It would be wholly pragmatic in its outlook, and would not get caught making ideological or symbolic stands. It would be free of the problems of path dependence: the pull of precedence, tradition and habit. However, by the same token, it would also be free of the normative constraints imposed by the need for democratic legitimacy. The dilemma of policy-making in the real political world is that progressive policies also need a wide public consent to be carried to power. But the public consent lies with the ideas and language established to found the policy consensus of the past. The path dependency of institutions is therefore not just a negative feature of institutional inertia; it is quite literally a necessary property of any constructive politics. All new policies and institutions have to be built on old ones; moreover, the language and culture of a particular problem and its political environment is not going to change overnight. France can learn indirectly about its own failings from Britain's experience and vice versa, but neither is going to be able to uproot another's solutions and successes and implement them in foreign soil. As I have shown, an attempted shift in the accepted language of public problems – giving it a new spin in order to bring a new policy line in – can go badly wrong. Turning the granting of cultural recognition into a *droit à la différence*, was a fatal mistake for anti-racism in France. Trying to undo the *race*-based focus of legislation in Britain might actually produce an end-result in which all ethnically specific anti-discrimination provisions are wound up in favour of a far less interventory, general 'Commission for Equality': as the CRE fears.

What this amounts to, in other words, is a bifurcation of rational, responsive policy-making and the open, party political democratic process. This indeed may be what has happened in France and Britain. Such a bifurcation can also have directly negative political effects. As the policy framework becomes less responsive and more ill-suited to the public problems at hand, it has to be justified on increasingly rhetorical grounds. Thus, as the politicians work to defend the consensus and all that is at stake in it, they depend increasingly on making dogmatic stands about sacred national values, virtues and ideals. The politics of the situation becomes more ideological, and less reasoned. This inflation of rhetoric in fact only masks the fact that – in the absence of pragmatic responsiveness and direct problem-solving producing new ideas and solutions – the policy-makers have become increasingly less able to do anything *except* talk symbolically. Indeed, it masks the general growing impotence of the state in the face of dilemmas which ironically it claims ever more strongly to be its own exclusive prerogative. Politicians, meanwhile, know very well that they can still trade in the strong nationalist ideological dimension of the framework, while also perhaps winning votes by criticising the apparent failure and powerlessness of practical state-led technocratic measures. Somewhere along the way, the foundation of legitimacy at the national policy level – the marriage of pragmatic responsiveness and the deliberative democratic building of public consensus – has been lost.

Can it be hoped that the nascent European political system will find a better liberal democratic balance? For sure, there are fine policy-makers and lobbyists in Brussels, not to mention sophisticated inter-governmental discussion and behind-closed-doors co-operation; there are high levels of institutional innovation; the European courts have created a whole new arena for rights-based and regulatory legal politics; there is no shortage of highly intelligent and well-studied policy-making going on in the corridors of the Commission.

But however rational European propositions are, there is also an enormous shortfall in legitimacy at this level. No attempt has been made to fashion a concerted vision that might be able to build a *European* public consensus on minority and migration questions. Without it, all the best international policy-making behind closed doors will come to nothing. The feeble amount of democratic involvement, and the patent fact that there is no encompassing policy framework at the European level, leaves the national languages and mind-set of existing policy frameworks unchallenged.[10]

The deepest irony in all this, is that it is precisely France and Britain – those countries that are most experienced in the policy dilemmas of immigration and integration – that are the least co-operative and constructive in the European arena. This is an alarming paradox for the cause of 'social learning' in policy-making at the European level. What is also apparent in the difficult relation of these old nation-states with Europe, is that the increasing fragmentation of state powers into their separate arms – the distinct democratic, judicial and techno-cratic arenas – opens all kinds of gaps and incoherencies in the policy process, when it is combined with the unevenly distributed separation of powers between national and the supra-national or regional levels. This anomalous situation offers further perfect opportunities for regressive political reaction, and short-sighted defection from international co-operation in the name of 'national interests'. The failing of the European Union to become a balanced, legitimate political system in its own right gives reason for concern that liberal democratic gains in the past at the national level in the area of immigration and integration could all too easily go into reverse. A more effective application of the European Union's regulatory powers would be a more direct route for shaping national policy-making in a progressive direction, but in the area of immigration and minority protection the EU has got little further than providing a means for Home Affairs ministries to swap the latest police monitoring techniques and statistics. Again, this is a symptom of the democratic deficit. All the effective political power in the EU is located in the Council of Ministers, and the inter-governmental agenda-setting meetings, not the Commission or the Parliament. As long as it is the politicians who have complete control over what happens in policy at the European level, there is unlikely to be any breakdown in the continued power of nation-states in Europe to set their own agenda on the politics of immigration and integration. The political impotence of the EU thereby only reinforces the ideological claims of the nationalist politicians sceptical of Europe. Its failure can even be taken to confirm the spurious nationalist historical arguments about cultural and historical particularities being ultimately resistant to the forces of international convergence. This is a problem characteristic of European politics generally, outside of this particular policy sphere. It is a dilemma which is fatally undermining even the strongest areas of policy convergence that seemed to be moving so fast at the beginning of the 1990s.

What is left is a dilemma of legitimacy at both levels: European and national. And policy itself is somewhere in limbo between the two. The seriousness of problems with unavoidable international or sub-national dimensions is not going to be enough to pull rational and progressive responses from reluctant national political systems, if a groundswell of public opinion and consent is not there: as I have underlined throughout, this has to be mobilised and shaped by ideas. The power of ideas – the language and theories used to identify and conceptualise the framework of public problems, create public perceptions and shape public opinion – is a key component of all liberal democratic politics, for better or worse. It should not be underestimated. Le Pen is a continual reminder of this in French political life. His presence reflects both the extent to which the language and conceptualisations everybody uses have been forged by his agenda, and how much politicians will continue to ignore progressive developments and local realities to reap rich electoral gains by adapting the populist lines he proposes. All the good work at the margins can still be wiped out by the instituting of sweeping new police and bureaucratic measures in the new, popularly approved, *Code de la Nationalité* and immigration controls, and the pervasive damage its symbolic justification in the intellectual work of the *Commission* and *Haut Conseil* has done. I would argue that the language and conceptual frame of the public problems is inescapable in its influence, and it is wrong to ignore it, as political and social scientists often do.

THE EUROPEAN DILEMMA

Political ideas are double-edged swords. The public philosophies of integration in France and Britain are no exception. The public invocation of an ideal of citizenship – and its component roots of equality, autonomy, civility and so on – is not only an example of the continued relevance of the post-enlightenment liberal tradition in western politics. It also imposes a normative language on everyday politics that can have mixed and sometimes regressive effects on actual practical outcomes. Most of the evidence from my study has been about the negative effect of big ideas: the mobilisation of an inflexible consensus through the seductive philosophical defence of a nation's 'core' values and virtues, and the restrictiveness of these frameworks. Yet, as I have stressed, big ideas are needed to mobilise public opinion in favour of progressive policy-making. Consensus cannot be built on rational policy propositions alone. The present-day European dilemma is the lack of such consensus building at the European level – a European vision and philosophy – that can compete with the power of the national frameworks. The problems with the French and British philosophies of integration is symptomatic of this far wider European political problem.

In many ways, this problem is reminiscent of the famous 'American dilemma' studied by Gunnar Myrdal, a study which throughout has been at the back of my own approach to contemporary problems in Western Europe. Myrdals's most famous contribution was to point out the social costs and damage incurred by the gap between the universal ideals of the American creed, and the realities of racial discrimination and inequality in the post-war USA. His work more than anything embodied the combination of the normative and practical empirical dimensions of social scientific work necessary for it to be politically engaged. Indeed, it was a study which played a significant part in providing both the ideas and the pragmatic factual framework for the later wave of civil rights and great society reforms in the USA, that were finally pulled through in the 1960s. These reforms combined the technocratic construction of model-based social policies and the regulatory framework of civil rights and legal intervention, with the strong build-up of an ideal philosophical consensus in public opinion on the values of racial equality and the need for change. This is a world that has to a large extent been lost: the American dilemma has returned, worse than ever. On the one hand, there is the apparent impotence of the Clinton administration to build coherent constructive policies in the face of mounting social breakdown, poverty and racial divisions; on the other, the resurgence of a populist, anti-state right-wing, armed with new and dangerous ideologies, and ready to roll back the state even more. The American dilemma may seem far off: but it contains a critical lesson for Europe.

Similar tendencies can be read from the contemporary picture of Europe I have made. The problems of immigration and minorities cry out for international regulation and norms, and co-ordinated, proactive policies. Yet the EU is technocratic, distant and politically weak, undercut by its ideological void and democratic deficit. At the national level, there is a resurgence in nationalist particularisms, coupled with a general suspicion of what states, international agencies and public policies can do. Across the board there is a general trade-off between permanently high levels of unemployment, poverty and rising social unrest, and the elite efficiency of market-led technocracy that steers clear of social policy. Populist politicians, armed with a combination of xenophobic and anti-democratic rhetoric, are able to trade in the great divisions this leaves behind.

My study has provided evidence to suggest the liberal political philosophies of integration in France and Britain – whatever their original progressive virtues – are now helping sustain this populist tendency. These philosophies are now tilting the balance of policy responses to ethnic dilemmas ever more in favour of ideological rhetoric, and against constructive and responsive adaptation to practical needs. The primary concern, then, must be that the outcome of their stubborn defence of national sovereignty and philosophical peculiarities may well result in the worst-case scenario for all. The signs are familiar. Any progressive European pooling of the problems is rejected, in defence of a nation-state withdrawing ever further from proactive policies. At the same time, instead of addressing the causes of integration failure – notably poverty, declining welfare and inequality – these states promote an increasingly centralised ideological consensus around cultural and value issues. In such circumstances the likely outcome in practice is likely to be *de facto* policy inactivity and *laissez faire*, coupled with a great deal of grand and pretty theorising about citizenship and the political cultural origins of national community. In short, the dominant face of post-1980s conservatism currently ruling in France and Britain. Under these conditions, the present-day American dilemma no longer seems so far off. Henceforth it may well be the European dilemma too.

Notes

1. Simon Hix, 'The study of the European Community. The challenge to comparative politics', *West European Politics*, vol. 17, no. 1 (1994).
2. Yasemin Soysal, 'Immigration and the emerging European polity' in S. S. Anderson and R. A. Eliassen (eds), *Making Policy in Europe: The Europification of National Policy* (London: Sage, 1993), and *Limits of Citizenship: Migrants and Postnational Membership in Europe* (Chicago University Press, 1994).
3. As well as Soysal, *Limits of Citizenship*, see Patrick Ireland, 'Facing the true fortress Europe: Immigrants and politics in the EU', *Journal of Common Market Studies*, vol. 29, no. 5 (1991).
4. Patrick Ireland, *The Policy Challenge of Ethnic Diversity: Immigrant Politics in France and Switzerland* (Cambridge, Mass. Harvard University Press, 1994); Marie Poinsot, 'The competition for political legitimacy at local and national levels among North Africans in France', *New Community*, vol. 20, no. 1 (1993).
5. John Rex and Beatrice Drury (eds), *Ethnic Mobilisation in a Multicultural Europe* (Aldershot: Avebury, 1994).
6. For example, Churches' Commission for Migrants in Europe, *The Comparative Approaches to Societal Integration Project: Final Report* (Brussels: CCME, 1996).
7. Simon Hix, 'The intergovernmental conference and the future of the third pillar' (Brussels: CCME Briefing Paper no. 20, 1995).
8. Soysal, Limits of Citizenship; Rogers Brubaker, *Citizenship and Nationhood in France and Germany* (Cambridge, Mass.: Harvard University Press, 1992).
9. See Miriam Feldblum, 'Reconfiguring citizenship in Europe: Changing trends and strategies', in Christian Joppke (ed.), *Challenge to the Nation State: Immigration in Western Europe and North America* (Oxford University Press, 1998).
10. See Andrew Geddes, 'Immigrant and ethnic minorities and the EU's democratic deficit', *Journal of Common Market Studies*, vol. 33, no. 2 (1995); and on the problem generally within the EU, Simon Hix, 'Parties at the European level and the legitimacy of EU socioeconomic policy', *Journal of Common Market Studies*, vol. 33, no. 4 (1995).

Bibliography

Ahsan, M. M. and A. R. Kidwai (eds) (1991) *Sacrilege versus Civility: Muslim Perspectives on 'The Satanic Verses Affair'* (Leicester: The Islamic Foundation).

Akhtar, Shabbir (1989) *Be Careful with Muhammad!* (London: Bellew).

—— (1990) *A Faith for All Seasons: Islam and Western Modernity* (London: Bellew).

Alba, Richard (1990) *Ethnic Identity: The Transformation of White America* (New Haven: Yale University Press).

Albert, Michel (1993) *Capitalisme contre capitalisme* (Paris: Seuil).

Alund, A. and C. U. Schierup (1991) *Paradoxes of Multiculturalism* (Aldershot: Avebury).

Andrews, Geoff (ed.) (1991) *Citizenship* (London: Lawrence & Wishart).

Anthias, Floya and Nira Yuval-Davis (1993) *Racialized Boundaries: Race, Nation, Gender, Colour and Class and the Anti-Racist Struggle* (London: Routledge).

Anwar, Muhammad (1986) *Race and Politics: Ethnic Minorities and the British Political System* (London: Tavistock).

—— 1989. 'Race relations policies in Britain: agenda for the 1990s' (Warwick: CRER Policy Papers in Ethnic Relations no. 21).

Appignanesi, Lisa and Sarah Maitland (eds) (1989) *The Rushdie File* (London: Fourth Estate).

Arato, Andrew and Jean Cohen (1992) *Civil Society and Political Theory* (Cambridge, Mass.: MIT Press).

Archbishop of Canterbury's Commission on Urban Priority Areas (1985) *Faith in the City: A Call for Action by Church and Nation* (London: Church House).

—— (1990) *Living Faith in the City* (London: Church House).

Arkoun, Mohammed (1992) *Ouvertures sur l'Islam* (Paris: Grancher).

Arthur, W. Brain (1988) 'Self-reinforcing mechanisms in economics', in Philip Anderson, Kenneth Arrow and David Pines (eds) *The Economy as an Evolving Complex System* (Reading, Mass.: Addison-Wesley).

Asad, T. (1990) 'Multiculturalism and British identity in the wake of the Rushdie affair', *Politics and Society*, no. 18.

Audard, Catherine (ed.) (1988) *Individual et justice sociale: autour de Rawls* (Paris: Seuil).

Baldwin-Edwards, Martin and Martin Schain (eds) (1994) *The Politics of Immigration in Western Europe* (London: Sage).

Balibar, Etienne and Immanuel Wallerstein (1988) *Races, nations, classes: les identitiés ambiguës* (Paris. La Découverte).

Ballis-Lal, Barbara (1990) *The Romance of Culture in an Urban Civilization: Robert E. Park on Race and Ethnic Relations in Cities* (London: Routledge).

Banton, Michael (1985) *Promoting Racial Harmony* (Cambridge University Press).

—— (1991) 'The race relations problematic', *British Journal of Sociology*, vol. 41, no. 1.

—— (1997) 'National variations in conceptions of racism', *Migration*.

Barker, Martin (1981) *Neo-Racism* (London: Junction).

Barry, Brian (1978 [1970]) *Sociologists, Economists and Democracy* (New Haven: Yale University Press).

—— (1990 [1965]) *Political Argument* (Berkeley and Los Angeles: University of California Press).

—— and Robert Goodin (eds) (1992) *Free Movement: Ethical Issues in the Transnational Migration of People and Money* (New York: Harvester Wheatsheaf).

Bastenier, Albert and Felice Dassetto (1993) *Immigration et espace public: la controverse de l'intégration* (Paris: L'Harmattan).

Bauböck, Rainer (1994) *Transnational Citizenship: Membership and Rights in International Migration* (Aldershot: Edward Elgar).

Baudrillard, Jean (1986) *L'Amérique* (Paris: Grasset).

Baumgartl, Bernd and Adrian Favell (eds) (1995) *New Xenophobia in Europe* (The Hague: Kluwers).

Baumgartner, Frank (1989) *Conflict and Rhetoric in French Policy Making* (Pittsburgh, P.: University of Pittsburgh Press).

Becker, Gary S. (1971) *The Economics of Discrimination* (University of Chicago Press).

Bellah, Robert, with Richard Madsen, William Sullivan, Ann Swidler and Steven Tipton (1985) *Habits of the Heart: Individualism and Commitment in American Life*, Berkeley and Los Angeles: University of California Press).

—— *et al.* (1992) *The Good Society* (New York: Knopf).

Belorguy, J-M. (1994) 'Evaluer les politiques de la ville,' *Territories*, no. 345–6 (Feb–Mar).

Benhabib, Seyla (1992) *Situating the Self: Gender, Community and Postmodernism in Contemporary Ethnics* (Cambridge: Polity).

Benveniste, Emile (1969) *Le vocabulaire des institutions indo-européennes* (Paris, 2 vols).

Berger, Peter and Thomas Luckmann (1966) *The Social Construction of Reality: A Treatise in the Sociology of Knowledge* (London: Penguin).

Berque, Jacques (1985) *L'immigration à l'école de la République* (Paris: La documentation française).

Birenbaum, Guy (1992) *Le Front national en politique* (Paris: Editions Balland).

Birnbaum, Pierre (1994) *Les fous de la République: histoires politiques des Juifs d'état de Gambetta à Vichy* (Paris: Seuil).

Blatt David (1995) 'Towards a multi-cultural political model in France? The limits of immigrant collective action 1968–1994', *Nationalism and Ethnic Politics*, vol. 1, no. 2.

Body-Gendrot, Sophie (1993) *Ville et violence: l'irruption de nouveaux acteurs* (Paris: Presses universitaires de France).

—— and Martin, Schain (1992) 'National and local politics and the development of immigration policy in the United States and France: A comparative analysis', in Donald Horowitz and Gerard Noiriel (eds) *Immigrants in Two Democracies: French and American Experiences* (New York University Press).

Bonnafous, Simone (1991) *L'immigration prise aux mots: les immigrés dans la presse au tournant des années 80* (Paris: Kimé).

Bouamama, Said (1991) *Vers une nouvelle citoyenneté: crise de la pensée laïque* (Lille: La boîte de Pandora).

——, Albano Cordeiro and Michel Roux (1992) *La citoyenneté dans tous ses états* (Paris: CIEMI/L'Harmattan).

Bourdieu, Pierre (ed.) (1993) *La misère du monde* (Paris: Seuil).

Bourne, Colin and John Whitmore (1993) *Race and Sex Discrimination* (London: Sweet & Maxwell, 2nd edn).

Boxill, Bernard (1992 [1984]) *Blacks and Social Justice* (Totowa, NJ: Rowman & Littlefeld).

Brubaker, Rogers (ed.) (1989) *Immigration and the Politics of Citizenship in Western Europe* (New York: University Press of America).

—— (1992) *Citizenship and Nationhood in France and Germany* (Cambridge, Mass: Harvard University Press).

Bulmer, Martin and Anthony Rees (eds) (1996) *Citizenship Today: The Contemporary Relevance of T. H. Marshall* (London: UCL Press).

Carens, Joseph (1987) 'Aliens and citizens: the case for open borders', *Review of Politics*, vol. 49, no. 2.

Castles, Stephen (1993) 'Migrations and minorities in Europe: perspectives for the 1990s. Eleven hypotheses', in John Solomos and John Wrench (eds) *Racism and Migration in Western Europe* (Oxford: Berg).

—— Heather Booth and Tina Wallace (1984) *Here For Good: Western Europe's New Ethnic Minorities* (London: Pluto Press).

—— and Mark Miller (1993) *The Age of Migration: International Population Movement in the Modern World* (London: Macmillan).

Centre for Contemporary Cultural Studies (1982) *The Empire Strikes Back* (London: Hutchinson).

Césari, Jocelyn (1994) *Etre musulman en France: associations, militants et mosqués* (Paris: Karthala).

Champsaur, Paul (ed.) (1994) *Les étrangers en France: contours et caractères* (Paris: INSEE).

Churches Commission for Migrants in Europe (1996) *The Comparative Approaches to Societal Integration Project: Final Report* (Brussels: CCME).

Club de l'horloge (1985) *L'identité de la France* (Paris: Albin Michel).

Cohen, Robin (1994) *Frontiers of Identity: The British and the Others* (London: Longman).

Cohn-Bendit, Daniel *et al.* (1993) *Towards a European Immigration Policy* (Bruxelles: Philip Morris Institute).

Coleman, James S. (1990) *Foundations of Social Theory* (Cambridge, Mass.: Harvard University Press).

—— (1993) 'The rational reconstruction of society', *American Sociological Review*, vol. 58, no. 1.

Colley, Linda (1992) *Britons: Forging the Nation 1707–1837* (New Haven, Cann. Yale University Press).

Commissariat Général du Plan (1988) *Immigration: le devoir d'insertion* (Paris: La documentation française, 2 vols).

Commission de la Nationalité (1988) *Etre français aujourd'hui et demain* (Paris: La documentation française, 2 vols).

Commission on Citizenship (1990) *Encouraging Citizenship* (London: HMSO).
Commission for Racial Equality (1985) *Immigration Control Procedures: Report of a Formal Investigation* (London: HMSO).
—— (1990) *Second Review of the Race Relations Act 1976* (London: HMSO).
—— (1990) *Schools of Faith: Religious Schools in a Multicultural Society* (London: CRE).
Commission Nationale Consultative des Droits de l'Homme (1993) *La lutte contre le racisme: exclusions et droits de l'homme* (Paris. La documentation française).
Connelly, William (1983 [1974]) *The Terms of Political Discourse* (Oxford: Robertson).
—— (1984) 'The dilemma of legitimacy', in William Connelly (ed.) *Legitimacy and the State* (Oxford: Blackwell).
Conover, Pamela and Donald Searing (1995) 'Citizens and members: Accomodation for cultural minorities' (Unpublished paper presented at ECPR, April 1995).
Cornelius, Wayne, Philip Martin and James Hollifield (eds) (1994) *Controlling Immigration* (Stanford University Press).
Costa-Lascoux, Jacqueline (1989) *De l'immigré au citoyen* (Paris: La documentation française).
—— and Patrick Weil (eds) (1992) *Logiques d'états et immigrations* (Paris: Editions Kimé).
Crick, Bernard (ed.) (1991) *National Identities: The Constitution of the United Kingdom* (Oxford: Blackwell).
Crouch, Colin (1992) 'Citizenship and community in British political debate' in C. Crouch and A. Heath (eds) *Social Research and Social Reform* (Oxford: Clarendon).
Crowley, John (1992) 'Consensus et conflits dans la politique de l'immigration et des relations raciales du Royaume Uni' in Jacqueline Costa-Lascoux and Patrick Weil (eds) *Logiques d'états et immigrations* (Paris: Editions Kimé).
—— (1992) *'Immigration, racisme et intégration*: Recent French Writing on Immigration and Race Relations', *New Community*, vol. 19, no.1.
—— (1993) 'Paradoxes in the politicisation of race: a comparison of the UK and France', *New Community*, vol. 19, no. 4.
—— (1995) *Immigration, 'relations raciales' et mobilisations minoritaires au Royaume Uni: la démocratie face à la complexité sociale* (Paris: IEP thèse du doctorat).
Dahrendorf, Ralf (1988) *The Modern Social Conflict: An Essay on the Politics of Liberty* (London: Weidenfeld & Nicolson).
—— (1990) 'Decade of the citizen', *Guardian*, 1st August.
—— (1994) 'The changing quality of citizenship', in Bart van Steenbergen (ed.) *The Condition of Citizenship* (London: Sage).
Davis, Mike (1990) *City of Quartz* (New York: Vintage).
—— (1992) *Beyond Blade Runner. Urban Control: The Ecology of Fear* (Westfield, NJ: Open Magazine pamphlet series, no. 23).
Debray, Régis (1989) *Que vive la République* (Paris).
Del Fabbro, Réné (1995) 'A victory of the street' in Bernd Baumgartl and Adrian Favell (eds.) *New Xenophobia in Europe* (The Hague: Kluwers).

Déloye, Yves (1994) *Ecole et citoyenneté: l'individualisme républicain de Jules Ferry à Vichy* (Paris: Presses de la fondation des sciences politiques).

Dench, Geoff (1986) *Minorities in the Open Society: Prisoners of Ambivalence* (London: Routledge).

Devlin, Lord (Patrick) (1965) *The Enforcement of Morals* (Oxford University Press).

Donald, J. and Ali Rattansi (eds) (1992) *Race, Culture and Difference* (London: Sage).

Dubet, François (1989) *Immigrations: qu'en savons-nous?* (Paris: La documentation française).

—— and Didier Lapeyronnie (1992) *Les quartiers d'exil* (Paris: Seuil).

Dummett, Ann (ed.) (1986) *Towards a Just Immigration Policy* (London: Cobden Trust).

—— (1992) 'Immigration: UK objectives for future European Community policy' (unpublished mimeo).

—— and Andrew Nicol (1990) *Subjects, Citizens, Aliens and Others: Nationality and Immigration Law* (London: Weildenfeld).

Dumont, Louis. (1983) *Essais sur l'individualisme* (Paris: Seuil).

—— (1991) *L'idéologie allemande: France–Allemagne et retour* (Paris: Gallimard).

Dunn, John (1984) *The Politics of Socialism: An Essay in Political Theory* (Cambridge University Press).

—— (1985) *Rethinking Modern Political Theory* (Cambridge University Press).

—— (1990) *Interpreting Political Responsibility* (Oxford: Polity).

—— (ed.) (1990) *The Economic Limits of Modern Politics* (Cambridge University Press).

—— (1993 [1977]) *Western Political Theory in the Face of the Future* (Cambridge University Press).

Duster, Troy (1990) *Backdoor to Eugenics* (London: Routledge).

Duyvendak, Jan Willem (1995) *The Power of Politics: New Social Movements in an Old Polity 1965–1989* (Boulder: Westview).

Dworkin, Ronald (1977) *Taking Rights Seriously* (London: Duckworth).

Edwards, John (1995) *When Race Counts: The Morality of Racial Preferences in Britain and the US* (London: Routledge).

Elster, Jon (1989) *The Cement of Society* (Cambridge University Press).

—— (1989) *Nuts and Bolts for the Social Sciences* (Cambridge University Press).

—— (1992) *Local Justice: How Institutions Allocate Scarce Goods and Necessary Burdens* (Cambridge University Press).

—— and Aanund Hylland (eds) (1986) *Foundations of Social Choice Theory*. (Cambridge University Press).

Etienne, Bruno (1989) *La France et l'Islam* (Paris: Hachette).

—— (ed.) (1991) *L'Islam en France* (Paris: CNRS).

Etzioni, Amitai (1993) *The Spirit of the Community: Rights, Responsibilities and the Communitarian Agenda* (New York: Crown).

Ewald, François (1986) *L'Etat providence* (Paris: Grasset).

Fanon, Frantz (1961) *Les damnés de la terre* (Paris: Gallimard).

Fassin, Eric (1996) 'Two cultures? French intellectuals and the politics of culture in the 1980s', *French Politics and Society*, vol. 14, no. 2.

Favell, Adrian (1993) 'James Coleman: Social theorist and moral philosopher?', *American Journal of Sociology*, vol. 99, no. 3.

—— (1996) 'Rational choice as grand theory: James Coleman's normative contribution to social theory', in Jon Clark (ed.) *James S. Coleman* (London: Falmer).

—— and Damian Tambini (1995) 'Clear blue water between "Us" and "Europe?", in Bernd Baumgartl and Adrian Favell (eds) *New Xenophobia in Europe* (The Hague: Kluwers).

Feldblum, Miriam (1998) 'Reconfiguring citizenship in Europe: Changing trends and strategies', in Christian Joppke (ed.) *Challenge to the Nation State: Immigration in Western Europe and the United States* (Oxford University Press).

—— (1999) *Reconstructing Citizenship: The Politics of Nationality Reform and Immigration in Contemporary France* (Albany, NY: State University of New York Press).

—— Ferrajoli, Luigi (1994) 'Dai diritti del cittadino al diritti della persona', in Danilo Zolo (ed.) *La cittadinanza: appartenenza, identità, diritti* (Roma: Editori Laterza).

Ferry, Luc and Alain Renaut (1985) *Des droits de l'homme à l'idée républicaine* (Paris: Presses universitaires de France).

—— and —— (1985) *La pensée 68: essai sur l'anti-humanisme contemporain* (Paris: Gallimard).

Findlay, Allan (1994) 'An economic audit of contemporary immigration', in Sarah Spencer (ed.) *Strangers and Citizens. A Positive Approach to Migrants and Refugees* (London: IPPR/River Oram Press).

Finkielkraut, Alain (1987) *La défaite de la pensée* (Paris: Gallimard).

Flew, Anthony (1984) 'The race relations industry', *Salisbury Review* (Winter).

Forbes, Ian and Geoffrey Mead (1992) *Measure For Measure: A Comparative Analysis of Measure to Combat Racial Discrimination in the Member Countries of the European Community* (Sheffield: Employment Dept).

Ford, Reuben (1994) 'Current and future migration flows', in Sarah Spencer (ed.) *Strangers and Citizens. A Positive Approach to Migrants and Refugees* (London: IPPR/River Oram Press).

Freeman, Gary (1979) *Immigrant Labour and Racial Conflict in Industrial Societies: The French and British experience 1945–1975* (Princeton, NJ: Princeton University Press).

—— (1992) 'Migration policy and politics in the receiving states', *International Migration Review*, vol. 26, no. 4.

—— (1992) 'The consequences of immigration politics for immigrant status: A British and French comparison', in Anthony Messina *et al.*, *Ethnic and Racial Minorities in Advanced Industrial Democracies* (London: Greenwood Press).

—— 1995. 'Modes of immigration politics in liberal democratic societies', *International Migration Review*, vol. 29, no. 4.

Furet, François, Jacques Juillard and Pierre Rosanvallon (1989) *La République du centre* (Paris: Calmann-Lévy).

Galleotti, Anna Elisabetta (1993) 'Citizenship and equality: the place for toleration', *Political Theory*, vol. 21, no. 4.

Gallisot, Réné *et al.* (1984) *La France au pluriel?* (Paris: l'Harmattan).

Galston, William (1991) *Liberal Purposes: Goods, Virtue and Diversity in the Liberal State* (Cambridge University Press).

Gaspard, Françoise and Farhad Khosrokhavar (1995) *Le foulard et la République* (Paris: La Découverte).

Gardner, John (1989) 'Liberals and unlawful discrimination', *Oxford Journal of Legal Studies*, vol. 9, no. 1.

Garrett, Geoffrey and Barry Weingast (1993) 'Ideas, interests and institutions: constructing the European Community's internal market', in Judith Goldstein and Bob Keohane (eds) *Ideas and Foreign Policy* (New York: Cornell University Press).

Geddes, Andrew (1995) 'Immigrant and ethnic minorities and the EU's democratic deficit', *Journal of Common Market Studies*, vol. 33, no. 2.

Gellner, Ernest (1992) *Postmodernism, Reason and Religion* (London: Routledge).

Genestier, Philippe (1991) 'Pour une intégration communautaire?', *Esprit* (Feb.).

Gerholm, Tomas and Yngve Georg Lithman (eds) (1988) *The New Islamic Presence in Western Europe* (London: Mansell).

Gilroy, Paul (1987) *There Ain't No Black in the Union Jack* (London: Hutchinson).

—— (1990) 'The end of anti-racism', *New Community*, vol. 17, no. 1.

Giordan, Henri (1982) *Démocratie culturelle et droit à la différence* (Paris: La Documentation Française).

Girardet, Raoul (1979) *L'idée coloniale en France de 1871 à 1962* (Paris: Pluriel).

GISTI (1994) 'Discriminations peu constitutionnelles', *Plein droit*, no. 26 (Oct–Dec).

Glazer, Nathan (1983) *Ethnic Dilemmas 1964–1982* (Cambridge, Mass.: Harvard University Press).

Glazer, Nathan and Ken Young (1986) *Ethnic Pluralism and Public Policy: Achieving Equality in the US and Great Britain* (London: Gower).

Goldstein, Judith and Bob Keohane (eds) (1993) *Ideas and Foreign Policy* (New York: Cornell University Press).

Goodin, Robert (1982) *Political Theory and Public Policy* (University of Chicago Press).

—— (1995) *Utilitarianism as a Public Philosophy* (Cambridge University Press).

—— and Philip Pettit (eds) (1993) *A Companion to Contemporary Political Philosophy* (Oxford: Blackwell).

Goulbourne, Harry (1991) *Ethnicity and Nationalism in Post-Imperial Britain* (Cambridge University Press).

—— (1991) 'Varieties of pluralism: the notion of a pluralist post-imperial Britain', *New Community*, vol. 17, no. 2.

—— (1992) 'New issues in black British politics', *Social Science Information*, vol. 31, no. 2.

Granovetter, Mark (1985) 'Economic action and social structure: the problem of embeddedness', *American Journal of Sociology*, vol. 91, no. 3.

Gray, John (1989) *Liberalisms: Essays in Political Philosophy* (London: Routledge).

—— (1993) *Beyond the New Right: Markets, Government and the Common Environment* (London: Routledge).

—— (1993) *Post-Liberalism: Essays in Political Theory* (London: Routledge).

—— (1993) 'Why the owl flies late', *The Times Literary Supplement* (15 Oct.).

much of the basis for conservative philosophy and its tradition in Britain.[63]

It should come as no surprise then, that the upshot of all this, ten years on with Labour now in power, is the serious threat of devolution – itself riding on the wave of Euro-inspired citizenship talk – which also demands internal constitutional change, a more explicit statement of rights and political identities, and a challenge to the idea of British political citizenship being based on subjecthood. None of these changes is going to happen in a direct, Jacobin manner. But a whole series of challenges to the existing institutional set-up have now been let out of the bag. If, the thinking goes, the Conservative Party destroys its own central philosophy and basis for ruling the nation – the careful incrementalism and balance that enabled them to pursue medium to long-term consequentialist and pragmatic outcomes – what else is there left but to re-conceive the nation in rational, constitutional and rights-based (deontological) terms? Such a redefinition of the nation could not but pass through a fundamental devolution to the periphery nations. This would now be most probably strongly supported in Scotland and Wales, with Ireland moving towards reunification. What is more, the Commonwealth is crumbling: both Canada and Australia are likely to vote for republicanism in the near future. Could it be, as with the Communist leaders in the Soviet Union of old, that the 'Queen' is in fact dead, but that nobody has noticed yet?

As a largely untouched relic of the old philosophy, race relations and multiculturalism now, unsurprisingly, might be looked at with a certain amount of nostalgia. Clearly, as an expression of the localised, devolved form of pluralism, it too has lost much of the basis for its equilibrating powers. One might expect the sectional mobilisation of the poor and disenfranchised Muslims to be the likely pattern for the future, rather than the smooth local representation of minority interests by interlocutory ethnic politicians. Perhaps future governments will be tempted to tamper with the old structure, set up for a political system that has largely been destroyed, and impose a new anti-pluralist centralism. In the sphere of education, this was already attempted in the last few years. This sphere saw the crude imposition of a national curriculum, Christian obligations, and a squeeze on the hitherto well-

—— (1994) 'Whatever happened to Englishness?', *The Times Literary Supplement*, (4 Nov.).

Griffin, James (1986) *Well-Being. Its Meaning, Measurement and Moral Importance* (Oxford: Clarendon).

Guiraudon, Virginie (1994) 'Atavisms and new challenges: (re) naming the enemy in contemporary French political discourse', *History of European Ideas*, vol. 19, no. 1–3.

—— (1996) 'The reaffirmation of the republican model of integration: Ten years of identity politics in France', *French Politics and Society*, vol. 14, no. 2.

—— (1998) 'Citizenship rights for non-citizens: France, Germany and the Netherlands (1973–1994)', in Christian Joppke (ed.) *Challenge to the Nation State: Immigration in Western Europe and the United States* (Oxford University Press).

Gusfield, Joseph (1981) *The Culture of Public Problems: Drinking-Driving and the Symbolic Order* (University of Chicago Press).

Gutmann, Amy (1985) 'Communitarian critics of liberalism', *Philosophy and Public Affairs*, vol. 14.

—— (1993) 'The challenge of multiculturalism in political ethics', *Philosophy and Public Affairs*, vol. 22, no. 3.

Habermas, Jürgen (1992) 'Citizenship and national identity: some reflections on the future of Europe', *Praxis International*, vol. 12, no. 1.

—— (1994) 'Struggles for recognition in the democratic constitutional state', in Amy Gutmann (ed.) *Examining the Politics of Recognition* (Princeton, NJ: Princeton University Press).

—— (1996) *Between Facts and Norms: Contributions to a Discourse Theory of Law and Democracy* (Cambridge, Mass. MIT Press).

Hacker, Andrew (1992) *Two Nations: Separate, Unequal, Hostile* (New York: Basic Books).

Hall, Peter (1986) *Governing the Economy: The Politics of State Intervention in Britain and France* (Cambridge: Polity).

—— (ed) (1989) *The Political Power of Economic Ideas: Keynesianism Across Nations* (Princeton, NJ: Princeton University Press).

—— (1993) 'Policy paradigms, social learning and the state: The case of economic policy making in Britain', *Comparative Politics*, vol. 25, no. 3.

—— and Rosemary Taylor (1996) 'Political science and the three new institutionalisms', *Political Studies*, vol. 44, no. 5.

Hall, Stuart and David Held (1989) 'Citizens and citizenship', in Stuart Hall and David Held (eds) *New Times: The Changing Face of Politics in the 1990s* (London: Lawrence & Wishart).

Hamlin, Alan and Philip Pettit (eds) (1989) *The Good Polity: Normative Analyses of the State* (Oxford: Blackwell).

Hammar, Tomas (ed.) (1985) *European Immigration Policy: A Comparative Study* (Cambridge University Press).

—— (1990) *Democracy and the Nation State: Aliens, Denizens and Citizens in a World of International Migration* (Aldershot: Avebury).

Hannoun, Michel (1986) *L'autre cohabitation: Français et immigrés* (Paris: l'Harmattan).

Hardin, Russell (1988) *Morality Within the Limits of Reason* (University of Chicago Press).

Hargreaves, Alec (1995) *Immigration, 'Race' and Ethnicity in Contemporary France* (London: Routledge).

Hargreaves-Heap, Shaun (1989) *Rationality in Economics* (Oxford: Blackwell).

Hart, H. L. A. (1968 [1963]) *Law, Liberty and Morality* (Oxford University Press).

Haut Conseil à l'Intégration (1993) *L'intégration à la française* (Paris: La documentation françise).

Hawthorn, Geoffrey (1991) *Plausible Worlds: Possibility and Understanding in History and the Social Sciences* (Cambridge University Press).

Haydon, G. (1987) *Education for a Pluralist Society: Philosophical Perspectives on the Swann Report* (London: London Institute of Education).

Heilbronner, Kay (1989) 'Citizenship and nationhood in Germany', in Rogers Brubaker (ed.) *Immigration and the Politics of Citizenship in Western Europe* (New York: University Press of America).

Held, David (ed.) (1993) *Prospects for Democracy: North South East West* (Cambridge: Polity).

Herrnstein, Richard and Charles Murray (1994) *The Bell Curve: Intelligence and Class Structure in American Life* (New York: Free Press).

Hiro, Dilip (1991) *Black British White British: A History of Race Relations in Britain* (London: Grafton).

Hirschman, Albert O. (1970) *Exit, Voice and Loyalty: Responses to Declines in Firms, Organizations and States*, (Cambridge, Mass.: Harvard University Press).

—— (1991) *The Rhetoric of Reaction* (Cambridge, Mass. Harvard University Press).

Hirst, Paul (ed.) (1989) *The Pluralist Theory of the State* (London: Routledge).

Hix, Simon (1994) 'The study of the European Community: The challenge to comparative politics', *West European Politics*, vol. 17, no. 1.

—— (1995) 'The intergovernmental conference and the future of the third pillar' (Brussels: CCME, Briefing paper no. 20).

—— (1995) 'Parties at the European level and the legitimacy of EU socio-economic policy', *Journal of Common Market Studies*, vol. 33, no. 4.

Hollifield, James (1992) *Immigrants, Markets and States: The Political Economy of Western Europe* (Cambridge, Mass: Harvard University Press).

—— (1994) 'Immigration and republicanism in France: The hidden consensus', in Wayne Cornelius *et al.*, *Controlling Immigration*. (Stanford University Press).

Hollis, Martin (1991) 'Friends, Romans, Consumers', *Ethics*, vol. 102 (Oct.).

Holmes, Colin (1988) *John Bull's Island: Immigration and British Society 1871–1971* (London: Macmillan).

Holmes, Stephen (1993) *The Anatomy of Antiliberalism* (Cambridge, Mass.: Harvard University Press).

Home Office (1976) 'A guide to the Race Relations Act 1976' (London: HMSO).

Honeyford, Ray (1988) *Integration or Disintegration? Towards a Non-Racist Society* (London: Claridge Press).

Horowitz, Donald and Gérard Noiriel (eds) (1992) *Immigrants in Two Democracies: French and American Experiences* (New York University Press).

Hurley, Susan (1989) *Natural Reasons: Personality and Polity* (Oxford University Press).

Hussenet, André (1990) *Une politique scolaire de l'intégration* (Paris: La documentation française).

Ireland, Patrick (1991) 'Facing the true fortress Europe: Immigrants and
politics in the EU' *Journal of Common Market Studies*, vol. 29, no. 5.

—— (1994) *The Policy Challenge of Ethnic Diversity: Immigrant Politics in France
and Switzerland* (Cambridge, Mass.: Harvard University Press).

Jazouli, Adil (1992) *Less annés banlieues* (Paris: Seuil).

Jelen, Christian (1991) *Ils feront de bons français: enquête sur l'assimilation des
maghrébins* (Paris: Robert Laffont).

—— (1996) *La France éclatée* (Paris).

Joly, Danièle (1995) *Britannia's Crescent: Making a Place for Muslims in British
Society* (Aldershot: Avebury).

—— (1996) *Haven or Hell? Asylum Policies and Refugees in Europe* (London:
Macmillan).

Joppke, Christian (1995) 'Towards a new sociology of the state: on Rogers
Brubaker's *Citizenship and Nationhood in France and Germany*', *European
Archives of Sociology*, no. 36.

—— (ed.) (1998) *Challenge to the Nation State: Immigration in Western Europe
and the United States* (Oxford University Press).

Jordan, Lucy (1991) *Cultural Interrelation in The Satanic Verses and the Rushdie
Affair* (Norwich: University of East Anglia MA Thesis).

Kacet, Salem (1993) *Droit à la France* (Paris: Belfond).

Katznelson, Ira (1973) *Black Men, White Cities* (Oxford University Press).

Kaus, Mickey (1992) *The End of Equality* (New York: Basic Books).

Keane, John (1988) *Democracy and Civil Society* (London: Verso).

Kepel, Gilles (1987) *Les banlieues de l'Islam* (Paris: Seuil).

—— (1991) *La revanche de Dieu: Chrétiens, Juifs, Musulmans à la reconquête du
monde* (Paris: Seuil).

—— (1994) *A l'ouest d' Allah* (Paris: Seuil).

Krasmer, Stephen (1993) 'Westphalia and all that', in Judith Goldstein and
Robert Keohane (eds), *Ideas in Foreign Policy* (New York: Cornell
University Press).

Kristeva, Julia (1990) *Lettre ouverte à Harlem Désir* (Paris: Rivages).

—— (1993) *Nations Without Nationalism* (New York: Columbia University
Press).

Kuhn, Thomas S. (1962) *The Structure of Scientific Revolutions* (Chicago
University Press).

Kureishi, Hanif (1991) *The Buddha of Suburbia* (London: Faber).

Kymlicka, Will (1989) *Liberalism, Community and Culture* (Oxford:
Clarendon).

—— (ed.) (1994) *Minority Rights* (Oxford University Press).

—— (1995) *Multicultural Citizenship* (Oxford University Press).

—— and Wayne Norman (1994) 'Return of the Citizen: A survey of recent
work on citizenship theory', *Ethics*, vol. 104 (Jan.).

Laacher, Smain (ed.) (1987) *Questions de nationalité: histoires et enjeux d'un
code.* (Paris: L'Harmattan).

Lacorne, Denis (1991) *L'invention de la République: le modèle américain* (Paris:
Hachette).

Lakatos, Imre and Alan Musgrave (eds) (1970) *Criticism and the Growth of Knowledge* (Cambridge University Press).

Lambert, Hélène (1995) 'Asylum seekers, refugees and the European Union: Case studies of France and the UK', in Robert Miles and Dietrich Thränhardt (eds) *Migration and European Integration* (London: Pinter).

Lapeyronnie, Didier (ed) (1992) *Immigrés en Europe: politiques locales d'intégration* (Paris: La documentation française).

Lapeyronnie, Didier (1993) *L'individu et les minorités: la France et la Grande Brétagne face à ses minorités* (Paris: Presses universitaires de France).

Laumann, Edward and David Knoke (1987) *The Organizational State: Social Choice in National Policy Domains* (Madison: University of Wisconsin Press).

Lawson, Roger, Katherine McFate and William Julius Wilson (1994) *Poverty, Inequality and the Crisis of Social Policy* (New York: Russell Sage).

Layton-Henry, Zig (1992) *The Politics of Immigration* (Oxford: Blackwell).

Leca, Jean (1983) 'Questions sur la citoyenneté', *Projet*, no. 173–4.

—— (1985) 'Une capacité défaillante d'intégration', *Esprit* (Jun.).

—— 1986. 'Individualisme et citoyenneté', in Pierre Birnbaum and Jean Leca (eds) *Sur l'individualisme: théories et methodes* (Paris: Presses de la foundation nationale de la science politique).

—— (1991) 'L'Islam, l'état et la société en France: de la difficulté de construire un objet de recherche et d'argumentation', in Bruno Etienne (ed) *L'Islam en France* (Paris: CNRS).

Leclerq, Robert-Jean (1989) 'Natures des revendications et des enjeux culturels portés par les minorités actives issues de l'immigration maghrébine en France pour la période 1978–1987', in Bernard Lorreyte (ed.) *Les politiques d'intégration des jeunes issus de L'immigration* (Paris: L'Harmattan).

Le Gallou, Jean-Yves and Club de l'horloge. (1985) *La préférence nationale: réponse à l'immigration* (Paris: Albin Michel).

—— and Jean-François Jalkh (1987) *Etre Français: cela se mérite* (Paris: Albatross).

Lequin, Yves (ed.) (1988) *La mosaique française: histoire de ses immigrés et l'immigration* (Paris: Larousse).

Lester, Anthony (1994) 'European human rights and the British constitution', in Jeffrey Jowell and Dawn Oliver (ed.) *The Changing Constitution* (Oxford: University Press, 3rd edn).

Lévinas, Emmanuel, ed. Séan Hand (1989) *The Lévinas Reader* (Oxford: Blackwell).

Lévi-Strauss, Claude (1983) *Le regard éloigné* (Paris: Plon).

Lewis, Philip (1994) *Islamic Britain. Religion, Politics and Identity Among British Muslims: Bradford in the 1990s* (London: Tavistock).

Lloyd, Cathie (1991) 'Concepts, models and anti-racist strategies in Britain and France', *New Community*, vol. 18, no. 1.

Lochak, Danièle (1988) 'Etrangers et citoyens au regard du droit', in Catherine Wihtol de Wenden (ed.) *La citoyenneté et les changements de structures sociales et nationales de la population française* (Paris: Foundation Diderot).

—— (1991) 'La citoyenneté: un concept juridique flou', in Dominique Colas (ed.) *Citoyenneté et nationalité perspectives en France et en Québec* (Paris: Presses universitaires de France).

—— (1994) 'Usages et mésusages d'une notion polémique: la référence à l'identité nationale dans le débat sur la reforme du Code de la Nationalité 1985–1993', in Jacques Chevallier *et al.*, *L'identité politique* (Paris: Presses universitaires de France).

Lorcerie, Françoise (1991) 'L'Islam au programme', in Bruno Etienne (ed.) *L'Islam en France* (Paris: CNRS).

—— (1994) 'Les sciences sociales au service de l'identité nationale. Le débat sur l'intégration en France au début des annés 1990', in Dénis Constant-Martin (ed.) *Cartes d'identité: Comment on dit 'nous' en politique* (Paris: Presses de la foundation nationale des sciences politiques).

—— (1995) 'L'université du citoyen à Marseilles', *Annales de la recherche urbaine*, no. 68–9.

—— (1996) 'La République à l'école de l'immigration', *Revue française de pédagogie*, no. 117 (Nov. – Dec.).

Lorreyte, Bernard (ed.) (1989) *Les politiques d'intégration des jeunes issus de l'immigration* (Paris: L'Harmattan).

Lukes, Steven (1985) *Marxism and Morality* (Oxford University Press).

—— (1992) 'What is left?', *The Times Literary Supplement* (27 March).

—— (1993) 'Five fables about liberty', in Stephen Shute and Susan Hurley (eds) *On Human Rights* (New York: Basic Books).

Lustgarden, Laurence (1980) *Legal Control of Racial Discrimination* (London: Macmillan).

Mabileau, Albert *et al.* (1989) *Local Politics and Participation in Britain and France* (Cambridge University Press).

MacDonald, Ian (1977) *Race Relations: The New Law* (London: Butterworth).

Marshall, Thomas H. (1992 [1950]) 'Citizenship and Social Class', in T. H. Marshall and Tom Bottomore, *Citizenship and Social Class* (London: Pluto Press).

Macedo, Stephen (1991) *Liberal Virtues: Citizenship, Virtue and Community in Liberal Constitutionalism* (Oxford: Clarendon).

MacIntyre, Alisdair (1981) *After Virtue: A Study in Moral Theory* (London: Duckworth).

MacKinnon, Catherine (1993) *Only Words* (Cambridge, Mass: Harvard University Press).

Majone, Giandomenico (1980) 'Policies as theories', *Omega*, vol. 8, no. 2.

—— (1989) *Evidence, Argument and Persuasion in the Policy Process*. (New Haven Conn. Yale University Press).

—— (1996) 'Public policy: Ideas, interests and institutions' in Robert Goodin and Dieter Klingemann (eds) *New Handbook of Political Science* (Oxford University Press).

Malewska, H. and G. Cachon (1988) *Le travail social et les enfants des migrants* (Paris: L'Harmattan).

Mann, Michael (1988) 'Ruling class strategies and citizenship', in Michael Mann, *States, Wars and Capitalism: Studies in Political Sociology* (Oxford: Blackwell).

March, James and Johan Olsen (1989) *Rediscovering Institutions: The Organizational Basis of Politics* (New York: Free Press).

Massey, Douglas and Nancy Denton (1993) *American Apartheid: Segregation and the Making of the Underclass* (Cambridge, Mass: Harvard University Press).

Mayer, Nonna and Pascal Perrineau (eds) (1996) *Le Front National à découverte* (Paris: Presses de la fondation nationale des sciences politiques, 2nd edn).

McCrudden, David, J. Smith and Colin Brown (1991) 'Groups versus individuals: the ambiguity behind the Race Relations Act', *Policy Studies*, vol. 12, no. 1.

Mendus, Susan (ed.) (1988) *Justifying Toleration: Conceptual and Historical Perspectives* (Cambridge University Press).

Mendus, Susan (1990) 'The tigers of wrath and the horses of instruction', in Bhikhu Parekh *et al.*, *Free Speech: The Report of a Seminar* (London: CRE).

Mény, Yves (1992) *La corruption de la République* (Paris: Fayard).

Messina, Anthony (1989) *Race and Party Competition* (Oxford University Press).

—— *et al.* (1992) *Ethnic and Racial Minorities in Advanced Industrial Democracies* (London: Greenwood Press).

Miles, Robert (1993) *Racism After 'Race Relations'* (London: Routledge).

—— and Annie Phizacklea (1984) *White Man's Country: Racism in British Politics* (London: Pluto Press).

—— and Dietrich Thränhardt (eds) (1995) *Migration and European Integration* (London: Pinter).

Miller, David (1989) *Market, State and Community* (Oxford: Clarendon).

—— (1995) *On Nationality* (Oxford University Press).

—— and Michael Walzer (eds) (1995) *Pluralism, Justice and Equality* (Oxford University Press).

Minc, Alain (1989) *La grande illusion* (Paris: Grasset).

—— (1993) *Le nouveau moyen age* (Paris: Gallimard).

Mishan, E. J. (1988) 'What future for a multi-racial Britain?' (pts 1 and 2), *Salisbury Review* (Jun/Sep).

Modgil, Sohan *et al.* (1986) *Multiculturalism: The Interminable Debate* (London: Falmer).

Modood, Tariq (1992) *Not Easy Being British: Colour, Culture and Citizenship* (London: Runnymede Trust/Trentham).

—— (1994) 'Establishment, multiculturalism and British citizenship', *Political Quarterly*, vol. 65, no. 1

——, Sarah Beishon and Satnam Virdee (1994) *Changing Ethnic Identities* (London: Policy Studies Institute).

Moruzzi, Norma Claire (1994) 'A problem with headscarves: contemporary complexities of political and social identities' *Political Theory*, vol. 22, no. 4.

Mouffe, Chantal (ed.) (1992) *Dimensions of Radical Democracy: Pluralism, Citizenship, Community* (London: Verso).

Mulhall, Stephen and Adam Swift (1996) *Liberals and Communitarians* (Oxford: Blackwell, 2nd edn).

Munoz-Dardé, Véronique (1994) *La fraternité: un concept politique. Essai sur une notion de justice sociale et politique* (Florence: EUI PhD thesis).

Murray, Laura (1994) 'Einwanderungsland Bundesrepublik Deutschland? Explaining the evolving positions of German political parties on citizenship policy', *German Politics and Society*, no. 33.

Myrdal, Gunnar (1994) *An American Dilemma: The Negro Problem and Modern Democracy* (New York: Doubleday).

Naïr, Sami (1992) *Le regard des vainqueurs: les enjeux français de l'immigration* (Paris: Grasset).

Nairn, Tom (1990) *The Enchanted Glass* (London: Picador).

—— (1981) *The Break-Up of Britain: Crisis and Neo-Nationalism* (London: Verso).

Neveu, Catherine (1993) *Communauté, nationalité et citoyenneté. De l'autre côte du miroir: les Bangladeshis de Londres* (Paris: Karthala).

—— (1994) 'Is "black" an exportable category to mainland Europe? Race and citizenship in a European context', in John Rex and Beatrice Drury (eds) *Ethnic Mobilisation in a Multicultural Europe*. Aldershot: Avebury.

Nicholls, David (1994) *The Pluralist State* (London: Macmillan, 2nd edn).

Nicolet, Claude (1982) *L'idée républicaine en France 1798–1924: essai d'histoire critique* (Paris: Gallimard).

—— (1992) *La République en France: état de lieux* (Paris: Seuil).

Noiriel, Gérard (1988) *Le creuset français: histoire de l'immigration XIXe–XXe siècle* (Paris: Seuil).

North, Douglass (1981) *Structure and Change in Economic History* (New York: Norton).

—— (1990) *Institutions, Institutional Change and Economic Performance* (Cambridge University Press).

Oakeshott, Michael (1975) *On Human Conduct* (Oxford University Press).

Olson, Mancur (1980 [1965]) *The Logic of Collective Action: Public Goods and the Theory of Groups* (Cambridge, Mass.: Harvard University Press).

Omi, Michael and Howard Winant (1993) 'The Los Angles 'race riot' and contemporary US politics', in R. Gooding Williams (ed.) *Reading Rodney King, Reading Urban Uprising* (New York: Routledge).

—— and (1994) *Racial Formation in the US from the 1960s to the 1980s* (London: Routledge, 2nd edn).

Ordeshook, Peter (1993) 'The development of contemporary political theory', in William Barnett *et al.*, *Political Economy: Institutions, Competition and Representation* (Cambridge University Press).

Oriol, Michel (1987) 'Sur la transposabilité des cultures populaires en situation d' émigration', in *L'immigration en France: le choc des cultures* (L' Arbresle Centre: Documentations Thomas More).

—— (1992) 'Islam and Catholicism in French immigration', in Donald Horowitz and Gérard Noiriel (eds) *Immigration in Two Democracies: French and American Experiences* (New York University Press).

Owen, D. (1992) *Ethnic Minorities in Britain: Settlement Patterns* (Warwick: CRER).

Parekh, Bhikhu (1989) 'The hermeneutics of the Swann report' in G. K. Verma (ed.) *Education for All: A Landmark in Pluralism* (London: Falmer).

—— (1989) 'Between holy text and moral void', *New Statesman* (24 Mar).

—— (1990) 'The Rushdie affair: research agenda for political philosophy', *Political Studies*, no. 38.

—— (1990) 'The social logic of pluralism', in Bhikhu Parekh *et al.*, *Britain: A Plural Society* (London: CRE).

—— *et al.* (1990) *Free Speech: The Report of a Seminar* (London: CRE).

—— (1994) 'Superior people', *The Times Literary Supplement* (25 Nov).

—— and Homi Bhabha (1989) 'Identities on parade: a conversation', *Marxism Today* (Jun).

Parsons, Talcott (1937) *The Structure of Social Action* (New York: Free Press).

Pastore, Ferruccio (1994) 'Familles entre les droits. Pour un encadrement de la problematique du statut personnel des familles immigrés des pays musulmans en Europe' (unpublished).

Paugram, Serge (1993) *La société francaise et ses pauvres* (Paris: Presses universitaires françaises).

Pearce, Brian, *et al.* (1990) *Law, Blasphemy and the Multi-Faith Society* (London: CRE/Inter-Faith Network of the UK).

Phillips, Anne (1993) *Democracy and Difference* (Cambridge: Polity).

—— (1995) *The Politics of Presence* (Oxford University Press).

Pinto, D. (1988) 'Immigration: l'ambiguité de la référence américaine', *Pouvoirs*, no. 47.

Pitken, Hanna Fenichel (1972) *Wittgenstein and Justice: On the Significance of Ludwig Wittgenstein for Social and Political Thought* (Berkeley, Calif.: University of California Press).

Pizzorno, Alessandro (1986) 'Some other kinds of otherness: a critique of rational choice theories', in A. Foxley *et al.*, *Development, Democracy and the Art of Trespassing: Essays in Honor of Albert O. Hirschman* (Notre Dame, Ill.: Notre Dame University Press).

Pizzorno, Alessandro (1991) 'On the individualistic theory of social order', in Pierre Bourdieu and James S. Coleman (eds) *Social Theory for a Changing Society* (Boulder, Colo.: Westview).

Pogge, Thomas (1989) *Realizing Rawls* (Ithaca, NY: Cornell University Press).

Poinsot, Marie (1993) 'The competition for political legitimacy at local and national levels among North Africans in France', *New Community*, vol. 20, no. 1.

—— (1994) *L' intégration politique des jeunes issus de l'immigration: du débat des idées aux actions collectives dans l'agglomeration lilloise* (Paris: IEP thèse du doctorat).

Poulter, Sebastian (1987) 'Ethnic minority customs, English law and human rights', *International and Comparative Law Quarterly* (Jul.).

Poulter, Sebastian (1990) *Asian Traditions and English Law* (London: Runnymede/Trentham).

Powell, Walter and Paul DiMaggio (eds) (1991) *The New Institutionalism in Organizational Analysis* (University of Chicago Press).

Preuß, Ulrich (1995) *Concepts, foundations and limits of European citizenship* (Bremen: Centre for European Legal Policy).

Putnam, Robert (1993) *Making Democracy Work: Civic Traditions in Modern Italy* (Princeton, NJ: Princeton University Press).

—— (1995) 'Tuning in, tuning out: The strange disappearance of civic America', *Political Science Review*, vol. 28, no. 4.

Rabinow, Paul (1989) *French Modern: Norms and Forms of the Social Environment* (Cambridge, Mass: Harvard University Press).

Rawls, John (1971) *A Theory of Justice* (Oxford University Press).

—— (1993) *Political Liberalism* (Princeton, N.J.: Princeton University Press).

Raz, Joseph (1986) *The Morality of Freedom* (Oxford: Clarendon).

—— (1990) 'Facing diversity: the case of epistemic abstinence', *Philosophy and Public Affairs*, vol. 19.

—— (1991) 'Free expression and personal identification', *Oxford Journal of Legal Studies*, vol. 11, no. 3.

—— (1994) 'Multiculturalism: a liberal perspective', *Dissent*, vol. 41, no. 1.

Renan, Ernest, ed. Joel Roman (1992) *Qu'est-ce qu'une nation? et autres essais politiques* (Paris: Presses poches).

Renaut, Alain (1991) 'Logiques de la nation', in Gil Délannoi and Pierre-André Taguieff (eds) *Théories du nationalisme* (Paris: Editions Kimé).

Rex, John (1985) *The Concept of a Multicultural Society* (London: CRER Occasional Papers in Ethnic Relations).

—— (1988) *The Ghetto and the Underclass: Essays on Race and Social Policy* (Aldershot: Avebury).

—— (1991) *Ethnic Identity and Ethnic Mobilisation* (Warwick: CRER Monographs in Ethnic Relations, no. 5).

—— (1991) 'The political sociology of a multicultural society', *European Journal of Intercultural Studies*, vol. 1, no. 1.

—— (1996) *Ethnic Minorities in the Modern Nation State* (London: Macmillan).

—— and Beatrice Drury (eds) (1994) *Ethnic Mobilisation in a Multicultural Europe* (Aldershot: Avebury).

—— and David Mason (eds) (1986) *Theories of Race and Ethnicity* (Cambridge University Press).

Rose, E. J. B. *et al.* (1969) *Colour and Citizenship: A Report on British Race Relations* (London: Oxford University Press).

Rosanvallon, Pierre (1992) *Le sacré du citoyen: histoire du suffrage universel en France* (Paris: Gallimard).

Rushdie, Salman (1988) *The Satanic Verses* (London: Penguin).

—— (1991) *Imaginary Homelands* (London: Penguin).

Sadran, Pierre (1992) *Le système administratif français* (Paris: Montechrestien).

Safran, William (1985) 'The Mitterand regime and its policies of ethno-cultural accomodation', *Comparative Politics*, vol. 18, no. 1.

—— (1990) 'The French and their national identity: the quest for an elusive substance', *French Politics and Society*, vol. 8, no. 1.

—— (1995) 'Nations, ethnic groups, states and politics: a preface and an agenda', *Nationalism and Ethnic Politics*, vol. 1, no. 1.

Saggar, Shamit (1991) *Race and Public Policy: A Study of Local Politics and Government* (Aldershot: Avebury).

—— (1991) 'The changing agenda of race issues in local government: the case of a London borough', *Political Studies*, no. 39, pp. 100–21.

—— (1993) 'Re-examining the 1964–70 Labour government's race relations strategy', *Contemporary Record*, vol. 7, no. 2.

—— (ed.) (1996) *Race and British Electoral Politics* (London: Prentice-Hall).

Said, Edward (1978) *Orientalism* (London: Routledge).

—— (1993) *Culture and Imperialism* (London: Chatto & Windus).

Samad, Yunas (1992) 'Book burning and race relations: political mobilisation of Bradford Muslims', *New Community*, vol. 18, no. 4.

Sandel, Michael (1995) *Democracy's Discontent: America in Search of a Public Philosophy* (Cambridge; Mass.: Harvard University Press).

Sayad, Abdelmalek (1984) 'État, nation et immigration. L'ordre national à l'épreuve de l'immigation', *Peuples Méditerranéens* (Apr.–Sep.).

—— (1991) *L'immigration ou les paradoxes de l'altérité* (Paris: De Boeck).

Scarman, Lord (Leslie) (1986 [1981]) *The Brixton Disorders 10–12 April 1981: Report of an Enquiry* (London: Penguin).

Schain, Martin (1988) 'Immigration and changes in the French party system', *European Journal of Political Research*, vol. 16.

—— (1993) 'Policy making and defining ethnic minorities: the case of immigration in France', *New Community*, vol. 20, no. 1.

—— (1995) 'Policy and policy making in France and the US: Models of incorporation and the dynamics of change', *Modern and Contemporary France*, vol. 3, no. 4.

Schattschneider, E. E. (1961) *The Semi-Sovereign People: A Realist's View of Democracy in America* (New York: Free Press).

Schlesinger, Arthur D. (1992) *The Disuniting of America: Reflections on a Multicultural Society* (New York: Norton).

Schnapper, Dominique (1991) *La France de l'intégration* (Paris: Gallimard).

—— (1992) *L'Europe des immigrés: essais sur les politiques de l'immigration* (Paris: Bonnin).

—— (1994) *La communauté des citoyens: sur l'idée moderne de nation* (Paris: Gallimard).

Schuck, Peter (1992) 'The politics of rapid legal change: Immigration policy in the 1980s', *Studies in American Political Development*, no. 6.

Scruton, Roger (1980) *The Meaning of Conservatism* (Harmondsworth: Penguin).

Scruton, Roger (1992) 'What is right?', *The Times Literary Supplement* (10 April).

Seguin, Philippe (1993) 'La République et l'exception française', *Philosophie politique*, no. 4, pp. 45–62.

Selbourne, David (1994) *The Principle of Duty: An Essay on the Foundations of Civic Order* (London: Sinclair-Stevenson).

Selznick, Philip (1992) *The Moral Commonwealth* (Berkeley, Calif. University of California Press).

Shepsle, Ken (1986) 'Studying institutions: some lessons from the rational choice approach', *Journal of Theoretical Politics*, vol. 1, pp. 131–49.

Silverman, Max (ed.) (1991) *Race, Discourse and Power in France* (Aldershot: Avebury).

—— (1992) *Deconstructing the Nation: Immigration, Racism and Citizenship in Modern France* (London: Routledge).

Sivanandan, Ambalavaner (1990) *Communities of Resistance: Writings on Black Struggles for Socialism* (London: Verso).

Skellington, Richard (1992) *Race in Britain Today* (London: Sage).

Skinner, Quentin (1989) 'Language and political change', in Terence Ball, James Farr and Russell Hanson (eds) *Political Innovation and Conceptual Change* (Cambridge University Press).

—— and James Tully (ed.) (1988) *Meaning and Context: Quentin Skinner and his Critics* (Cambridge: Polity).

Sleeper, Jim (1990) *The Closest of Strangers: Liberalism and the Politics of Race in New York* (New York: Norton).

Solomos, John (1989) 'From equal opportunity to anti-racism: racial inequality and the limits of reform' (Warwick: CRER Policy Papers in Ethnic Relations, no. 17).

—— (1989) 'Race relations research and social policy: a review of some recent debates and controversies' (Warwick: CRER Policy Papers in Ethnic Relations, no. 18).

—— and John Wrench (eds) (1993) *Racism and Migration in Western Europe* (Oxford: Berg).

Sooben, Philip (1990) *The Origins of the Race Relations Act* (Warwick: CRER Research papers in Ethnic Relations no. 12).

Sorman, Guy (1992) *En attendant les barbares* (Paris: Fayard).

Sowell, Thomas (1983) *The Economics and Politics of Race: An International Perspective* (New York: Morrow).

Soysal, Yasemin Nuhoglu (1993) 'Immigration and the emerging European polity' in S. S. Anderson and R. A. Eliassen (eds) *Making Policy in Europe: The Europification of National Policy* (London: Sage).

—— (1994) *Limits of Citizenship: Migrants and Postnational Membership in Europe* (University of Chicago Press).

Spencer, Sarah (ed.) (1994) *Strangers and Citizens. A Positive Approach to Migrants and Refugees* (London: IPPR/River Oram Press).

Spinner, Jeff (1994) *The Boundaries of Citizenship: Race, Ethnicity and Nationality in the Liberal State* (Baltimore, Md: Johns Hopkins University Press).

Steinmo, Sven, K. Thelen, and F. Longstreth (eds) (1992) *Structuring Politics: Historical Institutionalism in Comparative Perspective* (New York: Cambridge University Press).

Storey, Hugo (1994) 'International Law and human rights obligations, in Sarah Spencer (ed.) *Strangers and Citizens. A Positive Approach to Migrants and Refugees* (London: IPPR/River Oram Press).

Sunstein, Cass R. (1990) *After the Rights Revolution: Reconceiving the Regulatory State* (Cambridge, Mass.: Harvard University Press).

Swann Committee Report (1985) *Education For All* (London: HMSO).

Taguieff, Pierre-André (1988) *La force du préjugè: essai sur le racisme et ses doubles* (Paris: La Découverte).

—— (ed.) (1991) Les metamorphoses idéologiques du racisme et la crise de l'anti-racisme', in Pierre-André Taguieff (ed.) *Face au racisme* (Paris: La Découverte, 2 vols).

—— (ed.) (1991) *Face au racisme* (Paris: La Découverte, 2 vols).

—— (1996) *La République menacée* (Paris: Textuels).

—— and Patrick Weil (1990) 'Immigration, fait national et citoyenneté', *Esprit* (May).

Takaki, Ronald (1993) *A Different Mirror: A History of Multicultural America* (Boston: Little Brown & Co.).

Tamir, Yael (1993) *Liberal Nationalism* (Princeton, NJ: Princeton University Press).

Taylor, Charles (1989) 'Cross-purposes: the liberal-communitarian debate', in Nancy Rosenblum (ed.) *Liberalism and the Moral Life* (Cambridge, Mass: Harvard University Press).

—— and Amy Gutmann (ed) (1992) *Multiculturalism and the 'Politics of Recognition'* (Princeton, NJ: Princeton University Press).

Taylor, Michael (1987) *The Possibility of Cooperation* (Cambridge University Press).

—— (1996) 'Good government: On hierarchy, social capital and the limitations of rational choice theory', *Journal of Political Philosophy*, vol. 4, no. 1.

Todd, Emmanuel (1994) *Le destin des immigrés: assimilation et ségrégation dans les démocraties occidentales* (Paris: Seuil).

—— (1996) *L'invention de l'Europe* (Paris: Seuil, 2nd edn).

Todorov, Tzvetan (1989) *Nous et les autres: la réflexion française sur la diversité humaine* (Paris: Seuil).

Tribalat, Michèle *et al.* (1996) *De l'immigration à l'assimilation: enquête sur la population d'origine étrangère en France* (Paris: INED).

Tuck, Richard (1979) *Natural Rights Theories* (Cambridge University Press).

—— (1993) *Philosophy and Government 1572–1651* (Cambridge University Press).

Tully, James (1993) *An Approach to Political Philosophy: Locke in Contexts* (Cambridge University Press).

Ubbiali, Georges (1995) 'Towards the institutionalisation of prejudice?', in Bernd Baumgartl and Adrian Favell (eds) *New Xenophobia in Europe* (The Hague: Kluwers).

Unger, Roberto (1987) *Politics: A Work in Constructive Social Theory* (Cambridge University Press, 3 vols).

Van Parijs, Philippe (1991) *Qu'est-ce qu'une société juste? Introduction à la pratique de la philosophie politique* (Paris: Seuil).

Verma, G. K. (ed.) (1989) *Education For All: A Landmark in Pluralism* (London: Falmer).

Wacquant, Loïc (1992) 'Banlieues françaises et ghetto noir américain: de l'amalgame à la comparaison', *French Politics and Society*, vol. 10, no. 4.

—— (1993) 'De l'Amérique comme utopie à l'envers', in Pierre Bourdieu (ed.) *La misère du monde* (Paris: Seuil).

—— and William Julius Wilson (1991) 'Poverty, joblessness and the social transformation of the inner city', in Phoebe Cottingham and David Ellwood (eds) *Welfare Policy for the 1990s* (Cambridge, Mass. Harvard University Press).

Waldron, Jeremy (1993) *Liberal Rights* (Cambridge University Press).

Walzer, Michael (1981) 'Philosophy and democracy', *Political Theory*, vol. 9.

—— (1983) *Spheres of Justice* (New York: Basic Books).

—— (1984) 'Liberalism and the art of separation', *Political Theory*, vol. 12.

—— (1987) *Interpretation and Social Criticism* (Cambridge, Mass: Harvard University Press).

—— (1990) 'The communitarian critique of liberalism', *Political Theory* (Feb.).

Wayland, Sarah (1993) 'Mobilising to defend nationality law in France', *New Community*, vol. 20, no. 11.

Weber, Eugen (1977) *Peasants into Frenchmen: The Modernization of Modern France* (Cambridge, Mass.: Harvard University Press).

—— (1991) *My France: Politics, Culture, Myth* (Cambridge, Mass: Harvard University Press).

Weil, Patrick (1991) *La France et ses étrangers: l'aventure d'une politique de l'immigration* (Paris: Calmann-Lévy).

—— (1995) 'Racisme et discrimination dans la politique francaise de l'immigration 1938–1945, 1974–1995', *Vingtième siècle*, no. 47 (Jul.–Sep.).

—— (1996) 'Nationalities and citizenships: The lessons of the French experience for Germany and Europe' in David Cesarini and Mary Fulbrook (eds) *Citizenship, Nationality and Migration in Europe* (London: Routledge).

—— and John Crowley (1994) 'Integration in theory and practice: a comparison of France and Britain, *West European Politics*, vol. 17, no. 2.

Weldon, Fay (1989) *Sacred Cows* (London: Chatto & Windus).

Whelan, Frederick (1983) 'Democratic theory and the boundary problem', in J. Roland Pennock and John W. Chapman (eds) *Nomos 25: Liberal Democracy* (New York University Press).

Wieviorka, Michael (1991) *L'espace du racisme* (Paris: Seuil).

—— (ed.) (1996) *Une société fragmentée: le multi-culturalisme en débat* (Paris: La Découverte).

—— *et al.* (1992) *La France raciste* (Paris: Seuil).

Wihtol de Wenden, Catherine (1988) *Les immigrés et la politique* (Paris: Presses de la Fondation Nationale de la Science Politique).

—— (ed.) (1988) *La citoyenneté: les changements de structures sociales et nationales de la population française* (Paris: Foundation Diderot).

Wilson, William Julius (1980) *The Declining Significance of Race* (University of Chicago Press).

—— (1987) *The Truly Disadvantaged: The Inner City, the Underclass and Public Policy* (University of Chicago Press).

—— (1990) 'Race neutral policies and the Democratic coalition', *American Prospect*, no. 1 (Spring).

—— and Katherine O'Sullivan (1988) 'Race and Ethnicity', in Neil Smelser (ed.) *Handbook of Sociology* (New York: Sage).

Wright, Patrick (1985) *On Living in an Old Country: The National Past in Contemporary Britain* (London: Verso).

Yamgnane, Kofi (1992) *Droits, devoirs et crocodiles* (Paris: Robert Laffont).

Yonnet, Paul (1993) *Voyage au centre de la malaise française: de l'anti-racisme à la destruction du roman national* (Paris: Gallimard).

Young, Iris Marion (1991) *Justice and the Politics of Difference* (Princeton, NJ: University of Princeton Press).

Young, Ken and Naomi Connelly (1990) *Policy and Practice in the Multi-Racial City* (London: Policy Studies Institute).

Index

abode, right of (in Britain), 111,
    113–15
ad-hocracy, 135
achievement, levels of (among
    immigrants)
    in France, xvii, 57, 72, 191
    in Britain, x–xi, 191, 217–18
affaire du foulard, l', xv, xxv, 6, 75,
    153–4, 174–83, 221
Africans, xvi–xvii, 48, 49, 120, 172,
    209
    see also North Africans
agency (moral), idea of, 69, 82
    see also autonomy, responsibility,
        volonté
Algeria, Algerians, 49, 59–60, 65,
    67–8, 84, 102, 152, 157, 174,
    182–3
Alsace-Lorraine, 44
alterité, xxv, 73, 160–1
American Dilemma, An (Myrdal), 99,
    251–3
Americanisation, xviii, 189
Amin, Idi, x
Amsterdam, xviii, xix
Amsterdam Treaty, ix
ancien régime, xxv, 138–42, 231
anomie, xxv, 84, 179
    see also Durkheim
anti-discrimination legislation
    in France, xv, 186, 210
    in Britain, ix, xi, 8–9, 107, 118,
        120–1, 130, 211–16, 218, 243,
        248
    emergence of, 25, 31
    within European Union, ix,
        xiii–xiv, 30, 207, 210–12,
        244–5
    see also Race Relations Acts
anti-humanism, 57
anti-racism, 24
    and social movements, 24
    in France, 186, 247; *see also* SOS
        Racisme

radical, in Britain, vii, 12–13, 107,
    109, 118, 127, 130, 211–12,
    215–17, 220, 231–2
anti-relativism, 159, 192
anti-Semitism, 53, 57, 64
apartheid, 95
a priori (reasoning), xxv, 15, 112,
    132, 159, 173, 176, 186
    see also deontological, Kant
Arab world, 77, 174
    see also Mediterranean
Arkoun, Mohammed, 77
Aristotle, 80
Asians
    and achievement, x–xi, 191,
        217–18
    and cultural interests, 139,
        217–18, 228
    and discrimination, 213–14
    and education, 109, 130–2,
        228–9
    as racial category, 215–18
    in politics, 124, 126, 228
    population of, 120, 205, 213
    South East, xi
assimilation, idea of, 3, 8, 71, 95,
    104–5, 128–9, 173, 242
associations (immigrant), 47, 76–8,
    185, 244
Asylum and Immigration Appeals
    Act, xiii, 209–10
asylum seekers, *see* refugees
Australia, 4, 206, 234
autonomy (individual), idea of
    and citizenship, 2, 251
    in France, 69–70, 79, 81, 85, 87,
        100, 141, 176–81
    in Britain, 100, 140–2, 229
    see also freedom, liberty, Kant
Ayatollah, the, 224

Bangladeshi, x, 120, 221
banlieues, xv–xvi, xxv, 156, 174–5,
    177, 183–9